BEYOND the TANABATA BRIDGE

TRADITIONAL JAPANESE TEXTILES

Cat. 29 (detail)
Horse Trapping
see page 143

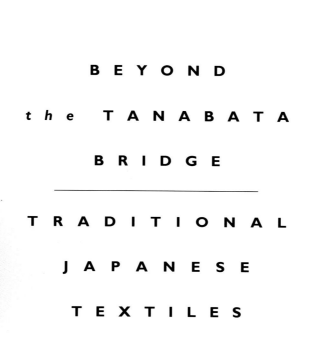

BEYOND *the* TANABATA BRIDGE

BRIDGE

TRADITIONAL

JAPANESE

TEXTILES

edited by William Jay Rathbun

THAMES AND HUDSON
IN ASSOCIATION WITH THE
SEATTLE ART MUSEUM

This publication and associated exhibition were supported by a grant from the National Endowment for the Arts. The exhibition will be shown at the Textile Museum, Washington, D.C., fall 1993, and the Birmingham Museum of Art, Alabama, spring 1994. Selections from the collection will be exhibited at the Seattle Art Museum at the conclusion of the tour.

First published in Great Britain in 1993 by Thames and Hudson Ltd, London

ISBN 0-500-01586-4

Designed by The Traver Company, Seattle
Printed and bound in Hong Kong
All photographs of objects in the collection of the Seattle Art Museum by Paul Macapia

CONTENTS

F O R E W O R D

J A Y   G A T E S
The Illsley Ball Nordstrom Director

From its earliest years, the Seattle Art Museum has been known for the excellence and depth of its collection of the arts of Japan. While the museum's holdings have grown and diversified over time, an area of particular strength is in traditional textiles. Startling in their capacity to embody aesthetic and social values, these woven arts from Japan suggest that culture's long history and rich tradition of producing textiles that can truly be considered an art form. Exquisitely quiet yet graphic communication, the fibers, color, weave, and style of these objects tell us both about their makers and the individuals for whom they were made — his or her place in society, including status, wealth, and associations.

Here in the commoner textiles of Japan, one can see the artistry lavished on the everyday, and that aesthetic distinction need not be reserved for the rich or elite or, for that matter, display in a museum. Imagining these often exuberant, sometimes breathtakingly elegant garments gracing the inhabitants of the faraway or long ago family farm or city street enriches our understanding of world cultures and enlarges our vision of the beauty possible in our daily lives.

The collection catalogued in this volume is the result of a fortunate partnership. William Rathbun, John A. McCone Foundation Curator of Asian Art, has brought his enormous energy and intelligence to bear on the growth of the museum's collection of Japanese art for over twenty years. In recognizing the need to develop our holdings in Japanese textiles he turned to C. Bagley Wright, a long-time trustee and patron of the museum whose leadership of and generosity to the museum over the years have been profound. It is to him that this volume is dedicated.

For this project Mr. Rathbun has enlisted the participation of some of the leading experts in the field of Japanese textiles. They include Louise Allison Cort, Arthur M. Sackler Gallery, Washington, D.C.; Mary Dusenbury, Spencer Museum of Art, Lawrence, Kansas; Richard Mellott, Asian Art Museum, San Francisco; Iwao Nagasaki, National Museum, Tokyo; Cynthia Shaver; and Amanda Mayer Stinchecum.

We are particularly grateful to the National Endowment for the Arts, a federal agency, for its generous support of this exhibition and catalogue, and to the enthusiasm of Thames and Hudson to bring it to a wider audience.

WILLIAM JAY RATHBUN
John A. McCone Foundation Curator of Asian Art

Ancient legend tells that among the gods the young princess Tanabata was the heavenly weaver and her husband, Kengyu, the celestial ox herder. Deeply in love, they neglected their duties, which angered the king, Tanabata's father, and in punishment he separated them, forever to dwell on either side of the Amagawa, or Milky Way. The king commanded myriad birds to form a bridge with their wings, and sent Kengyu across the Amagawa. Eventually, recognizing the suffering this separation caused the lovers, Tanabata's father relented, permitting the pair to meet once a year on the seventh day of the seventh month.

When at last they tried to meet, the lovers found the Amagawa so wide and its currents so tricky that it was impossible to cross unaided. Seeing their dilemma and filled with compassion for the lovers, the birds of heaven gathered again, hovering overhead to weave their outstretched wings to form a bridge, so that the lovers might meet. Thus every year, on the seventh day of the seventh month, the birds have gathered to form what is known as the Tanabata Bridge, so that the princess might cross the Amagawa to be with her husband.

This legend partly explains how, not long after the summer solstice, the stars Vega and Altair meet over the Milky Way; of more immediate interest, however, is the significance of weaving, and of women in relation to weaving, in early Japanese culture, which the legend clearly marks. The story, though probably more ancient, and of more distant origin, was first recorded in the annals of the Eastern Han dynasty (1st–3rd centuries) in China. Exactly when the legend traveled to Japan is not certain, but it was already a recognized romantic allusion in the earliest collection of poetry, the *Manyōshū* (ca. 7th century); the first celebration of the Tanabata Festival at the imperial court was recorded in 691.

Transmitted through the centuries in legend and poetry, the seventh day of the seventh month became a major festival day in Japan. Originating in the sinocentric imperial court of the Nara period (645–794), the celebration featured poetry contests and other genteel games. In medieval times (13th–17th centuries), it broadened to include flower arranging, archery, and incense contests. By the Edo period (1615–1868) the Tanabata Festival had become one of the *sekku,* or seasonal festivals which was celebrated at the shogun's palace in Edo as well as among the common people. Observances included the preparation of special foods and a launching of poem-papers into the bay at Shinagawa. The festivities at the Yoshiwara pleasure quarter were said to rival

The Tanabata Festival, ca. 1710, Okumura Masanobu, hand-colored print, courtesy of the MOA Museum of Art, Atami, Japan. This print commemorates the Tanabata Festival, which is still observed in Japan today. Above the clouds are the two star lovers separated by the flowing Milky Way, and the three magpies who are supposed to help the lovers cross it. Below, a girl plays a koto, with other musical instruments arranged about her. Behind, under ceremonial festooning, the various accoutrements of the Tanabata Festival are laid out on a table.

those of the imperial court in Kyoto. In the eighteenth century, when almost every household had a loom and young women were expected to become experienced weavers, the festival enjoyed special popularity, as young women entreated Princess Tanabata to aid them in becoming skillful at weaving and to find an adoring and faithful husband. Spiritually nourished on the Tanabata legend throughout childhood, every Japanese is familiar with this story, and today the festival remains one of the most charming and enthusiastically celebrated of all Japanese holidays. Currently it is a time when young couples, no doubt encouraged by department store chains, exchange gifts, disclose betrothals, and announce wedding dates.

This book travels the road beyond the Tanabata Bridge, exploring the everyday textile heritage of Princess Tanabata's role as heavenly weaver and, according to some accounts, also the celestial seamstress, and chronicles, through a cross section of examples, basic Japanese traditional textile media and techniques. It is a journey acknowledging the time-honored Japanese traditions of walking tours, travel diaries, and narrative handscroll-painting. It moves from the far north in Hokkaido through the main island of Honshu, to the Inland Sea area and Shikoku, on to the southern island of Kyūshū, and finally to the Ryūkyū Islands and Okinawa. This progress clearly establishes for the reader the distinctive regional character of certain techniques, while underscoring the interrelatedness of others.

Textiles provide unique insights to any society, but they are particularly valuable in understanding traditional cultures. In Japan, beginning in the early modern era, textiles, in the context of the phenomena of urbanization and a comparatively high standard of living, became an infallible barometer of social status and a gauge of technical expertise. As clothing, textiles enclose the individual's body, reacting with every gesture. They reveal deep-seated cultural preferences through color, motif, and garment shape. By these means textiles also send messages of the person's gender, age, social, political, and religious rank or association; they record an individual's occupation or special duties and also identify associations with particular groups.

This claim might be made for clothing at all times, but during the Edo period economic, commercial, and social conditions were newly conducive to a heightened personal expression through textiles. In the towns and cities, as flags and festival banners, as shop signs or doorway curtains, textiles announced the names and purposes of larger groups, and by their novel designs attracted the attention of passersby. Many of the qualities and some of the forms present in textiles of Japanese everyday life of the eighteenth and nineteenth centuries are very much alive today, in particular a taste for natural materials and a preference for traditional decorating techniques and — in the face of dwindling interest in wearing kimono — the enduring status of the informal kimono, the *yukata*. In commerce, the use of textiles became an agreeable cultural habit that persists to the present in *noren* (doorway curtain) and advertising banners.

Textile arts reached a high level of cultural distinction in the Edo period and the succeeding Meiji period (1868–1912) and were the focus of intense appreciation. The social and commercial importance of their role in turn encouraged a vigor and diverse aesthetic in the industry that supplied them. Born in part of religion, in part of peasant life, and in part as a response to a dynamic urban culture, Japan's commoner textile traditions evolved from the hands of anonymous weavers and decorators. Separated from the resources of palace workshops, unassuming weavers and dyers and patient needleworkers augmented native traditions by adapting foreign techniques, enlivened patterns by absorbing exotic motifs, and created innovative design solutions through ingenious artistry, technical prowess, and dedication of spirit.

It is not surprising that the elite classes could demand such highly complicated and diverse fabrics as sumptuous silk brocades, rich embroideries, and filmy gauze weaves. Commoners, however, working within often strictly circumscribed feudal guidelines for clothing material, color, and pattern, achieved flights of technical tours-de-force, creating with equal ease bold images and delicate detail with subtle nuance. Dyeing emerged as an art form in its own right, and while exuberant color was often proscribed by the puritanical shogunate or was economically out of reach, the urge among the general populace to use bright colors could not be entirely denied.

Through these centuries, commoners created a panorama of textile culture that compares favorably with the accomplishments of the aristocratic productions for drama, ingenuity, and visual beauty. In testimony to the aesthetic virtue of these traditions, fabrics and garments made for the upper classes selectively incorporated their techniques, materials, and motifs. The traditions of Okinawa reflect peculiar local circumstances, and that area's textiles cannot be interpreted as pure folk art.

This collection, the catalogue, and an exhibition organized by the Seattle Art Museum to be shown at the Textile Museum in Washington, D.C., and at the Birmingham Museum of Art, Alabama, chronicle these qualities of traditional Japanese textiles.

These garments and other fabric items in this collection appear for the first time in a major installation independent of other media. Thus presented, they reveal their vitality as a cultural expression with aesthetic power and technical virtuosity that has not previously been fully acknowledged. This catalogue seeks to present with scholarly discipline, in English, a basis for broader understanding of Japanese textiles, cutting through the perennial fog of folk tales and commercial hyperbole which until now has dogged presentations of this art.

The Seattle Art Museum has collected Japanese textiles since it opened in 1933. A series of textile stencils for the *katazome* paste-resist technique was among the items acquired in its first year of operation. The museum's collection focused, like those at other institutions, on the brocades and fancy embroideries associated with an elite class and includes a wide textile selection of fragments from the Todaiji and Horyūji, which are known to date from the seventh to twelfth centuries. In more recent years, attitudes of collecting have been tempered by a growing awareness of traditional folk crafts engendered by the Mingei movement. Established in the 1920s by the philosopher and collector Sōetsu Yanagi to preserve and respect the skills of Japanese crafts workers and their contributions to the life of the nation, the Mingei movement created a place in history for commoner textiles. The collections of Mingei museums in Japan testify to the success of the movement. A critical reappraisal of definitions of fine and applied art followed World War II. Collectors and museum curators in America consequently demonstrated a spreading acceptance of the mutually nonexclusive nature of both types of Japanese textiles, which eventually led to the development of several major collections. One of these was formed by Virginia and Bagley Wright, collectors and art patrons well known in the field of modern art, whose interests proved sufficiently broad that they acquiesced to my arguments, agreeing to purchase a core group of textiles in 1985. Almost immediately, the collection began to expand; over a five-year period the number of pieces more than doubled. In 1989, the Wrights made a gift of the collection to the Seattle Art Museum, the basis for this catalogue and exhibition.

In addition to the Wrights, other collectors, notably Frank D. Stout of Saint Helena, California, and Mary Wallace Johnson of Lake Oswego, Oregon, have been important contributors to the museum's collection. The Christensen Fund of Palo Alto, California, purchased much of the former Fifi White Collection, and in 1989, in recognition of our commitment to textile collecting and conservation, placed their collection on long-term loan with the Seattle Art Museum. Promised gifts of T. R. Welch of Seattle will further enrich the textile collection in the future. These collections form the single largest repository of Japanese folk textiles outside Japan and constitute a unique resource for the study and appreciation of this art.

It has been said — and is without doubt true — that a journey of even a thousand leagues begins with a single step. In this instance, that single step was the Wrights' textile purchase in 1985. Inspired by their acquisitions, as well as the interest their collection engendered among other enthusiasts, the present publication and exhibition began to take form. Along the way, many other people contributed to this exhilerating and concentrated effort, both in this country and in Japan. One of the most important of these is Betty C. Hoffman of Okinawa. Betty Hoffman has been an enthusiastic and unrelenting patron in Okinawan art circles for over twenty-five years. By the best of good fortune I met her at a critical moment in the development of this project, for she provided me an intensive introduction to many of the islands of Okinawa prefecture and to the many artists whom she has made her friends. It was in good part a result of her positive reinforcement of my own instincts that I found the strength to pursue a course which has led finally to this place. At a later date, Betty guided Museum Photographer Paul Macapia during a visit to Okinawa, generously sharing with him her respect and appreciation for the culture of her adopted home. She also counts as friends and colleagues several of this volume's essayists.

Colleagues at the Seattle Art Museum, while sharing the excitement of working with these wonderful textiles, have been asked over the years to solve many problems posed by such a complex project. Its success is largely due to their resourcefulness and good-natured cooperation. The project, although it was initiated before their arrival, has received continuing support from both Jay Gates, The Illsley Ball Nordstrom Director, and Patterson Sims, Associate Director for Art and Exhibitions. The Office of the Registrar, directed by Gail Joice, Associate Director for Museum Services, has been called upon continuously for the preparation of the textiles for photography, installation, travel, and conservation. For the associated exhibition, Exhibition Preparators, headed by Michael McCafferty, have worked diligently to devise appropriate mounts for safe and elegant installation and display. In preparing this book, Media and Publications Manager Helen Abbott, with editors Lorna Price and Paula Thurman, have struggled over many versions of the complex manuscript, coordinating the work of many authors and that of designer Anne Traver to provide an excellent format for the presentation of the material. Paul Macapia contributed his formidable talents in the photographs that grace the book, and Susanna Kuo created elegantly simple drawings. Assisting with the writing of the book, Michiyo Morioka brought to bear a daunting professionalism in research and scholarly rectitude in her writing. We are deeply thankful to her and to research assistants recruited from the University of Washington graduate art history program who worked with us over the years, most especially Julia Sapin-Yenne.

Our great appreciation goes to the essayists whose participation in this project lifted it into the realm of distinguished scholarship. Each has contributed a facet that in concert lends a special luster to the publication and exhibition for which we are truly grateful.

SIBERIA

HOKKAIDO

Sea of Japan

Aomori

TOHOKU

SHŌNAI

Sakata

Sendai

Yamagata

Niigata

Kanazawa

KANTO

CHUBU

Tokyo (Edo)

KOREA

Matsue

Kyoto

Nagoya

Pacific Ocean

Okayama

Osaka

CHŪGOKU

Nara

Korea Strait

Tsushima
Island

KINKI

Inland Sea

Shikoku
Island

Matsuyama

Fukuoka

IYO

Kurume

KYŪSHŪ

Hachijō Island

N

Ryūkyū Islands

Shuri
Naha

Okinawa Island

Miyako Island

THE TRADITION OF FOLK TEXTILES IN JAPAN

IWAO NAGASAKI

FOOD, SHELTER, AND CLOTHING ARE ESSENTIAL COMPONENTS OF DAILY life. In a sense, therefore, the history of clothing began almost simultaneously with the history of mankind. In Japan, textiles, dominated by the production of clothing, developed in numerous directions throughout the history of Japanese culture. The fragile nature of textiles, however, makes their preservation over the centuries very difficult. Thus, opportunities to study textiles of ancient periods through extant examples are severely limited. In Japan, we have preserved a range of textiles dating to various eras; some are over a thousand years old, but the group as a whole is not historically comprehensive.

The great number of textiles preserved at the Shōsō'in are from the seventh and eighth centuries and consist mostly of clothing and other items used by emperors, aristocrats, or priests. Early examples of common people's clothing and utilitarian objects are rare. Few textiles remain from the ninth through fifteenth centuries, and of those most were connected with Shinto and Buddhist functions. Many more textiles survive beginning with the sixteenth century, predominantly clothing of court nobles and the samurai, or military, class, Noh costumes, and *kosode* (kimono). Noh, established as stage art at the beginning of the Muromachi period (1392–1568) and from its inception patronized by the military class, provided its ceremonial and theatrical entertainment during the Edo period (1615–1868). Thus the Noh costume reflects not only a theater tradition but also the aesthetic taste of its patrons. Most extant examples of kosode, on the other hand, belonged to the wives and consorts of the military class or the wealthy townspeople class. Unlike the Noh costume, which adheres strictly to established tradition, kosode reflect fashions of the time. Neither represent the textile tradition of the commoners.

The designs and decorations of the commoners' textiles reveal a sense of freedom unconfined by tradition or the fashion of the time.

From the Edo period on, examples of folk textiles abound. They differ completely in fabric, weaving technique, and decoration from elegant Noh costumes or kosode of the upper classes. These are the garments and other articles that common people wore for working and used in daily life. Certainly the choice of fabric and weaving technique are influenced by use, but, partly for economic reasons, the designs and decorations of the commoners' textiles reveal a sense of freedom unconfined by strict adherence to either tradition or fashion of the time. The utilitarian nature of folk textiles has produced unique designs in Japanese textile art.

The folk textile tradition no doubt existed from ancient times, but the virtual lack of extant examples prevents us from accurately understanding its full scope and development. In terms of aesthetics, the most important group of folk textiles dates to the era after the mid-Edo period, and it will be the focus of this essay, along with associated folk crafts.

DURABILITY

Folk textiles clearly constitute a genre within Japanese textile art, but they elude strict definition. The very identity of the commoner class is broad and ambiguous, varying over time and place. In the feudal system of the Edo period, the social hierarchy ran from warriors, farmers, and artisans, down to merchants. Some lower-class samurai, however, although officially belonging to the highest social class, led lives not too different from that of artisans, while some merchants in big cities, despite being considered members of the lowest social class, enjoyed affluence surpassing that of upper-class samurai.

The difficulty of identifying commoners also makes it difficult to define their textiles. But the most important feature of commoners' clothing and other textiles is their durability, essential for those whose lives were centered on physical labor. This requirement conditioned the choice of textile fiber. *Asa* (a bast fiber and the fabric made from it), the most dominant fabric, is represented at the Shōsō'in by an early example of a garment worn by lower-class officials. It was widely used for the clothing of laborers during the ensuing Heian (794–1185) and Kamakura (1185–1333) periods. Even after the Edo period, asa garments were predominantly worn by commoners. The exception was *jōfu* (finely woven asa of high quality), which was used by women of the samurai and wealthy urban classes for their summer garments (*katabira*).

In addition to asa, from ancient times the Japanese used fabrics woven from the fibers of wisteria bark (*fuji*), arrowroot (*kuzu*), mulberry (*kōzo*), and Japanese linden (*shina*) for garments and other articles of daily use. An Edo-period work jacket (cat. 47) is made of wisteria fibers. Because of its durability in water, wisteria fiber is still used for bags to strain soy sauce and tofu and for bags women divers carry when collecting seaweed.

Leather, also because of its durability, was often used by commoners for work clothes such as woodcutters' coats and travel trousers, and people of all social classes used it for armor and footwear. Leather never became part of the regular clothing for upper-class people; as their lifestyle did not require rough labor, they had no need for such durable clothing.

Among folk textiles, one often finds examples of raw fabric processed to make it stronger and more durable. For instance, *kamiko*, made of specially treated paper, is windproof and cold-resistant but far less durable than asa and other plant-fiber fabrics. But *shifu*, which combines weft threads made of twisted, torn paper and warp threads of cotton, asa, or wisteria, is both warm and sturdy. It was produced from the latter part of the Edo period in the mountains of Yamagata prefecture and was used for work clothes. *Sakiori*, woven from wefts of torn strips of cotton fabric and warps of asa or cotton yarn, is an example of recycling as well as an application by which durability and warmth are improved. Sakiori was predominantly produced in San'in and Sado; on Sado Island, gold miners wore sakiori for its warmth and sturdy nature.

The illustrations in this chapter are details from a pair of folding screens in the collection of the Seattle Art Museum, *Scenes of Life in and around the Capital,* from the Edo period, second half 17th century, purchased with funds donated by Mildred and Bryant Dunn and by the Floyd A. Naramore Memorial Purchase Fund, 75.38. Each panel depicts various aspects of life in the great city of Kyoto, and the details shown here give a sense of the variety of activities and the garments worn at the time.

Sashiko originally may have been a recycling technique to salvage small, worn-out pieces of fabric. On recognizing that this stitchery technique improved durability, people began to apply it for that purpose. The emphasis on sturdiness demonstrates that durability was a prerequisite for folk textiles. In contrast, garments and textiles of the ruling class or the wealthy, from the seventh century through modern times, were mostly made of silk: decorative effect, achieved by weaving and dyeing techniques was more important than durability. Silk fiber allows various weaving techniques, making it possible to to produce delicate and intricate patterns such as *aya* (twill weave), *shusu* (satin weave), *sha* (gauze weave), and *ra* (fancy gauze weave). It also allows colorful designs through numerous dyeing techniques such as *itajime* (board-jammed dyeing or woodblock-resist dyeing), *rōzome* (wax-resist dyeing), and *yūzenzome* (multicolored paste-resist dyeing).

ECONOMIC FACTORS

Cotton as well as asa is an important material in folk textiles. In the fourteenth century, Japan began full-scale importation of cotton through China. Cultural exchange with China, kept to a minimum since the ninth century, was revitalized, and Japan again saw a vigorous influx of Chinese culture and goods. Among objects imported at that time were textiles that later became known as *meibutsugire* (celebrated fabrics). Most were woven silk — *kinran* (gold brocade), *donsu* (damask weave), and *sha* — but the so-called *kantō*-striped fabrics included cotton cloth as well. They were used for garments of the ruling military class and for Noh theater costumes. Tea connoisseurs later came to admire them and used them in the art of tea ceremony. Japan imported these textiles in great quantities, particularly during the Momoyama (1568–1615) and early Edo periods.

Once cotton production was established in Japan, cotton became widely available to Japanese commoners after the mid-Edo period. They

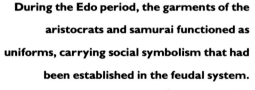

During the Edo period, the garments of the aristocrats and samurai functioned as uniforms, carrying social symbolism that had been established in the feudal system.

developed the stitchery techniques of sashiko and *kogin*, applied over indigo-dyed fabric, as well as various tie-dye techniques represented by Arimatsu *shibori* (in present-day Nagoya), and *kasuri* (ikat), which evolved with distinctive regional characteristics. The richness of cotton textile arts resulted from the availability of the material and demonstrates the importance of economic factors in the development of folk textiles.

Cotton and asa dominate the tradition of folk textiles. Their importance derives from both their durability and their economic efficiency. These fabrics remained relatively inexpensive because many of them could be manufactured at home, eliminating the cost of importing either raw fiber or finished fabric. During the Edo period, Edo and other cities had well-developed commodity-trading economies. Cotton merchants were numerous. Artisans and craftsmen in the cities, who were better off than farmers and fishermen, could purchase cotton fabric as well as cotton garments, which were now produced all over Japan. In contrast, in the farming and fishing communities, which lacked such advanced economies, home-manufacturing of textiles was essential. Sashiko and sakiori, techniques that recycled fabric, were used particularly in the northern area of Tohoku, where new cotton fabric and clothing were scarce.

Shiroishi (present-day Miyagi prefecture), Mino (present-day Gifu prefecture), and Tosa (present-day Kōchi prefecture) were regions where

high-quality paper was manufactured, giving local entrepreneurs the ability to produce kamiko inexpensively. During the late Edo period, elaborately decorated kamiko with dyed patterning of *sarasa* (colorful designs done by wax-resist dyeing or block printing, or a combination of the two) and *komon* (small overall designs done by stencil-resist dyeing) were sold in large cities as specialty products of local provinces. But originally kamiko was produced for use by common people as an inexpensive textile made from an abundant regional resource.

REGIONAL CHARACTERISTICS

The regional character of folk textiles is most clearly recognizable in the choice of material, as exemplified by sakiori and kamiko. An Ainu textile, *attusi,* is made from fiber taken from the bark of tall, deciduous trees, called *ohyō* (Ulmus spp.), commonly found in the Hokkaido and Tohoku areas. The fabric is woven on a primitive type of *izaribata* (literally, creep-along loom), a backstrap loom called *attusikarape* in Ainu, used by a weaver seated on the floor. Many examples of attusi are monocolored, retaining the color of the bark, but some are decorated with vertical stripe patterns in black, brown, and green. Attusi garments often had appliquéd cotton segments over which unique brace, swirl, and animal patterns were embroidered. Apparently cotton was considered a valuable material in Hokkaido until modern times and therefore was used only in small segments on garments. The combination of ohyō and cotton in attusi garments reflects a condition particular to Hokkaido.

The textiles of Okinawa are dominated by silk, asa, cotton, and *bashō*, a species of fiber-banana tree. Silk and asa were exclusively used for the clothing of aristocrats. *Tombian,* made from agave (*ryūzetsuran*), was also a specialty textile produced for Okinawan royalty. Cotton was not widely cultivated in Okinawa. Considered valuable, it was largely used for garments of the ruling class. Common people could use it only in *tisaji,* a scarf or kerchief woven by young women for their betrothed. Asa became inaccessible to the commoners of Okinawa after the Edo period, when it was reserved for gifts. At this point bashō, which could be easily cultivated in the Ryūkyū Islands, replaced asa in textile manufacture. This is another regional folk textile manufactured locally for economic reasons.

During the Edo period, the garments of the aristocrats and samurai functioned as uniforms, carrying social symbolism that had been established in the feudal system. Because of this, they display little regional character. Kimono worn by women of the wealthy classes were largely manufactured in Kyoto, and their patterns and designs reflected the fashion of the time as shown in the *hinagatabon* (style book of patterns currently in fashion) published in Kyoto. Thus regional differences were not clearly recognizable in such garments.

In contrast, clothing of the common people often displays designs and patterns distinctive to each region, such as those patterns in kasuri. *Kurume-gasuri* in Kyūshū often display designs combining pine, bamboo and plum, tortoise, bamboo and sparrow, peony and lion, Daikoku (one of the Seven Lucky Gods) and his mallet, or motifs of carp, castle, boat, and the old couple of Takasago, paragons of connubial fidelity. *Yumihama-gasuri* from the San'in area is a cotton ikat featuring family crests and other motifs resembling them. Tsugaru-kogin is a particular type of sashiko with complex geometric patterns; the designs vary among the northern, central, and southern areas of Tsugaru.

BEAUTY IN UTILITARIAN FUNCTION

Utility is another important factor characterizing folk textile tradition. Fiber, style, and technique are selected to satisfy the particular function for which the textile is used. The material and processing technique for the fireman's coat in this collection (cat. 17) and the *kappa* (travel coat; cat. 38) demonstrate this point. The fireman's coat, which must protect the body from heat and retain its strength when wet, is made from cotton fabric reinforced with sashiko stitchwork. The travel coat is made from paper treated with water-resistant oil, resulting in a lightweight, wind-resistant, and waterproof fabric ideal for its intended use.

Firemen wore their coats plain side out while fighting a fire. After quenching the blaze, they reversed their coats to display the bold and inspiring designs.

Workers engaged in manufacturing indoors as well as farmers working outdoors often wore upper garments with narrow sleeves and trousers that tapered toward the calf and ankle, which thus did not hamper their movement. In contrast, garments of the military, the court, and the wealthy display the ample and wide kosode sleeves and trousers fashionable in the leisure classes. The *happi* and *haori*, commoners' coats, are designed to be loose, with wide sleeve openings. Their front openings can be easily closed, with strings tied together or looped over buttons, without overlapping. The *jimbaori* (cat. 34), worn by samurai when riding horseback, has a long center-back opening; when the rider is mounted, the divided back falls to the left and right.

The sashiko-reinforced firemen's coats (cat. 15 and 16) were actually worn during firefighting activities. Inside they are decorated with an elaborately painted design. Firemen wore their coats plain side out while fighting a fire. During the peaceful Edo period, firefighting was one of the most dangerous occupations, and the large, elaborate designs of dragons and clouds or the thunder god were painted on firefighters' coats specifically to heighten their courage and lessen their fear. After quenching the blaze, firemen reversed their coats to display the bold and inspiring designs.

THE AESTHETIC BEAUTY OF FOLK TEXTILES

The utilitarian nature of folk textiles and garments by no means excluded decoration. From the Edo period on, decorative effects on such garments are far more interesting than those of the expensive textiles worn by upper-class people. The uniquely beautiful features of commoners' garments are intimately related to the techniques that produced them.

Sashiko stitchwork was applied initially in order to mend or reinforce old fabric or garments. But people began to create various patterns by stitching with regularity and planned variation. Work clothes and *noren* (door curtains) found in many regions display designs created by the addition of stitches in vertical, horizontal, and diagonal directions across what began as simple parallel-line stitchwork.

Kogin, which developed in the Tsugaru area in Tohoku, is generally a dark blue asa cloth decorated with sashiko in white cotton threads. It is believed that there are almost thirty basic patterns in the art of kogin. *Hishizashi*, appearing in the Nambu area, is light blue asa cloth stitched with white cotton thread. Its name derives from its basic motif, the lozenge (*hishi*). Both kogin and hishizashi achieved beautiful geometric patterns in sashiko, but they did not constitute an element of luxury nor were they a reflection of a leisurely lifestyle. Farmers, forbidden to wear cotton, out of necessity created many of these beautiful stitch patterns as a way of improving the durability and warmth of their asa work clothes. Kogin and hishizashi, both homemade textiles, display a precision and perfection of technique not found in articles created as merchandise for sale.

Some patterns incorporate symbols that become decorative motifs. Among the sashiko patterns, one finds interesting ideogram designs adorning the work clothing of farmers, fishermen, and children's clothes as well. Ideograms such as *hi* (sun), *ten* (sky), *mizu* (water), *tsuchi* (soil), *ta* (rice paddy), and *yama* (mountain), all important aspects of nature in agricultural communities, appear on farmers' work clothes. These stitched ideograms originally represented prayers and auspicious charms for everyday life. The hexagram (star-shaped) design, or woven bamboo pattern, was believed to expel evil spirits; it was applied to work clothes to protect the wearer from illness, accident, and natural disaster. *Hinode-mon* (sunrise pattern), which resembles a chrysanthemum, is symbolic of the sun's rays which reach all corners of the world; it is a wish that children grow strong and healthy under the bright sun.

The *hanten* and haori, coats worn by craftsmen, fishermen, and merchants, were originally marked with signs indicating the wearer's status; his guild, craft, or profession; and his employer's identity. Often representing abstract ideograms and symbolic motifs, they dazzle us when they are transformed into highly decorative motifs and bold designs. They have no parallels in the garments of upper-class Japanese. In the tightly controlled feudal society of Japan, this type of vigorous design was one way common people were permitted to express their aesthetic energy. This characteristic of strong design in clothing became increasingly noticeable in their garments and textiles after the Edo period, when the commoners and working classes enjoyed a lively society. Although decoration in folk textiles was a secondary element, emerging only in the process of fulfilling requirements for economy, utility, and durability, nevertheless, it developed into a full and unique style, employing techniques quite different from those used to create textiles for upper classes.

FOLK TEXTILE TECHNIQUES

Throughout Japanese history, complex weaving techniques such as *nishiki* (brocade), donsu, and kinran and delicate dyeing techniques such as *tsujigahanazome* and *chayazome* were never accessible to commoners. Those techniques could not fulfill the basic requirements of folk textiles. The intricate woven texture of nishiki and donsu is virtually impossible to achieve without using fine, smooth silk thread of uniform thickness. Such finely woven textiles were beyond the reach of the common people who, for economic reasons and the need for durable clothing, had to rely on cotton and bast fibers. In addition, tsujigahanazome and chayazome required complicated dyeing processes and high-quality fabric like silk and jōfu. They were not only too expensive but also geographically inaccessible to commoners because their production was limited to particular locations.

In contrast, some types were popular among both the elite classes and commoners, for instance, *shimaori* (striped weave), *shiborizome* (tie-dye), yūzenzome, and *komonzome*. Striped fabric was used for samurai garments and

as meibutsugire in the tea ceremony during medieval times, and after the mid-Edo period, it constituted an important element of commoners' clothing. Kasuri was sometimes used for *noshime*, a type of kimono worn by samurai on formal occasions and for some roles in Noh and Kyogen performances. But the most important products of kasuri were developed in regional folk traditions. The yūzen dyeing technique, perfected at the start of the eighteenth century, was used not only for kosode and katabira worn by women of the upper-class townspeople but was also used to decorate *futonji* (futon covers), noren, and banners for local theaters (*nobori*). Komonzome was seen widely in *kamishimo*, a samurai's vestlike formal garment with projecting shoulders and matching trousers. During the latter half of the Edo period, urban women and other commoners began to wear komonzome garments.

Although techniques were the same, the affluent used silk to produce fabrics with stripes and lattice patterns, while commoners used cotton. The yūzenzome kosode of upper-class women are characterized by colorful designs using many dyes and the delicate *itome nori* (rice-paste resist lines drawn like fine threads). Commoners' yūzenzome, although elaborate, was termed *tsutsugaki* (tube drawing) and was technically much simpler than yūzenzome. One finds different types of beauty and charm among textiles such as striped weave and yūzenzome, which were produced for both the upper classes and commoners. Sashiko, kasuri, and *chūgatazome* (stencil resist-dyeing which creates medium-size patterns) were the textiles developed specifically among the common people with the use of particular techniques, thus resulting in a unique beauty. *Aizome* (indigo dyeing) is another such example. Indigo dye is often found in shibori, katazome, and sashiko textiles; it is both inexpensive and durable and does not fade easily in water or sun. In addition, the more aizome is washed, the more its beauty is enhanced. Therefore its utilitarian nature contributes to the kind of beauty attainable only in folk textiles. Indigo was also believed to possess beneficial medicinal effects. Working-class people wore aizome fabric believing that it would keep off leeches in rice paddies and vipers in the mountains. It was also said that contaminated water could be purified by straining it through aizome cloth.

Figures of city dwellers depicted in Heian-period scrolls tend to wear clothing decorated with various patterns, while country folk usually wear undecorated, plain garments. During the Muromachi and Momoyama periods, as a result of an economy based on the use of currency, a merchant class possessing economic power eventually formed a new and wealthy social stratum in cities with commercial and industrial bases. Following the Edo period, the ruling class, represented by the *bakufu* (military government), established economic policies that promoted the development of urban economy. Great economic disparity came to exist between merchants and artisans living in urban areas and farmers engaged in agriculture in the countryside. In consequence, considerable differences began to emerge in the textiles used daily by these two groups of people. Even among the townspeople many social classes existed, ranging from merchants who were wealthier than samurai to artisans who led hand-to-mouth existences. The garments and textile goods used by these people reflect various differences according to their economic status and lifestyle.

The tradition of folk textiles became quite diversified during the Edo period. After that time, while the common characteristics of folk textiles persisted, the tradition also created a variety of textiles with differing emphasis and meaning for each characteristic. This very diversity makes folk textiles extremely appealing and interesting. Until recently, the tradition of folk textiles had been largely neglected; however, it is a field that fully deserves aesthetic appreciation and carries rich potential for future research.

Iwao Nagasaki is Curator of Japanese Textiles, Tokyo National Museum.

THE ART OF COLOR

MARY DUSENBURY

Scarlet is fleeting!
How can you compare it with
familiar robes
Dyed
acorn-grey

THESE LINES CONCLUDE A POEM FROM THE GREAT EIGHTH-CENTURY collection of Japanese verse, the *Man'yōshū* (Anthology of Ten Thousand Leaves). The poem condemns a minor provincial official, Owari Okuhi, for a love affair with a local belle while his faithful wife waits in the capital for his summons.[1]

The metaphorical use of color in this and other ancient poems assumes the reader's knowledge of the specific properties of the dye plants used to produce them. *Kurenai*, the bright scarlet of this poem, was obtained from the tiny petals of the safflower (*benibana, Carthamus tinctorius*) a member of the thistle family. Safflower was a fairly new dye material in Japan when this poem was written. Although the color was subject to fading, the clarity and range of the shades it produced, from the palest pink to a vibrant scarlet, were exciting to contemporary Japanese accustomed only to the deep, rich red of madder (*akane, Rubia cordifolia* L., *mugista* Miq.).

The most interesting group of medieval textiles is the armor. A lord's armor was designed to astound and dismay enemy forces as well as to impress his followers.

Safflower was imported from the Asian continent, along with the technical knowledge to grow and use it, probably in the mid-seventh century. The cultivation and harvesting of safflower were labor intensive and costly, and the dye process required an unusually high level of skill. The gray-brown of *tsurubami*, on the other hand, derived from the acorns of a native oak (*Quercus acutissima*). This dye material grew wild and was easy to gather. Moreover, the dye process was simple, and the results were predictable and lasting. Thus the eighth-century reader of this poem would have immediately understood the excitement and allure of the "woman from Saburu" from the color of her robes, which also conveyed the extravagance of the love affair. At the same time, to one familiar with the dye properties of the oak tree, reference to the gray robes of Owari Okuhi's wife eloquently suggests her patience and faithfulness.

Color has always been an important part of Japanese aesthetic sensibility. Literature is filled with allusions to costume and to color, and writers of all periods used the names of colors and dye plants metaphorically. Their audiences, until the twentieth century, understood the colors, the dye process, and the particular characteristics of each important dye plant; they also recognized and used classical references to color such as those in the *Man'yōshū* poem.

Samurai armor
Nambokuchō period, 1346
Bronze with lacquer, brocades, and leather
Honolulu Academy of Arts,
4264.1. Gift of Mrs. Lewis P.
Rosen in Memory of her
Husband, 1964

Like other aspects of aesthetic sensibility, Japanese color sense changed, sometimes radically, from period to period. At times, different color aesthetics provided a counterpoint within a single era. The magico-religious understanding of color that was characteristic of prehistoric Japan was overlaid in the Asuka (552–645) and Nara (645–794) periods with the rich complexity of color in Buddhist art and a Sino-Korean preference for clear, strong hues, used to indicate court rank. The subtle gradations, startling juxtapositions, and pure clarity of color at the Heian (794–1185) court were followed by a preference for simple, bold contrasts in the warring Kamakura period (1185–1333). Later the brilliance and splendor sought by Momoyama (1568–1603) daimyo were tempered by the subtlety of the muted colors advocated by their tea masters. A similar balance was struck in the late Edo period (1615–1868) between the somber elegance of the gold and silver foil brocaded costumes of the Noh theater, sponsored by the ruling warrior-class elite, and the subtle grays, rich browns, and deep indigo blues of the Kabuki stage, patronized by merchants and a lively urban populace.

Thus, over the centuries, Japanese dyers exploited the brilliance of intense color and explored the subtleties of a muted palette. Relying on a remarkably small number of basic dye materials, they responded with sensitivity to the changing demands of a sometimes diverse clientele.

Traditional methods of weaving and dyeing are carried on in Japan today. These details are from photographs of artisans at work taken by Paul Macapia in 1989.

The foundation of the dyer's craft was laid in the sixth and seventh centuries, when continental dye materials and procedures were introduced from Sui (581–618) and Tang (618–907) dynasty China, probably via the sinicized Korean kingdom of Koguryŏ (37 B.C.–A.D. 668). There is considerable evidence that color was highly significant in pre- and proto-historical Japan. Dye methods, however, were primitive. The widespread practice of *suriginu*, for example, involved simply rubbing or pounding fresh dye material into woven cloth. Since no bonding agent was used, the color washed out if the cloth got wet. It was the introduction of continental procedures that enabled dyers to produce a wide range of lasting colors.

The introduction of Buddhism to Japan in the sixth century brought with it a wave of continental influence that resulted in a major seventh-century reorganization of government and society, based on the model of Tang-dynasty China. Under a series of progressive rulers, Japan eagerly received cosmopolitan Tang culture.[2] Textiles played an important role in the rich material culture of Japan during this period. They were a major form of tribute payment and could be substituted for corvée service. Their colors and patterning were used to distinguish rank and to reflect authority. In order to foster the development of the textile arts and to ensure that the needs of the court were met, the government established various offices to oversee the production of textiles for the court. Among these was the Palace Dyeing

Office (Naisenshi),³ which was organized under the Ministry of the Imperial Household in 701.⁴

Although suriginu and other early methods of dyeing lingered, the methods employed by dyers in the Palace Dyeing Office reflected the skill and sophistication of their continental counterparts.⁵ The palace dyers had at their disposal all of the major dye materials used on the continent. To the indigenous palette of madder red, indigo blue,⁶ and a variety of yellows and browns, they added a purple obtained from the root of the gromwell plant (*murasaki* or *shikon*; *Lithospermum erythrorhizon* Sieb. & Zucc.) and two new reds, the safflower of the *Man'yōshū* poem and sappanwood (*suo*; *Caesalpinia sappan* L.).⁷ All three of these dyes have been very important from the time of their introduction.

Yellow was obtained from miscanthus grass (*kariyasu*; *Miscanthus tinctorius*), the bark of the Amur cork tree (*kihada*; *Phellodendron amurense*) and from gardenia hulls (*kuchinashi*; *Gardenia jasminoides* Ellis f., *grandiflora* Mak.). Browns and grays could be obtained from the bark or nuts of a variety of native plants. Acorns and chestnuts are mentioned most frequently in the literature and were also used with the addition of an iron mordant to produce black. Over-dyeing indigo with madder or sappanwood was another method of making black.

Palace dyers skillfully monitored the pH factor of their dye vats by using an increased alkalinity or acidity to produce a particular tone or shade of color. They used an alkaline solution made by leaching ashes in water (*aku*) to bleach the naturally off-white fibers, to gloss silk, and to act as a mordant (L., *mordere*, to bite), an agent used to assist in the chemical bonding of dye to fiber. They were aware of the chemistry of different types of ash, choosing, for example, ash from alum-rich woods such as camellia (*tsubaki*; *Camellia japonica*) to bring out the most desirable purple from gromwell roots.

Chinese dyers at the court of Chang-an recognized five official colors in addition to white. Each was made with a prescribed dye material whose legitimacy was traced to the Chinese Classics: yellow (gardenia hulls and bark of the Amur cork tree), purple (gromwell roots), red (madder roots), blue-green (fermented leaves of indigo with a yellow overdye for green), and black. These colors indicated court rank and, through an ancient and complex series of interrelationships, were intimately linked with an entire religio-philosophical system.⁸ Numerous admonitions throughout the Chinese Classics warn against substituting other dyestuffs for the "correct" materials. The order of the color-rank system remained remarkably stable in China for many dynasties, only changing to a significant extent in the Manchurian Qing (1644–1912).⁹

In 603, in imitation of Chinese practice, the regent Shōtoku Taishi (d. 621) established a system of official government ranks in Japan. As in

China, the ranks were to be distinguished by color. However, while the ranked colors (*kurai-iro*) of 603 were made with the "correct" materials, they were ranked in an order probably copied from the Korean court at Kudara (Koguryō): purple, blue, red, yellow, white, and black.[10]

Although certainly known in Japan, the Chinese concept of ritually correct colors does not seem to have interfered with the marked delight with which Japanese welcomed their newfound ability to create beautiful colors. As native skills in dyeing increased, so did the colors that were used to indicate the various court ranks. Palace dyers produced ever finer shades and tones of color from standard dye materials and were quick to exploit the potential of new materials, apparently quite unconcerned with philosophical orthodoxy. Safflower, for example, soon joined the ranks of court dye materials. Overdyes, forbidden in China for ceremonial or official garments, were popular at the Heian court. Green was a consistent favorite, but rank lists also included more unusual composites such as "grape" (*ebizome*). Even a cursory reading of the rank listings suggests that colors proliferated, and the rank order was changed at frequent intervals simply for the opportunity to accommodate newly developed shades, to introduce a new color, and generally to add visual beauty, novelty, and interest to the court. As is generally true of royal colors everywhere, the lists as well as the regulations for nonofficial costume offer a fairly accurate reflection of the scarcity and expense of the material or the difficulty of dyeing with it, as well as the perceived beauty of the color itself.

The move to the newly established capital of Heiankyō in 794 marked the beginning of a period of national isolation during which the Japanese assimilated the earlier flood of continental culture. The world of the Heian court was geographically circumscribed and small in scale, and its aristocrats, increasingly unconcerned with affairs of state, concentrated their energies on aesthetic pursuits of poetry, love-making, music, literature, ceremonies, incense, festivals, and dress. They were close observers of nature as it appeared to them in the gardens of the capital and in its immediate environs, viewing nuances of seasonal change with a Buddhist-inspired wistful sorrow at the passing of time and of all things. A subtle evocation of feeling formed the core of aesthetic expression even in dress, particularly in the colors and color combinations that a man or a woman chose to wear on a particular occasion.

The Heian lady carefully chose and arranged her robes in skillfully shaded or contrasting colors to echo the season, the occasion of the day, her mood, feelings, or even to convey a message.

The woman's formal costume, the *nyō-bo-hitoe* (colloq., *junihitoe*), was composed of many layers of solid-colored silk kimono-type garments, some lined, worn one over the other so that most showed only as layered edges at the neck, sleeve, and hem openings. The Heian lady carefully chose and arranged these robes in skillfully shaded or contrasting colors to echo the season, the occasion of the day, her mood, feelings, or even a message or image she wanted to convey to others. At first such color arrangements were quite personal. Later they became standardized, each combination was named (*kasane no irome*),[11] and sets were produced that indicated some of the different layers by the addition of multiple hems and collars on a single garment. Costumes worn out of court were considerably simpler, but as is amply evident from descriptions in contemporary literature,

Takegawa II, from
Genjimonogatari-emaki
(Tale of Genji)
Late Heian period, early 12th century
Portion of a hand scroll, ink and colors on paper
Tokugawa Reimeikai Foundation, Tokyo

such as the early eleventh-century *Genjimonogatari* (Tale of Genji) by Murasaki Shikibu, attendant of Shōshi, consort of the emperor Ichijō (r. 986–1011),[12] the same attention was paid to color and its combinations.

Pale lavenders, dark purple, layers of pure white, yellow, spring green, gradations of translucent pinks, crimson, sky blue, and deep sappanwood red formed the palette from which the court lady chose the colors of her costume. Dark or somber colors were considered inauspicious and unattractive and symbolized an enforced or self-imposed separation from the court. They were used for aristocratic costumes only in time of mourning or exile and by those who had taken Buddhist vows.[13]

We have learned a surprising amount about dye materials and dye technology in the Heian period from contemporary literature, paintings, and official documents, as well as from the few extant textiles. The *Engishiki* (Procedures of the Engi Era), compiled in 927 to document matters of court procedure, deals with the colors used to indicate rank and includes dye materials and even recipes. These passages, although sometimes tantalizingly elliptical about procedural details, reveal a dye technology capable of catering to the finely tuned color sense and discriminating demands of the court.[14]

The Heian-period emphasis on color may be seen as a natural extension of the earlier interest that the Japanese had taken in the aesthetic possibilities inherent in the color-ranking system. This emphasis, however, may also have had a certain practical base. While even remote provinces were able to produce fine, plain-woven silk cloth, only a few produced the more complex textiles that required specialized weaving and dyeing skills, elaborate looms, and access to precious dyestuffs. Thus most of the tribute silk sent as tax payments from the provinces arrived as bolts of white cloth that were dyed in the piece after they reached the capital.

Dyeing was a household occupation in aristocratic residences. It was supervised by the mistress of the household, whose aesthetic judgment and technical skill determined the quality of the colors and color combinations that were the focus of so much public scrutiny at court, and which could make or break a reputation. Contemporary literature suggests that the imperial offices responsible for the dyeing and construction of palace textiles were also headed by an accomplished noblewoman, who was sometimes brought into the palace as a lady-in-waiting specifically for that purpose.[15]

The Heian period is often considered to be Japan's Classical period, a recurrent point of reference for literature and other arts during the next thousand years. This was certainly true for the dyer's art. The purity and clarity of Heian colors and the skill of its dyers are still admired and emulated by fine dyers today.

The wars that characterized much of the medieval period in Japan led to a decline of court culture and attendant arts, including a dramatic loss of basic dyeing skills. The sections of an early seventh-century embroidered Buddhist panel (the Tenjikoku mandala of Chūgūji) that were repaired professionally in the Kamakura period, for example, are now more faded than the unrepaired original work.

The most interesting group of medieval textiles, appropriately, is the armor. A lord's armor not only served to protect him but was consciously designed to astound and dismay enemy forces as well as to impress his followers. Armor was made of horizontal rows of small metal or lacquer plates held together by a multitude of flat silk braids arranged to form bold patterns of strong color, often a deep indigo blue offset by madder crimson. The importance of color is illustrated by an old story in which the lord of Kaga, overwhelmed by the power of the crimson banners of his enemy, lord of the neighboring territory of Tajima, sent spies across the border to kidnap madder dyers.[16]

Despite continued bouts of civil war, the Muromachi period (1392– 1568) saw a general increase in productivity, the growth of towns and trade, the emergence of a merchant class, and an extensive renewed contact with the outside world, including Ming-dynasty China (1368–1644), India, southeastern Asia, and even Europe.[17]

The growth of a market economy led to the establishment of commercial dye houses, while outside trade made new dye materials available for their use. Indigo processing and dyeing methods were refined and have remained essentially unchanged up to the present. Large growing fields were established in suitable locations,[18] and the fermented leaves were processed into highly concentrated mudlike bricks (*sukumo*), which lasted indefinitely and could be transported easily throughout the country.[19]

The Muromachi period also saw the rise of an aesthetic that favored imagery of old age, winter, desolation, the withered and the cold, ideas embodied in the expressions *sabi* and *wabi*. This aesthetic was developed most fully at the Higashiyama retreat (Ginkakuji, the Silver Pavilion) of the third Ashikaga shogun, Yoshimasa (1436–90), by men such as the Zen Buddhist priest and poet Shinkei (1407–75), the Noh master Zeami (1363–1443), and the shogun's tea master, Murata Shukō (d. 1502). Tea masters replaced colorful paintings with monochrome ink landscapes and austere calligraphy and introduced the use of Korean utilitarian ware and rough native pottery. The textile colors associated with this aesthetic were subdued, complex, and subtle.

The civil wars of the fifteenth and sixteenth centuries were finally brought to a close by a succession of three powerful warlords who rose from the ranks of the military and gained leadership by force. In their patronage of

Gold and straw, brilliance and rusticity, existed side by side and vied for aesthetic supremacy in an extraordinary visual counterpoint during the Momoyama period.

the arts, Oda Nobunaga (1534–82), Toyotomi Hideyoshi (1536–98), and Tokugawa Ieyasu (1542– 1616) favored ostentatious displays of power, wealth, and splendor, delighting in bold patterns, bright colors, luxurious and sometimes outlandish clothing, and a profuse use of gold in paintings and other objects they commissioned. At the same time, they continued to patronize the finest adherents of the medieval aesthetic. The late sixteenth century saw the culmination of the aesthetic of sabi and wabi in the work of Sen Rikyū (1521–91), chief tea master to both Oda Nobunaga and Toyotomi Hideyoshi.

Thus in the brilliant Momoyama period was a short-lived but extraordinary aesthetic counterpoint where gold and straw, sophistication and rusticity, existed side by side and vied for aesthetic supremacy. Hideyoshi, for example, loved to hold extravagant tea parties, for which he had built a portable teahouse of pure gold. His tea master, meanwhile, designed ever smaller and sparser spaces constructed of such commonplace materials as wood, thatch, and clay, in which he displayed hanging scrolls of monochrome ink and subdued textiles of browns and grays. In 1591, Hideyoshi ordered Rikyū to commit ritual suicide. Although contemporary research suggests that their conflict was primarily political, this suicide has often been described as the result of an aesthetic impasse. Rikyū's death marked the end of the predominance of the medieval aesthetic, although the Way of Tea as Rikyū interpreted it has had a profound and lasting effect on Japanese aesthetics up to the present. Two or three of the most beautiful, complex, and subtle grays and browns from the groups known as "actor's colors" and the "forty-eight browns and one hundred grays" of the late Edo period are known by his name.

The Edo period was characterized by almost constant conflict between the rising merchant class and the Tokugawa shogunate, an interplay that directly and dramatically affected the development of the textile arts. A long series of sumptuary laws forbidding the use of luxury fabrics, bright colors, and complex weaves gradually led to the development of a variety of plain-woven fabrics of common materials such as *asa* (hemp, ramie), cotton, and rough silk patterned by various dyeing techniques rather than by complex weave structures. Ironically, these *kasuri* (thread-resist), *katazome* (paste-resist/stencil), *tsutsugaki* (freehand paste-resist), and *shibori* (tie-dye) textiles, as well as simple striped and checked fabrics dyed in a range of subdued colors, are now regarded by many critics more highly than the late Edo satins and brocades produced by looms sponsored by the shogunate and its retainers.

As the Edo period opened under the authoritarian military government established by Tokugawa Ieyasu in Edo (present-day Tokyo), private Kyoto workshops were firmly established at the hub of a thriving textile industry that catered to the demands of a widening samurai and merchant clientele. In the atmosphere of growing prosperity that pervaded much of the seventeenth century, merchants as well as aristocrats and members of the privileged military class patronized the most famous weaving and dyeing establishments. Sumptuary laws were widely ignored or circumvented. The striking black, red, and gold *kosode* that characterize the brief Keichō period (1596–1615), for example, were enjoyed by both samurai and merchants alike.

The height of merchant patronage of extravagant textiles took place at the turn of the century during the flamboyant Genroku era (1688–1703, or culturally approximately 1675–1725), a fifty-year period that saw the first flowering of a distinctive bourgeois culture with its own literature (the novelist Saikaku Ihara, 1642–93), drama (Chikamatsu Monzaemon, 1653–1724, who wrote plays for the popular theater, both Bunraku and Kabuki), and the "floating world" of the pleasure quarters, Yoshiwara in Edo, Shinmachi in Osaka, and Shimabara in Kyoto.

A story from the Genroku era conveys the spirit of the age. On a certain day, according to one version, the wives of three famous merchants gathered in Kyoto's fashionable Higashiyama district for a costume competition. The wife of Naniwaya Juemon of Osaka wore a safflower-scarlet kosode with depictions of Kyoto's most famous scenic spots embroidered in silver and gold on a ground of figured satin. The wife of Ishikawa Rokubei of Edo wore a kosode decorated with a profusion of scattered coral beads representing *nanten* (*Nandina domestica*) berries, a plant that appears frequently in literature as well as in the gardens of Japan. The acknowledged winner of

Merrymaking under the Cherry Blossoms (top)
Kanō Naganobu
Momoyama period, early 17th century
Six-fold screen; ink, colors, and gold on paper
Collection of the Tokyo National Museum, Registered National Treasure

Noh costume (above)
Early Edo Period, 17th century
Ink and silver on silk
Asian Art Museum of San Francisco, The Avery Brundage Collection, B62 M74

the competition, however, was the wife of the master of the old merchant house of Nakamura in Kyoto, who wore a costume designed by the famous artist Ogata Kōrin (1658–1716), an old family friend. Over a pure white under-robe, she wore a simple black kosode bound with an obi of antique gold brocade.[20]

The ostentation and unimaginative cultural referents of the Osaka kosode, the assured charm of the entry from Edo, and the understated elegance of the Nakamura kosode express the variety of aesthetic sensibilities typical of the vibrant diversity of the Genroku era.

Conservative reform in the early eighteenth century included more stringent and strictly enforced sumptuary laws. By the end of the century, prohibitions on materials and techniques, enforced by severe fines and long imprisonment, had a major effect on the textiles commissioned by merchants. Woodblock prints from the late eighteenth and early nineteenth centuries depict a populace dressed in striped, kasuri, shibori, and katazome garments in subtle yet lively gradations of blues, browns, blacks, and grays — a color aesthetic closely associated with the Kabuki stage.

Bursting from the wings to assume a dramatic entrance pose, an actor would let the color reverberate throughout the theater to the cheers of the audience.

In periods when the theater was under strict surveillance, famous actors vied with each other to introduce new shades and tones of the permitted hues. Bursting from the wings to assume a dramatic entrance pose, an actor would let the color reverberate throughout the theater to the cheers of the audience. The next day, the dyehouse responsible for the color would be deluged with orders by enthusiastic patrons. Many of these colors, named for the actor who introduced them, have been preserved in contemporary woodblock prints.

Dye recipes were complex, as the creation of a wide range of colors from a strictly limited number of dye materials required considerable skill and ingenuity.[21] Complexity also served to protect a popular color from theft by a rival dyehouse. Recipes were transmitted orally and were so carefully guarded that many have been lost. Today we know less about producing the palette of the late Edo period than we do about reproducing the colors used at the Heian court.

The late Edo period saw a widespread popularization of the textile arts, and many of the same styles, patterns, materials, and techniques were found in both urban and rural areas. Most of the cotton and asa textiles used in the cities were produced in the countryside, often by women working at home in the agricultural off-season, although by the end of the period well-organized workshops had developed in many areas. Most of these textiles were dyed a deep indigo blue by local professional indigo dyers.[22]

The Tokugawa shoguns continued to patronize silk weavers throughout the Edo period. Early eighteenth-century improvements in the production of raw silk thread and the development of virtuosic weaving and dyeing skills are reflected in the brocades and satins of the late Edo period. Like many other arts supported primarily by the Tokugawa, however, these textiles often appear stultified and repetitious in comparison with those of Momoyama and early Edo.

The actor Bando Mitsugoro V as a warrior dueling at night (top)
Kunisada Utagawa
Edo period, probably 1823
Woodblock print
Spencer Museum of Art, 00.1478

Portrait of actors Ichikawa Danjurō VII and Iwai Hanshirō V struggling with Minamoto banner (above)
Kunisada Utagawa
Edo period, probably 1827
Woodblock print
Spencer Museum of Art, 00.1485

The textiles created by and for the general populace, on the other hand, display a rich diversity, the product of a curious combination of historical factors that included the strict prohibitions on material and color imposed by the shogunate, the available wealth of a vigorous merchant class, and the input of the rural populace. The liveliness, balance, quietude, and vibrant yet subtle colors of the textiles from this period are understood by many Japanese to be an expression of a deeply felt native sensibility. Recently (and sooner in the West than in Japan) they have also been evaluated as among the finest examples of Japan's rich textile tradition.

Mary Dusenbury is Curatorial Associate at the Spencer Museum of Art, Lawrence, Kansas, and doctoral student in Japanese art, University of Kansas.

Acknowledgments:
I would like to thank Stephen Addiss, Jerry Dusenbury, and Patricia Fister for their helpful criticisms; Margaret Childs for guidance in Classical translations; and Seiki Nagasaki, professor emeritus at Kyoto University of Arts, who introduced me to the depth and richness of this field of study.

1. This is the final stanza of a poem by Otomo no Yakamochi (716–85), governor of Etchū (present-day Toyama), addressed to one of his scribes; see *Man'yōshū*, in vol. IV of *Nihon koten bungaku taikei* (The Great Compendium of Japanese Classical Literature), vol. VII, Book 18, poem no. 4109, p. 289.

2. Many of the goods that flowed into Japan from the continent have been preserved in the Hōryūji and in the Shōsō'in Repository of the Tōdaiji in Nara. Among them are more than 180,000 textiles, an invaluable source for the study of seventh- and eighth-century fabric in the greater Tang cultural area.

3. An alternate pronunciation of the Chinese characters used for the name of this office is *uchi no some no tsukasa*. See *Genshoku senshoku daijiten* (Fundamental Encyclopedia of Textiles), (Kyoto: Tankōsha, 1977).

4. See Yukihiro Tsunoyama, *Nihon senshoku hatten-shi* (Origins of Weaving and Dyeing in Japan), (Tokyo: Tabata Shoten, 1968).

5. The Palace Dyeing Office might originally have been managed by a continental craftsman, as were many other government offices and workshops at that time.

6. *Nihon akane* or "Japanese madder" (*Rubia cordifolia* L. var. *mungista* Miq.) now grows wild in Japan. It was probably used from at least the late prehistoric period to dye textiles. A late third-century Chinese document, the *Wei-shi* (History of Wei), lists gifts sent from the Japanese priestess-ruler Himiko to the Chinese emperor and includes textiles that clearly seem to have been dyed with indigo and madder. See *Gishi Wajin den* in the *Wei-shi*, in *Iwanami bunko no. 4370* (Tokyo: Iwanami Shoten, 1974), p. 37ff.

A poem in the eighth-century *Kojiki* (Record of Ancient Matters) suggests that madder was originally imported from the continent. If this interpretation is correct, it means that "Japanese madder" was not native, but was brought from the continent by early immigrants, probably in the Yayoi period (ca. 300 B.C. to A.D. 300). On the other hand, the poem might refer to either of two other madder species, *Rubia cordifolia* L. and *Rubia tinctorum*; both have also been used in Japan and are much better dye plants than Nihon akane. It is not clear which species was used at the Nara court, but it seems likely that court dyers had access to the same species of madder used by continental dyers.

Indigo: The textiles mentioned in the *Wei-shi* were dyed with *yama-ai* or "mountain indigo" (*Mercurialis leiocarpa* Sieb. & Zucc.). The court dyers, on the other hand, probably worked with a better species brought from the continent, *tade-ai* (*Polygonum tinctorium* Lour.), the species still used in Japan today.

7. Gromwell was native to Japan, but probably had not been cultivated or used as a dye material before this time. Safflower was imported from the continent and cultivated. Sappanwood, which grows in the warm climate of southeastern Asia, was imported in the form of dried wood chips. Sappanwood is comparatively easy to use, but it requires considerable knowledge and skill to produce consistently good colors and to control the shades and tones of gromwell purple and safflower red.

In the mid-1970s, the Nao Tanaka dye shop in Kyoto devoted several issues of its quarterly journal *Senshoku to seikatsu* (Textiles for Living), to specific traditional dye materials. See *Benibanazome* (Safflower Dyeing), 2 (Summer 1973); *Nihon no ai* (Indigo of Japan), 10 (Fall 1975); and *Murasakizome* (Murasaki Dyeing), 11 (Winter 1975).

8. The *Shu ji* (Book of History), ca. sixth century B.C., in an account of the unifying, nation-building activities of the mythical First Emperor, forges a conjunction among the most important components of the universe, including the Five Directions, the Seasons, the Five Elements, and the Five Colors:

East-Spring-Wood-Blue/Green
South-Summer-Fire-Red
West-Autumn-Metal-White
North-Winter-Water-Black
Center-Earth-Yellow

See James Legge, *The Chinese Classics* (Oxford: The Clarendon Press, 1861–72); and Wing-tsit Chan, *A Source Book of Chinese Philosophy* (Princeton, New Jersey: Princeton University Press, 1963).

Purple seems to have been added to the spectrum of ritually "correct" colors at least by the Han dynasty, and was always associated with very high rank. It was undoubtedly added for aesthetic reasons, as the only references to it in the Classics that this author is aware of link it with frivolity and extravagance (Legge, *Confucian Analects*, 1861, p. 94, for example). Justification for its inclusion linked it somehow to the yin-yang theory, suggesting that it symbolized the unity that transcended the duality of yin and yang and thus expressed the ultimate harmony of the universe. This certainly seems to be appropriate attire for those surrounding the Son of Heaven, but there appears to be some justification after the fact about the designation of the color purple as a ritually correct color. Helen Minnich cites this interpretation, basing her comments on an eighteenth-century lexicon compiled in Japan by Kiyoshi Hasegawa; see her *Japanese Costume and the Makers of its Elegant Tradition* (Rutland, Vermont: Charles E. Tuttle, 1963).

9. For example: In the third month of summer "orders are given by the officers of women's (work), on the subject of dyeing…that the white and black, the black and green, the green and carnation [red], the carnation and white, be all according to the ancient rules, without error or change; and that their black, yellow, azure [blue], and carnation be all genuine and good, without any presumptuous attempts at imposition. These furnish the materials for the robes used at the sacrifices in the suburbs and the ancestral temple; for flags and their ornaments; and for marking the different degrees of rank as high or low." See James Legge, ed., Ch'u Chai and Winberg Chai, *Li Chi: Book of Rites* (New Hyde Park, New York: University Books, 1967), vol. 1, p. 278.

For a discussion of color and rank in ancient China, see Hsi-pao Chou, *Zhong-guo gu-dai fu shi shi* (A History of Costume in Ancient China), (Beijing: Zhong-guo xi-ju, 1984).

10. Information on the ranked colors may be found in Ujō Maeda, *Nihon kodai no shikisai to some* (Color and Dye in Ancient Japan), (Tokyo: Kawade Shobōshinsha, 1975), and Seiki Nagasaki, *Iro no Nihonshi* (A History of Color in Japan), (Tokyo: Tankōsha, 1977).

11. Several books illustrating and discussing the color combinations used for women's court costume were published in the late 1980s. One of the best is Seiki Nagasaki, *Kasane no irome* (Layered Colors), (Kyoto: Kyoto Shōin, 1988).

The layered colors, as they were codified, were based on three documents: the *Masasuke shōzoku-shō* (Notes on Costume), written by Minamoto Masasuke in the late Heian period, the *Jokan kazari-shō* (A Costume Compendium for Court Ladies of Official Rank), by Ichijo Kaneyoshi in Muromachi, and the *Dongeinden shōzoku-shō* (The Dongeinden Costume Compendium), attributed to Shinshū Nigū in the second quarter of the sixteenth century. Nagasaki reproduces, illustrates, and discusses each of these documents.

12. Two English translations of the *Genjimonogatari* are available: Murasaki Shikibu, *The Tale of Genji*, Arthur Waley, trans., (London: G. Allen and Unwin, 1925–34, republished New York: The Modern Library, 1960), and, more recently, a translation by Edward Siedensticker (New York: Alfred A. Knopf, 1986).

Both offer a general sense of how color is used in *The Tale of Genji*, but neither takes Murasaki Shikibu's use of color as seriously as do modern Japanese critics who have explored the rich complexity of Heian color in considerable depth. The *Nihon koten bungaku taikei* (Great Compendium of Japanese Classical Literature), Tokubei Yamagishi, ed., (Tokyo: Iwanami shoten, 1969) edition of the *Genji* gives explicit headnotes and commentary on color terms. For a more general discussion of the role of color in Heian literature see Aki Ihara, *Heian-chō bungaku no shikisō* (Color in Heian Literature), (Tokyo: Chūō Kōronsha, 1982).

13. An interesting and important exception is a rich brown created and reserved for the retired emperor, who often took Buddhist vows. *Korozen* was a complex color dyed, in part, with rare and costly cloves imported from southeastern Asia.

14. There are, for example, over half a dozen recipes for purples from gromwell. Ingredients listed for this purple are approximately the same in each recipe, but the amount of prepared dyestuff, vinegar, ash, and even firewood differ for varying shades, intensities, and tones of purple, and, for each variant, differ again depending on whether plain woven silk, figured twill, or silk thread was being dyed, and whether the latter was reeled or pulled.

The *Engishiki* passages on color are discussed in the two books cited in n. 10. The section on purple from the fourteenth scroll is quoted in Maeda, *Nihon kodai no shikisai to some*, p. 174ff.

15. Genji's protegée Tamakatsura is taken into the palace for this purpose; see Seidenstricker, *Tale of Genji*, chaps. 22-31.

The office apparently kept Tamakatsura very busy: "It was now the Eleventh Month, a time of Shinto festivals, which kept her busy. She had offices at Rokujō, where she was visited by a steady stream of chamberlains and ladies-in-waiting. His Excellency the general [her new husband], hoping that he was not making a nuisance of himself, spent his days with her. She did in fact think him rather a nuisance." (p. 492)

16. Kazuko Takimoto, unpublished manuscript; see Mary Dusenbury with Kazuko Takimoto, *Textiles of Old Japan: Color and Dye* (San Francisco: San Francisco Craft and Folk Art Museum, 1986).

17. Portuguese, Spanish, and Dutch traders and missionaries visited Japan beginning in the mid-sixteenth century. Early in the Edo period the Tokugawa government closed the country, allowing only minimal contact with the Dutch and Chinese at the port of Nagasaki in Kyūshū.

18. Today there are still large growing fields and processing stations in the Tokushima area of Shikoku.

19. By the Edo period, deep, conical, fermentation vats were set into the tamped earth floor and heated, probably as they are today, with a small fire set in the middle of each set of four vats. Scholars differ on the advent of *shōaizome* (dyeing with sukumo in heated vats). For a discussion, see Monica Bethe, "Color: Dyes and Pigments," in *Kosode: 16th-19th Century Textiles from the Nomura Collection*, by Amanda Mayer Stinchecum (New York: Japan Society and Kodansha International, 1984), pp. 217-18.

20. The story exists in several versions, and all suggest scorn of ostentation and emphasize the understated elegance of the Kyoto woman. This version follows Seiroku Noma, *Japanese Costume and Textile Arts* (The Heibonsha Survey of Japanese Art), Armins Nikovskis, trans., (Tokyo, New York: Weatherhill / Heibonsha, 1974), p. 87f.

In a version cited by Seiki Nagasaki, *Iro no Nihonshi*, p. 173f, the wife of Nakamura Kuranosuke of Kyoto changed repeatedly from a pure white to a pure black kosode, dressing her maid in embroidered brocade.

21. *Araragi* (red yew), *zakuro* (pomegranate), *ume* (plum), *cha* (tea), *yashabushi* (alder), *gobaishi* (gall nuts), *chōji* (cloves), and *yamamomo* (mountain peach) with the addition of alum, *aku* (ash lye), and/or an iron mordant, all produce colors in the gray-brown-black range.

22. Indigo produces a full range of blues including *ai*, a clear sky blue, *kon*, a deep "indigo" blue, and *kachi*, a very dark blue-black. Used with skill, indigo is long-lasting, fades little when exposed to light, and strengthens plant fibers such as cotton and asa. By the late Edo period, most towns and many villages had a professional indigo dyer who sometimes kept over thirty working vats of differing ages and intensities. Dyeing was a lengthy process involving multiple dippings, airing for an all-important stage of oxidization, and redipping. A few of these indigo workshops still function today.

BAST FIBERS

LOUISE ALLISON CORT

ONTEMPORARY JAPAN PRODUCES SOME OF THE WORLD'S FINEST fabrics from machine-processed natural fibers and synthetic yarns. From this perspective, the survival of bast-fiber textiles seems paradoxical. In one respect, they are luxury goods: like linen, the bast fiber best known in the West, certain Japanese bast-fiber fabrics sell for exorbitant prices, a reflection of the increasing monetary value of the intensive hand-labor that underlies their harvesting and processing, and that is dignified, in some instances, by the government designation of Intangible Cultural Property. Kimono and *obi* sewn from such fabrics approach the cost of Paris couturier fashions. In another guise, certain other bast fibers are relics from the past: coarse, stiff, naturally brown in color, and resistant to dyes, they survive only through the loving attention of small groups of dedicated makers, and their meaning lies in their nostalgic value rather than in any practical requirement.

Bast fibers did not always occupy this marginal position among Japanese textiles. Until quite recently — in certain areas, within living memory of elders — bast-fiber textiles played much more central roles, which ranged across a wider spectrum of use and cost. Even in the past, certain bast-fiber fabrics such as the finest thread-banana cloth (*bashōfu*) or ramie (*jōfu*) were luxury goods whose use was restricted to the noble and the wealthy. Indeed, what is perceived in awe today as the "intensive labor" required to produce luxurious bast-fiber fabrics was simply the minimal effort applied in earlier eras; far higher standards prevailed to measure the finest quality of such fabrics, which to the naked eye are indistinguishable from silk and which required an almost unimaginable — certainly today an unaffordable — patience. At the other extreme, certain coarse bast-fiber cloth was always treated as utility cloth for bags and household furnishings.

In a manner that anticipates the printmaker M.C. Escher, diagonal panels of sinuous dragons and clouds interlock with images of hares and wooden mortars and pestles.

Vanished for good, replaced by cotton and synthetics, is the central role of homemade bast-fiber yardage for the everyday garments of commoners, especially farmers and laborers in the mountains. Until cotton began to be cultivated widely in Japan, the women of rural and mountain households collected, processed, and wove bast fibers to clothe all the household members. Indigo-dyed cotton became typical commoners' clothing only relatively recently; the mistaken impression of its predominance arises from the fact that most surviving cotton garments date from the nineteenth century. Even then, in remote areas where terrains were inhospitable to cotton cultivation or where cash to buy market cloth was scarce, bast-fiber clothing continued to be worn. Brown, not blue, was once the identifying color of Japan's peasantry, just as white was the privileged color of its elite.

Among bast-fiber textiles, the distinction between luxury and utility parallels differences in physical characteristics among different subcategories of the fibers. Virtually all "bast fibers" are recovered from the phloem, the vascular-system tissue located in the inner bark of the stems of dicotyledonous plants. (Technically *bashō*, which is usually discussed as a bast fiber, is a leaf fiber, rather than a stem fiber, of the thread-, or fiber, banana plant, *Musa liukiuensis*). They consist of elongated cell bundles which, when separated from the surrounding soft tissue by the process of controlled rotting (called retting) and split into constituent elements, hold their shape and can be manipulated as "threads."[1]

Brown, not blue, was once the identifying color of Japan's peasantry, just as white was the privileged color of the elite.

The bast-fiber threads from grasses differ significantly from those of vines and trees. Grass-bast fibers, known collectively in Japan as *asa* and represented by hemp (Jap., *taima*; *Cannabis sativa*) and ramie (Jap., *chōma* or *karamushi*; *Boehmeria nivea*[2]), seem to have been cultivated in fields from the time of their introduction to Japan.[3] Bleaching of ramie in particular produced a lustrous white fabric that figured importantly as a ground for luxurious, pictorially dyed fabrics such as the *chayatsuji* and *hontsuji*, which were worn as summer garments by women in the court and in high-ranking warrior households. The bast fibers of various plants that grew wild on the mountain slopes, including the trees *kōzo* (*Broussonetia kazinoki*) and *kaji* (*Broussonetia papyrifera*) in the paper mulberry family, and the vines wisteria (*fuji*, *Wistaria chinensis*) and *kuzu* (*Pueraria hirsuta*), tended to have tougher fibers that did not yield their natural brown color to available bleaching procedures.[4] Moreover, whereas hemp and ramie fibers could be lightly twisted or spun into a continuous thread, most vine- or tree-bast fibers were so stiff that the individual fibers had to be split and joined end to end by more elaborate twisting or even tying. (The same process must be used for thread banana.)

Accordingly, certain bast fibers with the greatest potential for refinement of color and texture — ramie and thread-banana — tended to develop as regional specialties that were marketed throughout the country. (Bashōfu was a product of the Ryūkyūs, but after the Satsuma domain seized control of the island kingdom in 1609, the cloth was sent to Japan as tribute and also distributed through the market system.) Other bast fibers that yielded serviceable but coarse cloth — hemp, wisteria, kōzo — were used locally for clothing fabric, but the cloth also was distributed in the commercial market for such specialized uses as bags for squeezing sake lees.

In short, Japan once had a far more diverse pool of bast-fiber textiles. Bast from wisteria was processed and woven widely in western Japan until the early twentieth century and was used for work clothes, lining cloths for wooden or earthenware food steamers, tatami edging, and even gauze-woven fishing nets. The tree called *mada* throughout northeastern Japan and *shina* in the mountainous area of central Japan (*Tillia cordata*) provided sturdy brown fiber for weavers. The fiber of the related tree called *hera* was woven in northeastern Kyūshū and also used for rope and raincapes, and the tree was transplanted to the San'in coast for use in weaving sailcloth. While not strictly a bast fiber, the fuzzy coating of wild fiddlehead ferns (*zenmai*, *Osmanda regalis*) yielded a useful if painstakingly produced fiber for weavers in northeastern

Japan. The perennial grass called *irakusa* (*Urtica thungeriana*) was harvested in early autumn in many parts of the country for its white fiber. On the northern coast, a species of maple called *ureki* (*Acer crataegifolium*) yielded fiber for raincapes and cloth. Sometimes the choice of fibers was extremely site-specific, as in the use of kuzu on the Koshiki Islands off southern Kyūshū where flat land for growing asa was at a premium.[5]

The market accommodated and even encouraged such diversity. The *Kefukigusa*, a 1638 publication that enumerates all the special regional products obtainable within the great cultural and commercial metropolis of Kyoto, lists an abundance of bast-fiber textiles.[6] Among asa products, fine bleached ramie and hemp mosquito netting came from Yamato and Ōmi provinces (present-day Nara and Shiga prefectures) south of Kyoto; special-quality Ōmi ramie was known by the poetic name of *saimi* (fine and beautiful). Asa thread and coarser grades of mosquito netting came from provinces to the west.[7] Ramie yardage came from most of the provinces in eastern and northeastern Japan, whereas cotton was still limited to the warmer southern provinces. "Thick cloth" (*tafu*, made from tree-bast fibers, most often mulberry) came from Tamba, Tosa, and Satsuma provinces (Hyogo, Kōchi, and Kagoshima prefectures). Satsuma, as administrator of the Ryūkyūs, also distributed bashōfu as one of its own "famous products." The post-town of Kakegawa, in Tōtōmi province (Shizuoka prefecture), supplied *kuzufu*, made from glistening kuzu vine fiber and favored for use in warriors' jackets and trousers. The *Kefukigusa* was written in the early stages of organization of national market networks for regional products under the Tokugawa government (1603–1868); later surveys of major urban marketplaces would have located even more local specialties.

Most of the ramie yardage sold in Kyoto probably entered the city's famed dyeing workshops to be ornamented in polychrome *yūzenzome* with currently stylish motifs; the finished cloth was redistributed throughout the country, ready to be tailored into fashionable garments. Of the ramie garments discussed here, Kyoto workshops were almost certainly responsible for the dyed designs as well as the Chinese-style silk brocade on the warrior's jacket (cat. 33). Matching jackets of this cut, *kajibanten*, were worn during ceremonial drills by firefighting brigades of samurai assigned to the home castles and Edo mansions of military rulers (daimyo), and they were ordered through drapers in Kyoto who served as purveyors to the daimyo domains of fine cloth and other Kyoto products. Summer versions of the jackets were tailored of ramie or kuzu while winter ones were of cotton or wool (cat. 34); both featured the daimyo's family crest prominently on the back. (These delicate jackets contrast in cut and material to the heavy garments made for actual firefighting activities by townsmen and warriors, (cat. 15-17), although the dyed designs tend to be equally striking.) None but a Kyoto designer could have provided the complex and sophisticated mix of auspicious Chinese motifs for the ramie garment made to be worn by a male child of a warrior household (cat. 41). In a manner that anticipates the printmaker M. C. Escher (1898–1972), diagonal panels of sinuous dragons and clouds interlock with silhouetted images of hares and wooden mortars and pestles. According to Chinese folklore, the moon is home to a hare who extracts the elixir of immortality in a mortar. Where the hare figures "enter" the dragon-and-cloud motifs, the wavelike appendages of the undulating dragons help to create a third motif, a hare leaping over waves, an image popular with warriors. Only a superior quality of ramie could have served as ground for the finely drawn designs.

Kyoto workshops also designed the specialized ramie costumes for the comic theater known as Kyogen (cat. 26). Performed in interludes between longer and more somber performances of Noh, the major theatrical form patronized by the warrior class during the Edo period, Kyogen plays mocked the perennial conflicts between masters and servants. The finely dyed ramie Kyogen costumes parodied the coarser hemp garments worn by real servants. Their large figurative motifs, such as turnips (cat. 26), suggest the simple-mindedness that usually characterizes the would-be "clever" servants. The kimono to be worn by an actor-merchant (cat. 61), made of the sort of plaid provincial silk favored by real merchants for everyday wear, contains panels of "humble" hemp embroidered in gold with sheaves of harvested rice, emblematic of wealth.

In contrast to the dyes of many hues that were the specialty of Kyoto workshops, provincial textiles dyers tended to use indigo. Well-born women never left their homes without covering their heads with an overgarment, a *kazuki*, which served the purpose of a cloak and veil. The ramie kazuki (cat. 24 and 26) probably afforded proper modesty to the wives of prominent merchants in provincial cities, where the crisply dyed motifs in shades of indigo were also executed.

Indigo was the dye used for ikat or *kasuri* patterning on many distinctive regional styles of ramie such as Echigo jōfu and Ōmi jōfu. Ōmi jōfu was a familiar fabric for everyday garments in Kyoto since it was produced in adjacent Ōmi province. In addition to the white-on-indigo kasuri, blue- or brown-on-white kasuri fabric was also made, and today elderly Kyoto citizens still remember wearing it during their childhood summers.

The production of Ōmi jōfu, recorded as early as the fifteenth century, typified the procedures that generated many fine-quality regional bast-fiber textiles. Merchants based in the highway town of Takamiya coordinated the cottage-industry process, buying raw asa in the mountains of eastern Ōmi and distributing it to women specialists who spun and twisted it as warp thread. Other merchants collected untwisted weft threads prepared by farm women and wives of townsmen and poor samurai in towns throughout southern Ōmi. (The Ōmi pottery center of Shigaraki produced unglazed stoneware cylinders in which the prepared threads were coiled; Shigaraki "ramie buckets" became favored found objects as tea-ceremony utensils.) The threads were delivered to specialists to have the kasuri patterns bound and dyed, then to weavers, usually young women. Brokers transferred the woven cloth for washing (and if undyed, for bleaching) to finishers who were concentrated in the Ōmi town of Yasu.[8] After 1600 Takamiya lay within the Hikone domain, which sent annual tribute of Ōmi jōfu to the shogun in Edo.

Various grades of "Takamiya cloth" were used by all classes of people in Ōmi, including warriors, Shinto priests and Buddhist monks, townspeople, and farmers. Similarly, in the Ryūkyū Islands, thread-banana fiber was prepared into bashōfu of varying qualities to serve everyone from king to peasant. Records of Chinese observers in the fourteenth through sixteenth centuries indicate that bashōfu garments were worn in summer, while ramie

Cat. 61 (detail)
Kimono, perhaps for dance
Yoke: Edo period, late 18th century
Body: Meiji-Taishō period, early 20th century, from Hachijō Island
Yoke: bast fiber (asa) cloth with metallic thread couching and silk thread embroidery
Body: silk cloth with woven plaid pattern (koshi), 89.142

(Oki., *bu*) was preferred for winter in the subtropical climate.⁹ A Korean document of 1546 recorded that three different grades of bashōfu were made from the varying qualities of fiber in the thread-banana plant, and that "the finest grade is white as snow, smooth and flawless as a beautiful woman's skin."¹⁰ Each piece of the thread-banana stalk — formed of leaf sheaths wrapped tightly in concentric layers, opening into "leaves" only at the very top — has fiber on both surfaces, sandwiching a pulpy center, but only the long fibers on the outer surface are used for weaving. (The short fibers of the inner surface formerly were used by papermakers.) Furthermore, the quality of the fiber is best on the innermost layers, where it is protected from the elements. An 1872 report on bashōfu production identified six different grades of fiber, indicating the great skill with which maximum diversity was teased from a single resource. The three outermost layers were graded for use as heavy thread, cords, and ropes. The fourth layer from the outside was used for work clothes, the fifth for everyday garments, and the sixth for garments for formal occasions. Only the three innermost leaf-sheaths on a given plant yielded the finest grade of fiber.¹¹

The very finest quality of banana-fiber cloth was woven in Shuri, the royal capital, and was not traded on the market but sent to the court. Shuri bashōfu was dyed in brilliant shades of yellow, red, blue, and green. Various ikat patterns were employed, as were complex woven designs — gauze weaves and floating-warp patterns — probably borrowed from techniques used in weaving Chinese silks. Plain-weave thread-banana cloth was patterned colorfully with the Okinawan stencil-resist technique called *bingata*.

Okinawan warriors wore unlined bashōfu garments for everyday use in summer and unlined ramie for formal occasions (in winter the corresponding fabrics were cotton and lined silk). The ramie garment with silk stripes (cat. 62) may well have been a warrior's costume, since commoners were not permitted to wear silk under Edo-period sumptuary laws. Commoners wore cotton or bashōfu in winter and bashōfu in summer.¹² Only plain-weave bashōfu was permitted. The only patterns allowed were blue or reddish brown stripes (narrower for men than for women, and for elders than for young people), except for dark, small-figure printed patterns (imitating kasuri, but less time-consuming) permitted to women for formal occasions.¹³ Only after the end of Tokugawa rule in 1868 did commoners adopt the full range of Okinawan textile-decorating techniques, and they developed their own hierarchy: double ikat for formal garments (cat. 63); simple ikat, checks, and stripes for everyday ware; and stripes or plain cloth for work clothes.¹⁴

Okinawan bashōfu was receptive to a wide range of decorative treatments, although their deployment varied along the social hierarchy. Certain other bast fibers, coarser and more resistant to dye, depended for embellishment upon additive techniques including appliqué and embroidery. Often the embellishing materials were brought from outside and were limited in supply, testing the skill of the embellishers to use them to maximum effect. Peasant women of the far northern end of Honshu, in the Tsugaru and Nambu regions of what is now Aomori prefecture, quilted together layers of local indigo-dyed hemp or ramie with densely spaced ornamental stitches of asa thread to produce garments that were visually arresting at the same time as they were warm and durable (cat. 5). Whenever possible, the women

Cat. 63. (detail)
Unlined robe
Meiji period, late 19th-early 20th century, Okinawa
Ryūkyūan construction
Fiber-banana *(bashō)* cloth with cotton warp stripes and weft ikat, 89.100

enlivened the hemp with patches of ikat-dyed jōfu (cat. 9) or replaced them with kasuri- or *shibori*-patterned cotton, stitching with white cotton thread (cat. 7). These precious fabrics were brought by coastal trading ships that returned south loaded with rice grown in the Tsugaru region facing the Japan Sea coast. Garments from Nambu, which had less to offer the traders, were more often restricted to the local hemp.[15]

Still farther north, the indigenous Ainu population of Hokkaido Island used the bast fiber from the tree of the elm (*Ulmus*) family known as *ohyō* to make the robe called *attush*[16] (Jap., *atsushi*). The bark was stripped from the living tree before it began its spring growth; the inner bark was soaked and washed and then split into threads that produced a dense, warm, yellowish brown fabric.[17] Most surviving attush, however, show use of fabrics from the south, which had been traded for animal furs and skins, dried fish, and other goods. Some ohyō fabrics include cotton warp stripes. Elaborate bilaterally symmetrical patterns were rendered over much of the garment in a combination of appliqué and chain-stitched embroidery and incorporate indigo-dyed cotton, red silk, or even remnants of tie-dyed and embroidered kimono that once clothed elegant urban women and were later sold to rag dealers; Russian cotton chintzes also appear. Sometimes the whole body of the garment replaces ohyō with Japanese striped, plaid, or kasuri-patterned cotton recovered from second-hand clothing (cat. 1 and 3).

The juxtapositions are striking to the modern eye, but the Ainu makers were concerned with fabricating the kind of god-pleasing "ornament" that was the very basis of their identity as "humans" (*ainu*).[18] Evidence from Ainu epic literature suggests that the patterns represented flames, and the robes were most impressive when worn in multiple layers.[19] In one epic sung by a woman, the protagonist relates:

Cat. I (detail)
Ainu robe (*attusi*)
Late Edo-early Meiji period,
19th century
Elm bark fiber (*ohyō*) cloth
with cotton cloth appliqué
and cotton thread chain-
stitch embroidery, 89.136

...day after day,
I remained staring
after the many needle paths,
after the countless needle paths,
and in the paths of my needle
there would take form
many swirling patterns,
countless swirling patterns.
The upper clothing racks
and the lower clothing racks
would bend down under the weight
of the beautiful robes
which I had embroidered.
There was a brilliant glittering
over the clothing racks
where hung the beautiful robes
which I had embroidered.[20]

The bark was stripped from the tree before spring growth; the inner bark was soaked and then split into threads that produced a dense, warm, yellowish brown fabric.

The price paid for augmented ornament was high, however; the attush in this catalogue were produced by a declining Ainu population racked by contagious diseases resulting from contact with the Japanese; between 1822 and 1854, the total Ainu population fell from 24,339 to 18,805.[21]

Against all odds, production of bast-fiber textiles continues in many parts of Japan, carried on in remote areas by elderly women and men who will not abandon the skills they know until they die, or else by younger women who have learned the skills and are determined to continue them. Thanks to modern communication systems, groups of weavers making *tafu* in an isolated mountain village on Shikoku Island and weaving *shinafu* in northeastern Japan are in contact with each other, sharing their lore, problems, and goals. They struggle with the question of how to make their fabrics accessible and meaningful in a transformed world, yet all of them find personal meaning in the continuation. One textile historian reflected:

> As I held the [tafu] grain bag that had been in continuous use for fifty or sixty years and that even now was undamaged, I felt as though I were looking at the character of the person who wove the cloth so well. Even if tafu is reproduced using the same processes as in the past, the life of the past when such cloth was worn is unlikely to return. Nevertheless, from the warmth of this natural fiber that could stand up to use over decades, and from the manner of living of those people who gave themselves devotedly to association with it, I felt that I had many things to learn.[22]

Louise Allison Cort is assistant curator for ceramics, Arthur M. Sackler Museum, Smithsonian Institution, Washington, D.C.

1. Ludwig Weindling, *Long Vegetable Fibers* (New York: Columbia University Press, 1947), p. 15; Gordon Cook, *Handbook of Textile Fibers — Natural Fibers*, 4th ed. (Watford, England: Merrow, 1968), pp. 3-4.

2. Ramie has recently become familiar as a commercial fiber that is used alone for crisp, linenlike fabric or mixed with cotton in heavier knits. The current sources of ramie are the People's Republic of China, the Philippines, and Brazil (Lisa Belkin, "A Loophole Lets Fiber Surge," *The New York Times*, September 6, 1986).

3. The introduction of grass-bast fibers into Japan seems closely related to the introduction of wet-field rice cultivation; evidence for the transmission of the latter from the Korean peninsula (based on the strain of rice) by the third century B.C. is now known at sites in northern Kyūshū.

4. Grass-bast fibers could be bleached in salt water (for example, the jōfu of the Noto Peninsula or Ryūkūan bashōfu) or on snow (Echigo jōfu and Ojiya *chijimi*, both ramie fabrics from Echigo province [modern Niigata prefecture]). The usual bleach for tree-bast fibers was lye from wood ash; today stronger chemical bleaches render the paper mulberry fibers snow-white.

5. Takeuchi Junko, "Ki no nuno, kusa no nuno" (Cloth from trees, cloth from grasses), *Aruku-miru-kiku*, 184 (June 1982), pp. 20-30.

6. Takenouchi Waka, ed., *Kefukigusa* (Tokyo: Iwanami Shoten, 1976), pp. 157-87.

7. Asa had long been in demand in Japan's urban centers; the document of A.D. 927 known as the *Engishiki* (Institute of the Engi Era) lists offerings of asa as tribute from twenty-six of the sixty-six provinces.

8. Moriyoshi Watanabe, *Ōmi asa-shi* (History of Ōmi Asa), (Tokyo: Yuzankaku, 1975), pp. 95-108. A special issue of the Japanese publication *Senshoku to seikatsu*, 26 (Autumn 1979) features textiles of Ōmi.

9. Kunisuke Akashi, *Senshoku monyoshi no kenkyū* (Research on the History of Design Motifs), (Kyoto: Shibunkaku, 1976), p. 373.

10. Akira Tonaki, "Kijoka no bashōfu" (Banana-fiber cloth of Kijoka), in *Kijoka no bashōfu*, Ningen kokuho shiriizu (Living National Treasure series), (Tokyo: Kodansha, 1977), vol. 41, p. 36.

11. Kiyotaro Tsujiai, *Ryūkyū bashōfu* (Banana-fiber Cloth of the Ryūkyūs), (Kyoto: Kyoto Shoin, 1973), pp. 59-62.

12. Ibid., pp. 20-23.

13. Nihon Minzoku Gakkai, *Okinawa no minzokugakuteki kenkyū* (Ethnographic Research on Okinawa), (Tokyo: Minzokugaku Shinkokai, 1973), pp. 114-15.

14. Tonaki, "Kijoka no bashōfu," p. 34.

15. Kiko Horiuchi, "Tsugaru to Nambu no sashiko" (Quilting of Tsugaru and Nambu), *Senshuko no bi*, 9(1981), pp. 89-90.

16. Donald L. Philippi, *Songs of Gods, Songs of Humans: The Epic Tradition of the Ainu* (San Francisco: North Point Press, 1982), p. 31.

17. Takeuchi, "Ki no nuno," pp. 26-28.

18. Kichiemon Okamura, "Yoki no bi" (Bewitching Beauty), *Senshoku no bi*, 29(1984), pp. 96-97; Philippi, *Songs of Gods*, p. 4.

19. In a formulaic phrase, the hero wears *o-uhui nikap attush* ("elm bark fiber coat with its hem in flames"; Philippi, *Songs of Gods*, p. 31). It is described thus: "He wore sixfold/magnificent robes/fastened under his belt,/ and he wore sixfold/magnificent robes/hanging loose" (ibid., p. 35).

20. Ibid., p. 254.

21. Ibid., p. 3.

22. Takeuchi, "Ki no nuno," p. 31.

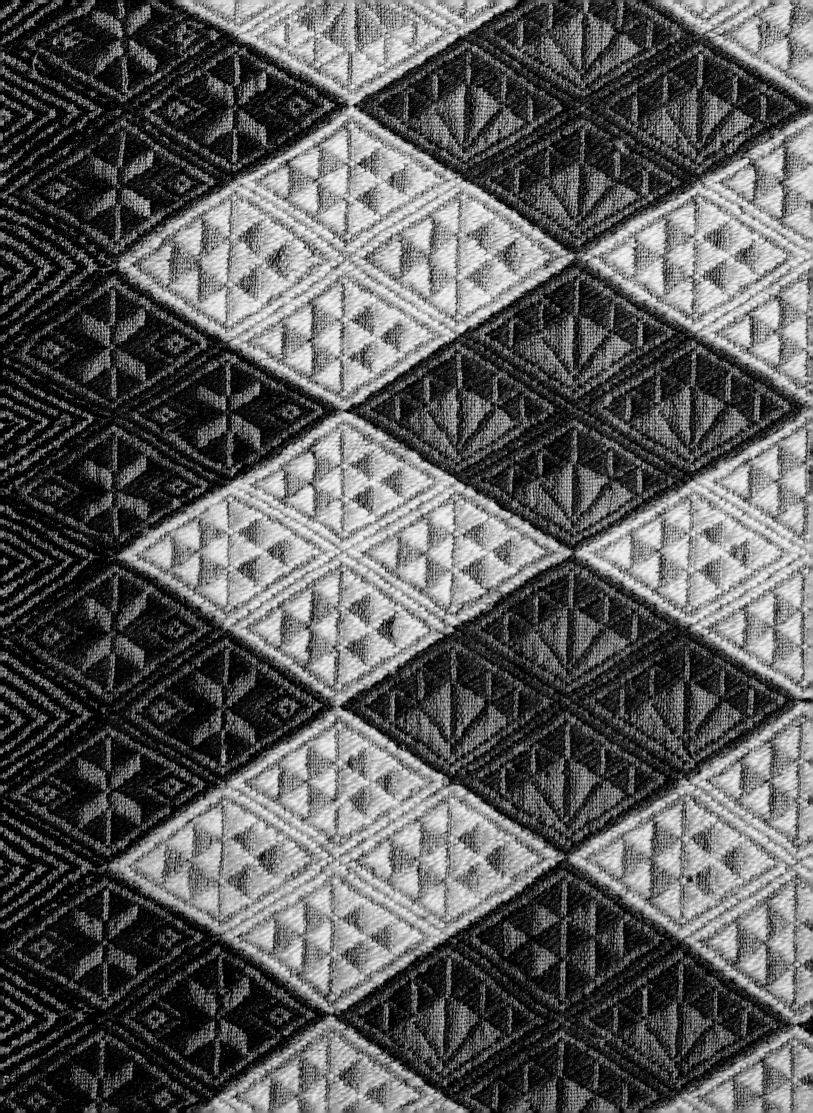

SASHIKO:
A STITCHERY
OF JAPAN

CYNTHIA SHAVER

THE TERM *SASHIKO* (FROM *SASU*, TO PIERCE), WHICH REFERS TO THE stitching of one or more layers of cloth with a simple running stitch, can also apply to the completed fabric. Initially the sashiko technique was probably a way to recycle or extend the life of the cloth. Among the textiles in the Shōsō'in is an eighth-century "distant mountain"-pattern monk's robe covered with a purple silk running stitch. This stitch is not integral to the structure of the robe. A development of an earlier ritual robe, this one has evolved to the point that the stitches have lost their original function of strengthening the garment and attaching the patches of cloth; rather they have been retained to give the appearance of the original concept, the monk's "robe of rags," a symbol of his material poverty and renunciation of worldly things. This eighth-century robe is the oldest example of sashiko extant in Japan.

Sashiko was done throughout Japan, primarily by women. It is not known to have been a commercial technique, with the possible exception of some firemen's clothing. Made by and for people who were too poor to buy new cloth, sashiko developed from necessity rather than as a luxury. With a few exceptions, the art of sashiko was not highly competitive; that is to say, the product was not regarded as a statement of fashion.

Made by and for people who were too poor to buy new cloth, sashiko developed from necessity rather than as a luxury.

Originally a practical technique for making cloth thicker, warmer, and more durable, sashiko can also be purely decorative. Overstitched clothing is both strong and warm; therefore it was reasonable to reinforce the cloth by overstitching before it wore out. Today sashiko is done on new garments and textiles intended for sale in folk-craft shops.

Sashiko stitching is typically applied with white cotton thread on an indigo-dyed fabric. Most sashiko uses a doubled strand of thread, although it can be done with a single strand. The length of the stitch varies with the number of layers being sewn together. Skill and practice are needed to keep the stitches straight and even in length. Stitches number from around four to ten per inch (2.5 cm). Sashiko was done on balanced weave textiles — cloth with warps and wefts of the same thickness and weight of thread. Although the ground-fabric threads were not usually counted, the stitches were. Within a pattern, the same number of stitches and their length is consistent for each line. Many patterns have straight lines that intersect at right angles, so counting the stitches made precise patterns. At the point of intersection,

Cat. 6 (detail)
Apron (maekake)
Meiji period, late 19th century
Quilted (sashiko) cotton cloth and bast fiber (asa) cloth with counted stitch embroidery (hishizashi), 89.131

either the stitching threads cross, creating a pattern, or the threads define a space that reads as a star or the center of a flower, for example.

Sashiko can form one repeating pattern or a combination of several patterns. The most notable sashiko styles developed in Tohoku, the northern part of Japan's main island (including Aomori, Iwate, and Yamagata prefectures). Historically, most of the cloth in this area was made from ramie or hemp; the climate of much of Tohoku was not suitable for growing cotton. The people were restricted to using these fibers because the cost of bringing in cloth from a different region was prohibitive. In addition, government laws restricted the use of certain fibers within social classes.[1] Regional and technical distinctions of sashiko styles within the Tohoku area often reflect differing social and economic distinctions.

Cat. 7 (detail)
Farmer's coat
Meiji period, ca. 1900, Tsugaru
Quilted *(sashiko)* recycled cotton cloth with thread-resist decoration *(shibori)*; sleeves and trim of striped cotton cloth, 89.147

TSUGARU SASHIKO

An "embroidered" kimono (cat. 5), a tie-dyed kimono (cat. 7), and a stencil-dyed vest (cat. 8) are from the Tsugaru area on the Japan Sea side of Aomori prefecture. Tsugaru is a mountainous area with a wet climate quite suitable for growing rice. This circumstance provided considerable economic stability and helped the area become prosperous. The people had a cash economy and so were able to trade with the more cosmopolitan southern area around Edo (Tokyo); the expense of acquiring cloth from other regions in Japan was not an obstacle. Ramie, hemp, and cotton were used for the base fabric, often with a variety of techniques (tie-dye, ikat, stencil dyeing).[2] Combining fabrics dyed by different techniques is typical of the Tsugaru area. The thread of Tsugaru sashiko was white cotton in a horizontal or vertical running stitch, or a combination of both. The main color of the base fabric was dark indigo blue. The darkness of indigo depended on how many times the fabric was dipped in the dye vat. The Japanese used a group of indigo dye vats and multiple dippings rather than continuous dipping in one strong solution. A large quantity of indigo was needed to achieve a deep color, but people of this area were affluent enough so that the greater expense for indigo did not concern them. The sashiko was done over two layers of fabric, usually with new cloth on the outside and old cloth on the inside. Most of the sashiko clothing of Tsugaru were kimono (i.e., an outer wrap such as a coat) or vests.

Kogin stitching developed from sashiko and is found only in Tsugaru. It is a counted-thread embroidery based on the diamond unit, and is laid over and under an odd number of warps. To create the elongated diamond (unlike the 90-degree diamond), the base fabric must be an uneven weave, with more warps than wefts per inch. Kogin stitching uses a straight, horizontal running stitch. The base fabrics woven for kogin stitching were generally loose, allowing the stitcher more easily to count the warp threads. "Kogin" can refer to both the act of stitching and the finished fabric. Kogin (from *koginu* or *kogino*), a word native to the Tsugaru peninsula, originally referred to a rough woven cloth dyed with indigo, with or without stitches.[3] Fabrics with stitching were called *sashikogin*. Kogin stitching was done on ramie or hemp fabrics. In the Tsugaru area, ramie grew wild but eventually was cultivated, as was hemp.

Cotton threads appear after the Kyōhō era (1716–36), they are softer and easier to sew than ramie or hemp thread.[4]

There are three regional styles of kogin garments: east, west, and three-stripe. These distinctions refer to east of, west of, or at the mouth of the Iwaki River, which runs through the center of the Tsugaru peninsula. East kogin garments display a combination of large patterns, and west kogin garments use a combination of small patterns with horizontal stripes on the shoulders. The three-stripe style has different patterns within the pectoral areas and three stripes on the back. The cat's-foot pattern (*neko no ashi*) and the linked-swastika pattern (*sayagata*) were particular to the east side, and the abacus stitch (*soroban zashi*) to the west side. A kimono in this collection (cat. 5) is an example of east kogin.[5]

NAMBU SASHIKO

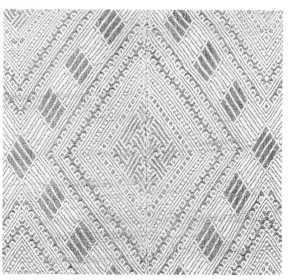

Cat. 5 (detail)
Kimono
Late Edo-early Meiji period,
19th century, Tsugaru
Yoke, shown here: bast fiber
(asa) cloth with cotton thread
embroidery (kogin)
Body: bast fiber (asa) cloth,
89.89

The sashiko of the Nambu area of northeast Aomori and northern Iwate prefectures is bright and simple. The land is very dry and not conducive to rice culture, a key factor that contributed significantly to a region's wealth; hence Nambu was quite poor. The base fabric of Nambu sashiko is a light blue ramie or hemp.[6] The light color (produced by only a few dippings in the indigo vats) was an economy measure. A deep blue fabric, usually cotton, was often layered over the shoulders and edges of a garment. This two-layered area as well as the entire garment was stitched with a dark blue cotton, ramie, or hemp thread. The contrast of the dark blue shoulder panels and thread on a light blue base fabric creates a very light, spare design. The sashiko was done in a simple horizontal running stitch and was used on trousers, kimono, and vests.

Hishizashi, another type of sashiko, comes from the Nambu area around Hachinohe. It is a counted-thread embroidery based on the diamond unit, as is kogin, but it is sewn over and under an even number of counted warps. The colorful hishizashi apron (cat. 6) is done by this method. Originally three colors were used in this technique: the base fabric a light blue ramie or hemp, and the stitching with dark blue as well as white cotton threads.[7] Only one layer of fabric was ever used.

Hachinohe was a port or gateway to Hokkaido in the north and Edo and Osaka in the south. Its location on the trade route assured the availability of many different items, such as cloth and dyes. In the early twentieth century, aniline dyes and wool yarns were introduced to the Nambu area.[8] The land around Hachinohe was very dry, a landscape of brown and buff tones. The contrast of the bright aniline-dye colors and the browns of the land was quite striking. Examples of these brightly colored aprons are often considered garish by Westerners; as a result, this category of sashiko is rarely seen outside Japan. Like all the sashiko of Nambu, hishizashi was used on a variety of garments, sometimes covering them entirely.

SHIMOKITA SASHIKO

The sashiko of the Shimokita peninsula in Aomori prefecture was made by and for the people of the fishing industry. It was typically a dark blue cotton stitching on dark blue cotton fabric. The needle is pushed perpendicular to the base fabric, coming out of the fabric with each stitch,[9] in contrast to the method of running the needle in and out of the fabric several times with each thrust for other types of sashiko. The Shimokita technique used more thread for the sashiko and gave the garments a dense, heavy feeling. This area was economically sound in the nineteenth century, and people could afford extra thread for stitching as well as the large quantity of indigo needed to dye the thread and the base fabric a deep color.

SHŌNAI SASHIKO

The characteristic feature of sashiko of the Shōnai plain, in Yamagata prefecture, is its geometric designs. This style developed at the same time as Tsugaru kogin, that is, in the late eighteenth century.[10] The base fabric is a plain, dark blue cotton, and the sashiko stitching, over one or two layers of fabric, is either white or dark blue cotton. A vest in this collection (cat. 12) is a typical district garment of Shōnai. It has two stitch patterns of seven stitches per inch, "mountains" and "persimmon flower." Both are characteristic of the Shōnai plain sashiko. These patterns are composed of straight lines intersecting at right angles. The designs are relatively easy to execute by counting the stitches in each line of pattern. The horizontal lines were stitched first, and then the vertical lines.

Cat. I5 (detail; interior)
Commoner's firefighting coat
(hikeshi banten)
Late Edo-early Meiji period,
mid-I9th century
Quilted (sashiko) cotton cloth
with freehand paste-resist
decoration (tsutsugaki), 89.81

SASHIKO OF FIREMEN'S CLOTHING

The sashiko of firemen's coats and their other occupational clothing is particular to the use of the garment rather than to the district of origin. Firemen's coats consist of two or three layers of cotton stitched with a vertical running stitch over the entire garment, generally with six or seven stitches per inch. Fires in Edo were fought by four classes of firefighters: samurai, feudal lords, retainers, and townspeople. Only the latter (machibikeshi) wore stitched garments. This group of firefighters was established in 1718, and their typical outfit gradually developed over time. It might include underwear, a hood, a short and a long coat, trousers, and mittens. The entire outfit was covered with sashiko stitching. Kuniyasui Sakai reports:

> They put on quilted protective underwear, a quilted long coat which covers their bodies through their knees, a regular coat over it, long socks on their feet, quilted mittens on their hands, and a "cat" hood which covers the whole head and chest except eyes and has especially thick cloth at the top. [Arriving at the scene of the fire] they poured water over themselves.... A total weight [of soaked clothing] at this time was said to be about 70 pounds.[11]

The water of the drenched clothing, evaporating in the heat of the fire, kept the firefighters cool as they approached the blaze with long hooks to pull the structure down and prevent the fire from spreading. The fabric of this clothing was cotton and predominantly dark blue, as was the stitching thread. Sometimes, however, the base fabric is brown or gray.[12] The shirt-length underwear was one layer of cotton with a vertical sashiko stitch. On the lower third of the underwear, the stitching was often done in large X-shaped patterns. The hood and mittens were two layers of cotton, generally with four stitches per inch. The trousers were one layer of fabric with dense *sashiko* stitching over the legs.

From its conception, sashiko was a practical technique, an economic necessity in extending the life of a garment or cloth. Initially no sashiko was done solely for decorative purposes. Regardless of the sashiko style, the garments were never made for sale. Second-hand clothing was not considered an option, so the wearer reflected the pride of the stitcher, someone within the family. In this way, the stitching could boast of the maker's skill and mental ability. With kogin and hishizashi, the stitching had precise rules, partly governed by the counting of the stitches. This led to a more formalized style of stitching. A woman's dowry would always include five to seven finished kogin. These kogin were thought to reflect the attitudes and mental skills of a potential bride. With an economically successful marriage at stake, a stitcher would strive to make the sashiko better than anyone else. Traditionally done only on kimono, today one can find kogin embroidery on door curtains, placemats, bags, and slippers. As government regulations relaxed and people became wealthier, cotton and wool were brought to the area, and stitched garments became old-fashioned and represented poverty. For the last sixty years, sashiko has been found on new garments and textiles made from a variety of materials including synthetic and metallic threads. Today it is found for sale in folk-craft shops and is also incorporated into designer clothing, adapting to use in a modern, technological world.

A dowry would always include five to seven finished kogin, which were thought to reflect the attitudes and mental skills of a potential bride.

Cynthia Shaver is a private dealer and appraiser specializing in Japanese folk textiles. She has traveled extensively in Japan and lectures and writes about Japanese folk art.

1. Charles Terry, trans., *Japanese Life and Culture in the Meiji Era*, ed. Keizo Shibusawa (Tokyo: The Toyo Bunko, 1969), 5, Life and Culture, p. 21: "In 1643, the government issued a proclamation concerning farmers' clothing, which limited...ordinary farmers to hemp [ed. note: and ramie?] and cotton...." I assume the character being translated as 'hemp' is asa, which refers to a bast fiber such as hemp (*Cannabis sativa*) or ramie (*Boehmeria nivea* Hook & Arn.) and can be read either way. This is a common confusion, and mistakes are often made.

2. Toshiko Horiuchi, "Tsugaru to Nambu no sashiko" (Sashiko from Tsugaru and Nambu), *Senshiku no bi* (Textile Art Magazine) 9(1981), p. 90.

3. Kageo Muraoka, "Tsugaru no kogin" (Sashi-kogin from Tsugaru), *Kogei* (Craft) 14(1932), p. 21. Muraoka and other scholars have said that the first kogin were reported to be hemp or ramie thread on a base fabric of hemp or ramie.

4. Ibid., p. 27.

5. Ibid., p. 35.

6. Horiuchi, "Tsugaru to Nambu," p. 89.

7. Muraoka, "Tsugaru no kogin," p. 46.

8. Ibid.

9. Horiuchi, "Tsugaro to Nambu," p. 90.

10. Muraoka, "Tsugaro no kogin," p. 27.

11. Kuniyasui Sakai, *Edo no hanabana towazu katari* (Speaking on All Matters of Edo Firefighting), (Tokyo: Nikkeijigyo Shuppansha, 1980), p. 100.

12. An example in which the stitching thread changes from blue to brown to give the effect of a striped base fabric is in the collection of Harold and Gertrud Parker, Tiburon, California.

KATAZOME, TSUTSUGAKI, AND YŪZENZOME

RICHARD MELLOTT

O F THE VARIOUS TECHNIQUES DEVISED IN JAPAN TO DECORATE TEXTILES, three resist-dye methods, *katazome*, *tsutsugaki*, and *yūzenzome*, have played a particularly important role from the Edo period (1615–1868) to the present. Their origin, however, begins much earlier, during the Kofun period (250–552), when various methods of weaving and dyeing were imported from the Asian continent. Other more complex and sophisticated techniques for working textiles were subsequently introduced during the Asuka and Nara periods (552–794).

By the latter half of the third century, according to a Chinese report entitled *Wei-zhi* (History of the Wei [period]), the Japanese were using various plants to obtain dye colors — indigo (*ai*) for blue and madder (*akane*) for red. Although no examples of dyed cloth survive from this early period, it is believed that solid colors were then the rule; at any rate, there is as yet no evidence to indicate that these very early fabrics might have been patterned.

Beginning in the sixth century and continuing through the eighth, a wide variety of new dyes and dye techniques as well as numerous weaving methods were introduced from China to the recently centralized Japanese state, situated within the Nara basin. From surviving examples in the collection of the Hōryūji temple and the Shōsō'in, we know that many new types of patterned weaving, such as brocade (*nishiki*), twill (*aya*), and others, began to be produced in an almost unlimited variety of patterns. As for new patterned-dyeing techniques, the most important advancements included three types of resist-dye materials, the so-called *sankechi*: block-resist dyeing (*kyōkechi*); tie dyeing (*kōkechi*); and wax-resist dyeing (*rōkechi*).[1]

In the sixteenth century, when Portuguese traders arrived, textiles from Southeast Asia and India began to be seen in Japan.

These three methods of patterned dyeing, although they do not appear to have continued in an unbroken line up to the Edo period, must be seen as one source upon which the later katazome, tsutsugaki, and yūzenzome techniques were ultimately based. Block-resist dyeing (kyōkechi) appears not to have survived past the eighth century, and it is only within the last twenty years that anyone has tried to recreate this technique.[2] Tie dyeing (kōkechi), however, seems to have survived at least into the Heian period (794–1185), as it became popular among ordinary people and then reappeared during the Muromachi period (1333–1568) whence it continued to the present. Wax-resist dyeing (rōkechi), both stenciled (*suri-e*) and drawn (*kaki-e*) techniques, went out of fashion during the early Heian period, only reappearing during the Kamakura period (1185–1333) and then in greatly modified form.[3]

Cat. 31 (detail)
Festival banner *(nobori)*
Meiji-Taishō period, late 19th-early 20th century
Cotton cloth with freehand paste-resist decoration *(tsutsugaki)* and hand-painted pigments and ink decoration, 89.162

Other sources of influence for the development of these three techniques were, no doubt, imported fabrics brought to Japan from China and elsewhere after Japan began to trade with continental neighbors during the Kamakura period. At first, small quantities of cloth from Song and later Yuan China (eleventh to fourteenth centuries) entered Japan and were highly coveted by military lords, high-ranking priests, and aristocrats. After relations were established with Ming China (1368–1644), larger quantities of cloth entered the country. In the sixteenth century, when Portuguese traders arrived, textiles from Southeast Asia and India began to be seen in Japan. Japanese weavers and dyers did not succeed in mastering the new techniques of Ming China and elsewhere until the end of the sixteenth and the beginning of the seventeenth centuries, but once they did, they began to produce a variety of weave-patterned as well as dye-patterned textiles, including gold and silver brocades, damasks, figured satins, patterned gauzes, and stenciled, painted, and embroidered designs. They also began to combine these new techniques with older ones to suit the needs of their affluent clients. It is from this revitalized textile industry that the katazome technique emerged and subsequently, tsutsugaki and yūzenzome as well.

KATAZOME

Katazome literally means "dyeing with a stencil." The earliest examples of cut-paper stencil-dyed material (other than those few Nara period pieces mentioned previously) are found on armor of the Kamakura period. Softened deerskin with small stencil-dyed patterns was used to cover the breastplate, visor, and other parts of the helmet as well as other areas where the metal was exposed. These stencil-dyed patterns are believed to have been done with either a metal stamp or a cut stencil.

Some scholars have suggested that the use of cut-paper stencils was reintroduced into Japan from China during the sixteenth century together with the new weaving techniques mentioned above.[4] At this time in China, an insoluble paste made from ground soybeans and slaked lime was used as a resist, since dyeing was done by immersing the cloth in a dye bath. In Japan, however, the paste composition was modified to better serve the needs of the Japanese. Rice was substituted for soybeans because it was more plentiful, could be removed from the cloth by boiling in water, could be easily adapted to a wide range of humidity levels, and also made a paste of a smoother consistency more suitable for finely cut stencils and the reproduction of finer, more detailed designs.

Cranes, bamboo, cherry blossoms, turtles, iris, chrysanthemums, maple leaves, bush clover, lions, water, ice, fans, peonies, squares, triangles, rectangles are commonly encountered motifs.

One of the oldest surviving medieval examples using cut-paper stencils is a kimono made of hemp fiber with a small-pattern design (*komon*), said to have belonged to Uesugi Kenshin (1530–78).[5] Succeeding generations of samurai and other wealthy nobles began to have their formal attire, especially *hakama* and *kamishimo*, made from komon-dyed fabric.[6] At the beginning of the Edo period, with the establishment of Edo as the capital, a great new demand arose for komon-designed cloth for kimonos. By the mid-Edo period, however, fashions had changed dramatically, and while komon patterns continued to be used for formal attire, especially among prosperous merchants, a new variety of larger-patterned stencil-dyed design became popular.

The katazome-dyed textiles of the late Edo, Meiji (1868–1911), and Taishō (1912–26) eras include a seemingly endless variety of patterns ranging from minute dots to large family crests. Cranes, bamboo, cherry blossoms, turtles, iris, chrysanthemums, maple leaves, bush clover, lions, water, ice, Japanese written characters, fans, peonies, pine, squares, triangles, rectangles, and lozenge patterns are only a few of the commonly encountered motifs. The majority were intended for use as repeated patterns in the dyeing of yards of cloth for bedding, articles of clothing, banners, or for other special uses, such as *noren* (door curtains).

The process of katazome dyeing today has probably not changed much since the seventeenth century. First, a stencil is placed over a piece of cloth, and a resist paste is applied through the cut paper onto the cloth. The stencil is then removed. When the paste is dry, a sizing liquid is brushed over the entire piece of cloth. Again, this is allowed to dry before a colored dye is brushed onto the cloth surface. (If the cloth is to be dipped into a dye bath, as with indigo dyeing, then usually the reverse of the cloth is also stenciled with the same resist pattern that appears on the front. Without this precaution the rice paste may begin to dissolve in the dye vat and the dye would then bleed into the resisted areas.) This procedure may be repeated as many times as is required to achieve the desired color. Only the areas of cloth free of resist paste take on the dye color. When the dye is dry, the paste is washed away, leaving undyed areas to form the pattern against the dyed background.

The cut-paper stencils used today are, in all likelihood, very similar in construction to those developed in the sixteenth century. They are made from two to four layers of handmade *kōzo* paper (mulberry fiber) laminated with the juice of unripe persimmons. After drying, the sheets are hung in a room filled with wood smoke for about two weeks. In this atmosphere the tannin in the persimmon juice alters to make an exceptionally durable paper that is very strong and nearly waterproof. Stencil paper made in this manner will withstand hundreds of dye applications.

TSUTSUGAKI

Another method of dyeing cloth using rice-paste resist and applied colors is known as tsutsugaki in Japan, literally meaning "drawing with a tube." As with katazome, the precise date when tsutsugaki-decorated textiles began to be produced in Japan is unclear. A number of Muromachi-period garments decorated with this technique have survived, as evidence that it began at least this early.[7] Since most of these pieces were costumes for the Noh theater or kimonos for wealthy patrons, it is believed that during the first phase of tsutsugaki production the technique was reserved exclusively for garments of the upper classes. By the early Edo period, with the consolidation of the government under the control of the Tokugawa family, strict new regulations were enacted that forbade, among other things, the outward display of luxuriously decorated textiles. These sumptuary laws curbed the spread of the tsutsugaki technique, at least in the early decades of the Edo period. Three chief factors — the successful cultivation of cotton during the seventeenth century, the widespread popularity of cotton fabric among all classes of society, and the ease of dyeing it by this technique — gradually caused weavers and dyers throughout Japan to become familar with tsutsugaki. Certainly by the end of the Edo period, tsutsugaki dye shops could be found in almost every village. The subsequent Meiji and Taishō eras saw an absolute boom in the production of tsutsugaki-decorated fabrics.

Naturally, the types of garments, fabric, and decoration varied depending upon the class of society for which the product was designed. The imperial court, wealthy samurai, and religious leaders required fine silk and linen kimonos, some with boldly dyed designs (*katsugi*), others with exquisite, highly refined dyed designs (known as *chayazome*), and plain silk kimonos ornamented only with dyed family crests. In addition, they used a large variety of ceremonial costumes with various decorations, among them Noh costumes (*kataginu*, *suō*, and hakama); fire brigade processional outfits (hakama and kamishimo); and campaign jackets to wear over armor (*jimbaori*), and others. For domestic purposes they used banners, noren, futon covers, furniture covers, and more, all decorated with resist-dyed designs. As the merchant class gradually accumulated wealth and power during the latter half of the Edo period, its members too began buying luxury textiles formerly available only to the upper classes. Most of the items mentioned above became very popular within the households and businesses of prosperous merchants. Farmers and commoners could seldom afford fine kimonos; however, they could afford most of the other household textiles. In fact, it was the local dye shops in smaller towns throughout Japan that pushed the tsutsugaki technique to new heights of achievement, especially in the decoration of futon covers and *yogi* (a padded futon in the shape of a kimono).

Cat. 23 (detail)
**Bedding cover *(futonji)*
Meiji period, 19th century
Cotton cloth with freehand
paste-resist decoration
(tsutsugaki), 89.144**

Bold traditional and original designs were created to please the dyers' ever-growing clientele. Since most elaborately decorated futon covers and yogi were made for celebrations, such as weddings, their motifs are usually of an auspicious nature. Among a great many designs the most common are: phoenix in a paulownia tree, symbolizing peace and the traditional virtues of sincerity, righteousness, and truthfulness, all qualities hoped for in a new marriage; the so-called three friends — pine, bamboo, and plum — symbolizing longevity, fidelity, and integrity, also appropriate for a wedding gift; cranes (longevity, good fortune); tortoise (longevity, stability); and rabbits in waves (conception). Simple family crests were also a favorite motif.

Phoenix in a paulownia tree symbolize peace and the virtues of sincerity, righteousness, and truthfulness, all qualities hoped for in a marriage.

The dynamic and energetic depiction of these popular designs varied from region to region and from shop to shop; today it is possible to make only broad, speculative generalizations about the origins of specific examples unless, of course, their origin can be documented. In general, those country tsutsugaki textiles with bright colors and active, complicated designs (cat. 23) have been found mostly in western Japan, especially in Kyūshū and Shikoku. In Izumo, Tohoku, and parts of western Japan facing the Japan Sea, the artisans seemed to favor more restrained, clear designs done in one or two shades of indigo. In the large cities, especially Edo and Kyoto, it seems a full range of tsutsugaki textiles were made, but dyers there specialized in more sophisticated designs done on silk or *asa*.

The process of making tsutsugaki textiles is straightforward, but it requires time and patience. It is likely that the sequence of production has not changed much since the seventeenth century. First the textile is washed and cut and sewn into the desired size and shape. Then the cloth is stretched on a frame using bamboo poles, which makes the surface smooth and wrinkle-free. The design is sketched onto the stretched cloth with a pencil or a piece of charcoal. Next, rice-paste resist made of water, lime, and rice flour is drawn over the previously sketched lines using a tube (*tsutsu*).

The tube typically has two parts: a cone-shaped chamber made of paper treated with persimmon juice and a metal or bamboo tip with an opening. As the chamber is squeezed, paste is extruded through the tip. The width of line varies with the size of the tip's opening. When the design has been completed, rice bran is sprinkled over the paste to hasten drying. Then resist paste is drawn on the textile's verso in exactly the same pattern, insuring a clean, dye-free design under the paste on both sides of the fabric. Then the piece is allowed to dry. If certain design elements are to be colored with dye other than the blue of indigo, the other colors are brushed on at this stage. The fabric is then coated with a liquid or mordant made from ground soybeans and water, to help fix the dyes. Finally, a coating of rice paste is applied over them on both sides of the fabric.

When the garment is dry, the stretcher is removed, and the piece is immersed in the dye bath. In the case of an indigo dye bath, the number of times the cloth is immersed determines the darkness of the blue color; it is possible to preserve a light blue color by covering it with paste after the first or second immersion and then proceeding to dip the piece many more times in order to obtain a darker surrounding color. After the piece is allowed to dry completely, it is placed in hot water to soak until the rice paste softens. Then the remaining paste is scraped off, and the piece is again soaked in hot water. Finally, it is stretched again and allowed to dry. From beginning to end, depending upon the weather and other factors, the process takes about twenty days to complete.[8]

Cat. 21 (details)
Coverlet in kimono form (yogi)
Late Edo-early Meiji period, 19th century
Cotton cloth with freehand paste-resist decoration (tsutsugaki), 89.143

YŪZEN

Yūzenzome means "dyeing in the style of Yūzen." Miyazaki Yūzen was a Kyoto fan painter who is given credit for perfecting this technique during the late seventeenth and early eighteenth centuries. He did so in order to decorate various textiles with extremely fine, precise lines and in multiple colors, something not possible when using the tsutsugaki method. As we shall see, however, the two techniques share many similarities, a fact of which Yūzen was no doubt aware. Of the several significant differences, however, the most basic is that unlike all tsutsugaki textiles, which are dipped in a dye vat, no yūzen-decorated textiles are dyed by immersion.

In the yūzenzome process as it is done today, the artisan employs a bamboo-stick cloth stretcher to make a smooth surface, upon which he draws fine outline designs using light blue tracing fluid (*aobana*) made from the *tsuyukusa* plant (*Commelina communis*). He then covers these outlines with rice-paste resist using a tsutsu and immerses the entire cloth in a mordant made from ground soybeans and water in order to prevent the blurring of designs during dyeing. The cloth is then allowed to dry. Now the details of the design are painted in by the artist with brushes and various colored dyes; he then covers these colored designs with rice paste. The cloth next is brushed with dye to color the background, is steamed to fix the dyes, and finally, thoroughly washed to remove the tracing fluid and the rice paste.[9] After the cloth has had its final drying, various other details can be painted in, or sections may be embroidered to enhance the design. All in all, yūzenzome is a very time-consuming process; the end product is, therefore, a very costly one.

We have seen that katazome and tsutsugaki have their orgin at a much earlier time in Japanese history, when they were used by the more affluent classes of society. Only later, with the establishment of cotton cultivation and the resulting widespread use of cotton, did these two techniques become available to a broader spectrum of people. Cotton, then, can be seen as an important catalyst in the economics of these types of pattern-dyeing and their diffusion. Yūzenzome, by contrast, was only developed much later and specifically for decorating expensive garments for the wealthy classes, as it remains to this day.

Richard Mellott is Curator of Education, The Asian Art Museum of San Francisco.

1. Kaneo Matsumoto, *Jodai-gire: 7th and 8th Century Textiles in Japan from the Shōsō'in and Hōryūji*, trans. by R. Mellott and S. Kaneko (Kyoto: Shikosha, 1984), pp. 171-72.

2. In the late 1970s Mr. Gizo Tokuda, a Kyoto-based *obi* designer, began investigating the *kyōkechi* dyeing process. He studied first-hand original examples in the Shōsō'in collection, researched the scant published references, and then began experiments aimed at trying to reproduce this technique. He succeeded not only in recreating the process but also in making reproductions that appeared exactly like the Nara period fragments.

3. During the Nara period printed designs on textiles are thought to have been done by either pressing carved, inked blocks on fabric, or by placing it directly on an inked block and rubbing the back with a flat tool. It is not clear, but perhaps possible, that cut-paper stencils were also in use at this time.

4. See Eisha Nakano, *Japanese Stencil Dyeing* (New York: Weatherhill, 1982), p. 4.

5. Ibid.

6. Kamishimo are stiff upper garments worn on formal occasions over a kimono by daimyo and higher-class samurai.

7. Reiko Mochinaga Brandon, *Country Textiles Of Japan* (New York: Weatherhill, 1986), p. 31.

8. Ibid, pp. 35-37.

9. William G. Morton, "Yūzen," in *Kodansha Encyclopedia Of Japan* (Tokyo: Kodansha, 1983), p. 359.

KASURI

MARY DUSENBURY

Tiny points of light in a deep, blue sea flicker and realign themselves as an old woman bends in the rice fields. On a marriage futon (cotton bedding), a white crane, painterly in execution, is poised in flight over the ancient tic-tac-toe symbol of a well. Dancing patterns on a tiny, patched kimono tell the history of parents' and grandparents' clothing as a toddler plays.

RANGING FROM SIMPLE MOTTLED EFFECTS TO ABSTRACT GEOMETRIC motifs and freeform representations of the flora and fauna of Japan, the hazy white patterns of cool, sun-bleached *asa* (hemp, ramie) or soft cotton reserved against a deep indigo ground were a familiar sight in the late Edo (1615–1868), Meiji (1868–1912), and Taishō (1912–1926) periods. Old photographs and the descriptions of Western travelers attest that in the late nineteenth and early twentieth centuries, *kasuri* (thread-resist) textiles formed a strong visual element in the pageant of everyday life in both urban and rural Japan.

When Commodore Perry arrived in Japan in 1853, kasuri was being woven throughout the country. From the mid-eighteenth century on, its manufacture had provided off-season income in many agricultural areas, where women wove kasuri cloth for sale in the cities. Each region had developed its own distinctive characteristics, although in almost all areas the predominant dye was indigo, the fiber was either asa or hand-spun, short-staple cotton, and motifs were reserved in white against a dark ground. By the late eighteenth century, an improved agricultural economy and the ready availability of cotton had stimulated production.[1] More cloth stayed in local communities, and kasuri became a folk craft, a cloth designed and made in a community for its own use. At the same time, the commercial importance of kasuri grew as a wider and more affluent patronage was able to afford the fabrics whose cost had once limited their use to the *buke* (ruling warrior elite) and wealthy merchants. Spurred by a lively market economy, motifs proliferated in the nineteenth and early twentieth centuries, while a variety of technical innovations facilitated both the creation of freeform painterly designs and a more efficient production.

Kasuri textiles have long been admired for their quiet beauty and for the skill, ingenuity, and creative imagination they express.

Today kasuri textiles have become a symbol of traditional Japan for both Japanese and Westerner. In Japan, they have evoked many responses: shame during periods when Japan turned from its heritage to emulate the modern West, nostalgia as conditions within the country changed rapidly and inexorably, and, finally, pride, as a late twentieth-century industrialized nation has come to look anew at its rich cultural heritage. In the West, kasuri textiles have long been admired for their quiet beauty and for the skill, ingenuity, and creative imagination they express.

Technically, the word "kasuri" refers to thread-resist textiles, cloth in which warp and/or weft yarns are partially tied, bound, or compressed before they are dyed so that when they are stretched on the loom as warp and/or woven in as weft, the sections reserved from the dye form a predetermined pattern in the finished cloth.

"Kasuri," however, is not primarily a technical term. Unlike Western twentieth-century textile scholars, the Japanese have not traditionally classified textiles mainly by technique. "Kasuri" most often refers to plain-woven cloth of asa or cotton with white patterns reserved on a deep indigo ground, as described above. The most typical kasuri textiles developed in the mid- to late Edo period, mostly from Okinawan prototypes that began to enter Japan in the late sixteenth and the seventeenth centuries. The word evokes images of traditional rural costume and bed covers, although the history and development of the tradition were considerably broader and more complex.

"Kasuri" thus refers to a certain type of cloth defined not only by technique but also by material, pattern, color (even specific dye material), and use. It does not include a small group of silk-warp ikat imported into Japan in the seventh and eighth centuries, nor an important tradition of silk thread-resist aristocratic garments that developed in Kyoto in the sixteenth century before the introduction of Okinawan kasuri cloth. Although these garments are partially patterned by resist-dyeing sections of warp threads before weaving, they are not related to the southern tradition either in design, material, color, weave structure, or patronage. Neither they nor the Edo-period Noh costumes that developed from them have traditionally been identified as kasuri.

The word "kasuri," first used in Japan in the seventeenth century, was probably derived from the word *kashiri*, a term used to describe thread-resist textiles on the southern Ryūkyūan island of Yaeyama. "Kasuri" is also phonetically related to a number of words that describe the soft, hazy edges typical of the patterns it creates. *Kasuru* means to graze, abrase, or blur; *kasureru* describes the hazy beginning and end of a calligraphic brushstroke; *kasumeru* means to skim or brush lightly; and *kasumi* refers to mist and haze. All these phonetic associations suggest the subtle shading-off of the kasuri pattern into the background fabric.

Twentieth-century Japanese textile historians have not developed an all-inclusive technical term for these textiles, although, like their Western counterparts, they generally mention all Japanese thread-resist textile traditions in any discussion of the development of kasuri weaving in Japan. The nonspecialist, however, still looks bewildered if an Edo-period thread-resist Noh costume, for example, is referred to as kasuri. Accustomed to traditional terminology and methods of classification, the Japanese layperson does not make the technical connection between these two very different traditions, finding it difficult to associate the colorful, heavily brocaded silks of the Noh stage with simple blue-and-white work clothing. Luxurious silk textiles that employ thread-resist techniques for Noh costumes and aristocratic garments are classified with a different set of terms, yet all make use of the same technical means of achieving a pattern in the finished cloth.[2]

It is important to be aware that in using the word ikat as a general technique classification, we have adopted a Malay-Indonesian word into the English language to fill a vocabulary gap.

Dangawari kimono
Momoyama period, late 16th century
Silk; warp-way thread-resist dyeing
Kyoto National Museum

Most Western as well as some Japanese scholars use the Malay-Indonesian word "ikat" as a general technical classification. It is important to be aware that in doing this we have adopted a Malay-Indonesian word into English and defined it to suit our needs, to fill a gap in technical vocabulary within the English language. Different cultures classify things differently, and the way a society chooses to classify objects and ideas is important information in itself. Even if, as here, we choose to discuss a group of textiles drawn together by a common technology, we should be aware that this is simply one method of grouping objects; that it is not the only point of view; and that this method of classification may seem very awkward, puzzling, ignorant, or even comical to people from the culture that produced those textiles.

Here, I use the phrase "thread-resist" as a general technical term, reserving the word "ikat" for thread-resist textiles from southeastern Asia and "kasuri" for textiles traditionally so identified within Japan (including Okinawa).³ I discuss both major Japanese traditions of thread-resist textiles but will focus on those textiles customarily referred to as kasuri, the tradition most closely related to the textiles in this publication.

OKINAWAN ROOTS:
FOURTEENTH THROUGH SIXTEENTH CENTURIES

The roots of kasuri weaving reach through Okinawa, the ancient kingdom of Ryūkyū, to coastal and insular southeastern Asia. Thread-resist textiles were known in India at least by the eighth century. By the fourteenth century they were widely disseminated throughout the coastal regions and islands lying between India and the Ryūkyū archipelago, possibly including the island chain Yaeyama and Miyako, which had close cultural and economic ties with other parts of southeastern Asia and later became one of the main kasuri-producing regions of Okinawa.

Throughout the fourteenth and fifteenth centuries, ikat entered the Ryūkyūs as part of an extensive trade and tribute network⁴ conducted independently by several Ryūkyūan island confederacies. The *Rekidai hōan* (Records of Foreign Trade) lists ikat textiles among those sent as royal gifts to Shuri from Thailand in 1430 and Malacca between 1467 and 1481.⁵ Most Japanese and Okinawan scholars believe that ikat textiles and a knowledge of ikat weaving also entered the islands through the auspices of Ryūkyūan sailors, who often spent several months at a time in southeastern Asian trading ports.

The fourteenth century saw the establishment of a central capital at Shuri on the island of Okinawa and the beginnings of political unification of independent island confederacies. This process was spurred by King Satto (1349–1406), who was also responsible for establishing formal relations with China. In 1372 he sent a tribute mission to the new Ming dynasty (1368–1644), which established important cultural and economic ties that lasted for more than five centuries.

Ryūkyū was a maritime trading country at the intersection of several ocean currents that supported a series of ancient trade routes. Many of the items listed in inventories of tribute from Ryūkyū to the Ming court were trade goods from southeastern Asia (aromatic woods, incense, pepper, and sappanwood, a red dye material) and Japan (swords, fans, gold and silver articles, copper, tin, agate, and lacquer). The most important local products were horses, seashells (used for mother-of-pearl inlay in lacquer ware), and textiles.

Early tribute records are an important source of information about the development of Okinawan textiles, although the names of specific types of cloth remain open to various interpretations. Yoshitarō Kamakura, for example, states that the *Sheng je hsia pu* mentioned in early inventories probably refers to raw or glossed *bashōfu*, cloth woven of the inner bark of the upright, stalklike "leaf" of the *Musa sapientum*, fiber-banana tree. Other scholars interpret the records to suggest not only that bashōfu textiles were included in the tribute of 1372 but that some of them were patterned with a simple warp ikat.[6]

Thread-resist patterned textiles became very important in the Ryūkyūs; highly prized at court, they were also a major trade and tribute item. In time an elaborate code developed that restricted certain patterns and colors to particular members of the royal family and others to the aristocracy. Garments became a language expressing rank, social status, and occasion.[7]

Many scholars have pointed out that the patronage and supervision of the court at Shuri were important factors in the production of the superb eighteenth- and nineteenth-century kasuri textiles that are the pride of twentieth-century collections throughout the world. Much of the initial development of thread-resist weaving in Okinawa, however, took place in tiny hamlets on isolated islands such as Yaeyama and Miyako. On these islands, in the hands of women who were weaving cloth for their own families, a fundamental change occurred that transformed the southeastern Asian ikat heritage and laid the foundation for the development of both the Okinawan and the Japanese kasuri traditions.

The southeastern Asian ikat textiles that sparked the development of thread-resist patterning in Okinawa were composed along the vertical axis of the cloth. Like most ikat textiles in southeastern Asia today, they were warp-faced, warp-ikat.[8] In other words, the ikat patterning was in the warp and the unpatterned weft (horizontal) threads, almost hidden in the intersections of the closely packed warp, did not have a decorative function.

Okinawan thread-resist textiles became quite different from their southeastern Asian prototypes when weavers began to make use of weft as well as warp patterning and to manipulate the weft thread during the weaving process in order to create simple, painterly effects. Although very complex patterns can be tied into a warp, the weaver has no flexibility once that warp is on the loom.[9] Weft patterning is more flexible. Not only can the weaver change weft yarns at will, but she can manipulate the weft to a certain extent as she weaves. A slight shift at a selvedge, for example, changes the direction of the image being built. As the threads shift, the image they create changes. In the hands of skillful island weavers, simple rectangles of white on a natural or dark ground were transformed into images of the flora and fauna of the islands, motifs that were elegant in their simplicity, abstract yet quite recognizable.[10] Weft manipulation to create thread-resist patterns (*hikizurashi*, slide-pulling), virtually unknown in other parts of the world, is characteristic of the Okinawan kasuri tradition. It

Simple rectangles of white on a natural or dark ground were transformed into images of the flora and fauna of the islands, motifs that were abstract yet quite recognizable.

Cat. 53 (detail)
Child's kimono
Late Edo-early Meiji period, 19th century
Bast fiber *(asa)* cloth with weft ikat *(yokogasuri or e-gasuri)* and double ikat *(kasuri)*, 89.108

is probably the earliest and simplest prototype of the various devices that later Japanese weavers would employ to depict complex freeform motifs.

The development of thread-resist patterning in the weft also made possible the creation of independent images in both warp and weft as well as double images in which carefully planned reserved portions of warp and weft meet to form clearly defined motifs. In warp or weft patterning, the motifs appear in halftone where a reserved thread crosses one that has been dyed. In double patterning, both warp and weft threads have been reserved from the dye, and the pattern is sharper where the white sections meet. In the child's kimono (cat. 53) the ground motifs as well as the horizontal bars of the well pattern are in weft kasuri; the vertical bars are warp kasuri. Both appear in halftone. The corners of the well stand out where warp and weft thread-resisted sections meet. The pure white of these small double-kasuri sections adds a feeling of dimensionality to the whole composition. In this little garment, the weaver has balanced warp and weft motifs against double motifs, enjoying and employing the play of fully dyed ground, halftone motif, and fully reserved motif.

Okinawan weavers were able to develop weft and double thread-resist patterns because their looms differed from those of most of their southeastern Asian neighbors in one significant aspect: Okinawan looms, like the old Japanese *izaribata*, had a spacer, or "reed," that separated each warp or small group of warps from its neighbors. As a result, the warps did not necessarily bunch together to dominate the fabric. Rather, the weaver could control the balance of warp and weft and therefore could make effective use of weft patterning as well as warp patterning. In other respects Okinawan looms were quite simple. They were back-tensioned and had only simple heddling devices.

Weaving a kasuri textile—tying the warp and weft threads, aligning them on the loom, weaving the web, and watching the pattern emerge— is a time-consuming, concentrated activity.

Kasuri weaving required skill, experience, and patience but needed few tools beyond the two-harness, back-tensioned loom used historically throughout Japan and Okinawa. The thread is interlaced in a plain-weave structure (over-one, under-one). To make a kasuri textile, the warp and/or weft threads to be patterned were stretched taut and the areas to be reserved from the dye were tied tightly with a plant fiber that would shrink when wet.[11] On the southern Ryūkyūa islands, the warp was often wound around the outside of the house, supported by pegs inserted in the coral walls. The threads were then steeped in a heated dye vat, aired, and washed — a process repeated until the desired depth of color was achieved. If several colors were used, the weaver tied and retied sections of thread as necessary between dyeings.

The process of weaving a kasuri textile, tying the warp and weft threads, carefully aligning them on the loom, weaving the web, and watching the pattern emerge as each weft thread finds its place, is a time-consuming, concentrated activity. Over the centuries, important technical innovations and a whole new repertoire of motifs emerged from the meditative interaction of skillful weavers with the web of cloth before them.

Thus, on the tiny islands of the Ryūkyūan archipelago, the southeastern Asian ikat tradition was transformed, and a new tradition emerged. It incorporated ancient motifs and at the same time created new ones describing the flora and fauna of the islands and reflecting the imagination and skill of their weavers.[12]

INTRODUCTION OF KASURI TEXTILES
TO JAPAN FROM THE RYŪKYŪS:
SIXTEENTH AND SEVENTEENTH CENTURIES

In 1609, with the approval of the Tokugawa shogunate (1603–1867), Shimazu Iehisa, lord of the southern Japanese fiefdom of Satsuma, invaded Ryūkyū. In 1611 Ryūkyū became a vassal state and agreed to send Satsuma a heavy annual tribute of rice and textiles.[13] The Ryūkyūan government, in turn, taxed each island according to the resources and skills of its inhabitants, the internal needs of the government, and the external demands placed upon it. Changes in the tax structure after the invasion reflect an increased demand for textiles to meet the yearly tribute payments. In 1636, for example, the land tax was replaced by a poll tax on all able-bodied adults between the ages of fifteen and fifty on the southern island groups of Miyako and Yaeyama. The land tax had generally been paid in rice and millet, but the poll tax was to be paid in textiles. Since Miyako and Yaeyama were two of the primary kasuri-producing regions of the country, this change in the tax structure suggests not only a need for additional textiles in general but a specific demand for kasuri textiles within Japan.[14]

The quiet simplicity of the Okinawan textiles quickly gained popularity among aristocratic warrior families as fabric for *kosode* and other garments. These textiles were fresh and novel yet close enough to contemporary Japanese taste in material, color, design, and even the width of the fabric to be easily incorporated into traditional Japanese dress. The subdued colors and sparse, random design of seventeenth-century Okinawan fabric provided a counter-aesthetic to the sometimes gaudy display of the late sixteenth-century warlords Oda Nobunaga (1534–82) and Toyotomi Hideyoshi (1536–98). The Okinawan aesthetic was closer to that of the late medieval tea-master Sen Rikyū (1522–91) and certainly closer in spirit to the more frugal taste of the early Tokugawa regents.

A *haori* (jacket) said to have belonged to Tokugawa Tsunanari (1651–99), head of the powerful Ōwari branch of the ruling Tokugawa family, is the earliest extant kasuri textile of almost certain Okinawan provenance.[15] It probably is a good example of the Okinawan textiles that entered Japan in the seventeenth century as part of the annual tribute payments to Satsuma, as gifts to the Tokugawa rulers, and undoubtedly through independent trade as well.[16] The haori is woven of plant fibers, probably either ramie or bashō. Scattered motifs like thin, even brushstrokes appear singly and in small groupings on both the vertical and horizontal axes of the cloth. Although the motifs are set into a faintly described grid, they appear random and convey a feeling of spaciousness, a quality often found in later Okinawan textiles. Here the motifs provide a lively counterpoint to the quiet spaces of the ground, drawing attention to the simple beauty of the cloth itself and to the subtle variation of natural colors in the undyed ground. Most of the motifs and the grid are dyed a rich deep brown. Faint traces of blue, green, orange, yellow, and red, some of silk thread, add further variety and visual interest to the composition. Motifs on the Tokugawa haori are not pulled into place as was described above. There is no evidence of hikizurashi or apparent effort to create any sort of freeform pattern.[17]

The Tokugawa haori, tribute records, and a list of objects bequeathed by Tokugawa Ieyasu (1542–1618) to his sons (the *Sumpu onwakemono-chō*, compiled 1616–18)[18] provide some information on the type of Okinawan textiles that entered Japan in the early Edo period. From these sources we can deduce that the seventeenth-century kasuri textiles that entered Japan from Okinawa through the tribute assessment were subdued in color, made of a variety of native plant fibers, and employed warp, weft, and double thread-resist patterning to create simple geometric motifs on both axes of the cloth.

AN EARLY KYOTO TRADITION OF SILK THREAD-RESIST TEXTILES: HEIAN PERIOD (794-1185) TO SIXTEENTH CENTURY

The thread-resist textiles that entered Japan in the late sixteenth century from the Ryūkyūs were not the first known in Japan, nor even the first to be manufactured there.[19] When Okinawan kasuri was introduced to Japan in the second half of the sixteenth century, wealthy warrior and merchant families already had access to a sophisticated tradition of thread-resist textiles, which was centered in the capital city of Kyoto.

The first thread-resist textiles known to have been manufactured in Japan were wide, flat ceremonial sashes (*hirao*) that hung from waist to ankle as part of a courtier's formal costume in the Heian period.[20] Copied from Chinese court costume, hirao were also incorporated into the Bugaku dance costume and were used as adjuncts to the vestments of Buddhist priests. These plaited *karagumi* (literally, Chinese braid; technically, paired oblique twill interlacing) sashes had sections of threads reserved from the dye to create large blocks of background color that set off intricately worked central and border designs. The technique of reserving sections of thread from the dye to create pattern is usually associated with woven textiles, a two-element construction. Here it was used very successfully in a plaited, single-element construction. Today, eight hundred years later, hirao are still used in certain ceremonial costumes.

Dangawari kimono (details, above and right)

Several extant kosode of the late Muromachi (1392–1573) and Momoyama (1568–1615) periods were patterned by reserving large sections of warp threads from the dye in order to effect a change of background color. Although the hirao were plaited and the kosode were woven, the use of the thread-resist technique to achieve a shift of background color is identical in both types of textiles. The designer and weaver of a late sixteenth-century *dangawari* (rung-patterned) kosode, owned by an old Kyoto merchant family, used this simple technique to create a subtle and richly complex garment. The warp was tied and dyed in vertical bands to change the background color, at intervals, from soft green to rusty gold. Large blocks of solid color shift into narrow vertical bands set into the natural white of the silk. Woven into this ground, a figured twill appears sometimes as a large, allover pattern of formally arranged and highly stylized peonies and sometimes as startlingly intimate details telescoped into the narrow vertical bands of color. A kosode worn by the daimyo Uesugi Kenshin (1530–78) uses the technique in a similar fashion, although the effect is dramatic rather than subtle. The hemline and upper torso of the Kenshin kosode are dyed purple, a bold contrast to the off-white of the large central panel. A figured twill medallion pattern runs throughout.[21] The high level of sophistication of several of these kosode suggests a long period of evolution prior to the sixteenth century, but material evidence of this development and maturation is lacking.

The use of thread-resist dyeing in these and similar sixteenth- and seventeenth-century garments is very different in concept, material, appearance, and purpose than its use in southeastern Asia or Okinawa. In the Kyoto tradition, the technique was not used to create a motif but rather as a means of changing the ground color from section to section of the garment.

The very particular use of the thread-resist technique to effect a series of vertical color blocks in the warp in both the plaited hirao sashes and the woven dangawari kosode suggests that the sixteenth-century rung-patterned kosode were related to and possibly an outgrowth of the older tradition of block-dyeing hirao sashes. Both shared the use of the highest quality silk thread; both came from Kyoto; and both were made within a small and intimately related group of long-established Kyoto craftsmen who served all the upper echelons of Kyoto society — the court, the Kyoto nobility, the buke, and important merchant families.

The tradition of the late Muromachi and Momoyama rung-patterned kosode continued into the Edo period and was used for *shimekiri* (cut stripes), a name reflecting the same idea of sharp changes in background color, and for *noshime*, a man's formal inner kosode worn, for example, with the warrior's formal *kamishimo* (stiffened vest and trousers). The idea was further developed within the tradition of costume in the Noh drama, where it was used for heavily brocaded *karaori* and *atsuita*. Interestingly, despite a similar patronage in the seventeenth and eighteenth centuries, the dangawari garments had virtually no influence on the development of asa and, later, cotton kasuri weaving in Japan. In the eighteenth century, however, popular kasuri motifs, such as arrow patterns, began to appear within the block-resisted bands of shimekiri and noshime garments.

Although there are many extant examples of thread-resist dyed aristocratic secular and theatrical garments from the seventeenth century,[22] there are very few examples of kasuri textiles from the period. Once again, scholars must rely on local histories and trade documents to attempt to piece together the early development of kasuri weaving in Japan. Much research remains to be done, and scholars disagree on the specific dates of first production of kasuri in various parts of the country. However, the broad outline is fairly clear.

DIFFUSION, ASSIMILATION, AND DEVELOPMENT
OF KASURI WEAVING IN JAPAN:
SEVENTEENTH AND EIGHTEENTH CENTURIES

Early histories of kasuri suggested that the technique was diffused slowly throughout the country starting in Satsuma, moving through Kurume in northern Kyūshū, and from there northeastward in an orderly progression.[23] More recent research has disproved this theory and revealed a seemingly arbitrary and multifaceted situation. The *sankin-kōtai* system of forced attendance at the shogunal court[24] and complex inter-fief trade patterns, which employed both sea and land routes, played an important role in determining the flow of both kasuri cloth and technical knowledge from one part of the country to another. Commercial opportunity often spurred the initial development of kasuri weaving in Japan, at least kasuri weaving that can be traced in any way. Influences did not move only in one direction, as was suggested by early scholars. Currents and crosscurrents created a web of interrelationships that stimulated the development of new patterns. At the same time, economic competition led to technical innovations that increased production, facilitated complicated patterning, and encouraged the development of freeform painterly designs.

Several scholars have published lists of the dates of first production of kasuri in various parts of the country. Although the dates vary widely depending, as they do in many cases, on interpretation of ambiguous trade records, most scholars agree that there was little kasuri production within Japan itself before the eighteenth century, and that production was not widespread before the late eighteenth and first half of the nineteenth centuries. Most scholars now agree that kasuri was not woven in Satsuma until 1740, considerably later than in several other parts of the country.[25] Until the mid-eighteenth century, Satsuma continued to depend on tribute textiles from Okinawa, which were then dispersed to other parts of Japan, where they were known as *satsumagasuri*, or kasuri from Satsuma.

The isolated, mountainous, and relatively poor province of Echigo (present-day Niigata prefecture) on the Japan Sea was, surprisingly, one of the first and most important areas to produce kasuri cloth within Japan. Echigo provides a good example of the combination of factors that encouraged kasuri development. Located on the "backside of Japan" (Ura Nihon), this rice-producing region traded regularly, and independently, with Okinawa. Thus Echigo had direct access to Okinawan kasuri cloth as well as the contacts necessary to learn directly from its weavers, in much the same way that the Ryūkyūans had learned from their southeastern Asian neighbors in the fourteenth and fifteenth centuries. Echigo also had well-established marine ties, through the Inland Sea, with the important port and wholesale market of Osaka. Echigo was an agricultural area, snowbound many months of the year, and with its short growing season was too far north for double cropping. For some time its people had supplemented their farm incomes by producing asa cloth for the Osaka market in winter. Although geographically isolated, they seem to have quickly realized the growing popularity of kasuri patterns in the cities and incorporated them, at an early date, into the cloth they wove for sale to Osaka, Kyoto and, as the fame of their fine asa kasuri textiles spread, to Edo as well. Such commercial motivation probably also contributed to the comparatively early development of kasuri in other remote parts of the country. Some scholars state that Echigo started weaving kasuri cloth in the late seventeenth century, but others date the first production to the early eighteenth.[26]

Most kasuri fabrics sold in the cities were woven on farms by women working at home in the winter when the fields were dormant. Their production and their profit were greatly increased when cotton became available in the second half of the eighteenth century (see n.1). The comparative speed with which it was possible to spin cotton thread increased production, stimulated the development of new patterns, and made kasuri cloth available to a wider market.

Japanese scholars emphasize the fundamental role of *temae kasuri* (kasuri woven within a rural household for its own use or that of its immediate community) in the assimilation of kasuri as an indigenous textile. While credit is probably rightly given to women who wove for their families, the few clues that remain to trace the development of kasuri within Japan all point to the importance of the stimulation of a commercial market.

Few kasuri textiles remain from this period, and it is much more difficult to trace their history and development than that of the silk dangawari, noshime, and other thread-resist garments worn by the most powerful families in the country and preserved within the storehouses of the Noh theatrical companies that they patronized. Rural households, by contrast, did not have the luxury of treating clothing as a treasure to be preserved intact for future generations. When a garment was worn out, it was cut down and used for children's clothing or household items such as lunch bags. After more years of service, now soft and worn with age, the cloth was used to bundle a baby or, stitched and quilted into multiple layers, to scrub the floor. Many weavers, however, saved small bits of an end of the weaving to remember the pattern and share it with daughters, granddaughters, and a few old friends. They pasted these scraps onto old paper, often children's copy paper, stitched into *shimachō* (literally, stripe books). These pattern books remain a treasure trove of local history, providing visual and technical information about the textiles produced in a particular household in a particular time and place. Some include the work of two or three generations of weavers. Sadly, undated and unsigned, too many of these shimachō have lost their identities.

Many weavers saved small bits of an end of the weaving to remember the pattern and share it with daughters, granddaughters, and old friends.

By the late eighteenth century, kasuri weaving was established in many parts of Japan and rapidly gained in popularity among the townsmen of the lively urban centers of Kyoto, Osaka, and Edo. Strict government prohibitions on the use of luxury fabrics by the general populace greatly stimulated the development of kasuri weaving and of *katazome* dyeing (fabric patterned with stencil and paste resist). Even wealthy townsmen, prohibited from wearing brocades, damasks, and high-quality silk *shibori* (tied, stitched, and bound resist textiles), patronized the kasuri and katazome dealers.

As demand increased so did specialization, and the marketing system grew more complex. Asa or cotton weaving, depending on the location, became an integral and important part of the rural economy in many regions. Speed and skill in weaving were among the criteria for hiring female agricultural workers.[27] Middlemen began to reap such large profits that producers in some areas banded together to bargain collectively with them or to bypass the system altogether to sell directly to urban wholesalers.[28]

Late Edo-period woodblock printmakers gave a vivid sense of the widespread use of kasuri fabrics at this time. Katsushika Hokusai (1760–1849) in *View of Mt. Fuji from the Gohyaku Rakan Temple* depicts a group of fashionably dressed men, women, and children admiring the view.[29] Two women are dressed in elegant kasuri kosode, one with lively white patterns on a deep indigo ground, the other with a dark "well pattern" against a reserved ground. A young samurai lad is also dressed in kasuri, while other figures wear stripes, checks, katazome, and plain, dark fabric. Woodblock artists such as Utagawa Kuniyoshi (1797–1861) and Tōshūsai Sharaku (active 1794–95) depicted popular Kabuki actors in dashingly striped and kasuri-patterned garments. Worn by men and women alike, kasuri fabrics appeared now sophisticated and elegant, now debonair, dashing, and bold. Kasuri, katazome, and striped textiles set the tone of fashion in late eighteenth- and early nineteenth-century urban Japan.

Shimachō
Meiji-Taishō period, 19th and early 20th century
Scraps of cotton *kasuri* and striped cloth on used paper
Private collection, Japan

Five Beautiful Women (detail, below)
Hokusai Katsushika
Edo period, early 19th century
Hanging scroll, ink and color on silk
Margaret E. Fuller Purchase Fund, Seattle Art Museum, 56.246.
The woman in the bottom left corner of this hanging scroll is wearing a *kasuri* kimono.

DESIGN, PATTERN, AND TECHNICAL INNOVATIONS: LATE EIGHTEENTH THROUGH EARLY TWENTIETH CENTURIES

Under the stimulus of a lively and very competitive market economy, designs proliferated and became increasingly complex. By the late eighteenth and early nineteenth centuries, different regions had developed their own designs and production methods to make the products of their looms distinctive. Many Japanese kasuri textiles differed as much from their Okinawan prototypes as those of seventeenth-century Okinawa had from their southeastern Asian forebears.

One of the most striking characteristics of Japanese kasuri is the strong interest in realistic depiction and freeform painterly effects that developed in the nineteenth and early twentieth centuries. On garments, these motifs were usually small, as in the early nineteenth-century travel cape (*bōzugappa*) (cat. 50) and the kimono (cat. 52). Sometimes *e-gasuri* (picture kasuri) was interspersed with geometric patterns, as in the child's kimono (cat. 53). On quilts (futon), motifs were larger, the entire cover sometimes forming one composition (cat. 59).

Three mid-nineteenth-century technical innovations made this development possible. One was the *e-dai* (picture stand), also known as *osa-dai*,

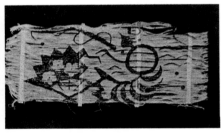

ezu-dai, *tane ito dai*, and *sumi ito dai*. The e-dai is a wooden frame with a bamboo comb (*osa*) on either side (an open-topped reed). The distance between the two osa is equal to the length of the weft thread required to weave one row of fabric (i.e., the width of the finished fabric plus weaving take-up). A cotton guide thread (*tane ito*) is wound from side to side through each slot in the two reeds until it forms a taut, false weft face the length of one pattern repeat. The pattern is painted on the surface of the tane ito with a brush and india ink, following the design printed or drawn on a piece of paper placed on the surface of the e-dai under the stretched threads, or with the aid of a paper stencil (*katagami*). The tane ito is then stretched out — often on a large warping frame — as a guide for tying weft threads for the textile. This technique is most commonly used to measure and tie weft threads but occasionally is used for warp threads as well.[30]

A second innovation was the *kobajogi*. Its basic purpose and principle is the same as that of the e-dai. *Koba* (very thin boards of paulownia) are stacked up and turned on edge. Each sliver of wood equals one weft thread. A pattern is printed or drawn on the edge of the stack, and the weft threads are then dyed using the numbered koba as a measure.

The third innovation, the *itajime* (literally, board-pressed) is a technique in which warp or weft threads are stretched in order and pressed tightly between pairs of boards that resemble the blocks used in printing ukiyo-e woodblock prints except that one of each pair is carved with a mirror

Picture stand (*e-dai*; left)
One of the mid-19th century technical innovations that contributed to the development of increasingly complex kasuri designs. Photograph by Mary Dusenbury.

Cotton guide thread (*tane ito*; right)
Formed on the *e-dai*, the *tane ito* is a false weft face the length of one pattern repeat and is most commonly used to measure and tie weft threads. Photograph by Mary Dusenbury.

image of the other. Either the design or the ground was carved out. If the design was left in relief, it appears as white against a dark ground. If, on the other hand, the design was carved out, the raised ground is reserved from the dye and the pattern appears as a dark motif against a white ground. After the threads were stretched and the boards positioned and clamped together, they were immersed in a dye bath, usually indigo. The dye penetrated the carved-out portions of the boards but was resisted from the uncarved or raised sections.[31]

The e-dai and the kobajogi were designed to give a dyer's freedom to the weaver. The itajime retains much of that freedom while speeding the overall process by eliminating the time-consuming stage of hand-tying the areas to be resisted from the dye. The e-dai was used primarily in Kurume in northern Kyūshū, Iyo, Bingo, and along the San'in coast. It was associated with cotton kasuri. The kobajogi was used primarily in Echigo and surrounding areas such as Ōmi and was associated with asa kasuri. The itajime is generally believed to have developed in Yamato near Nara, later spreading to Ōmi, the Noto peninsula, and Kurume. It was used for both asa and cotton.

Much scholarship remains to be done on the development of kasuri weaving in different parts of Japan. In the last decade, the Japanese government has created new regional museums that serve not only as repositories of local artifacts but also as research centers for local history. Future research may lead to a new interpretation of the development of kasuri weaving in different parts of Japan. It now appears, for example, that the itajime may have been used as early as 1826 in Ōmi, more than a decade before its supposed invention in Yamato.[32]

The San'in coast facing the Japan Sea (the present-day prefectures of Shimane and Tottori) was an important area for both katazome dyeing and e-dai kasuri weaving, and there is a close connection between these two types of textiles. Both dyers (generally men working professionally) and weavers (generally women working at home) worked with cotton, brought their thread or cloth to the same indigo dyers, and sold to the same market. Katazome and e-dai stencils resemble each other so closely that it is not always possible to tell them apart. There is no reason that they could not have been used interchangeably. Today old stencils are housed together in local collections, sometimes in the same case, and often unlabeled.

The itajime's close relationship to printing techniques gave it considerable freedom of patterning, but it was most useful for producing multiples at comparatively high speed. It also provided an easy method of producing dark patterns on a light ground, for which the region around the old capital, Nara, became very well known.

REGIONAL DIFFERENCES
(SANCHIMONO, LOCAL PRODUCTS)

The invention of the e-dai, kobajogi, and itajime in the early decades of the nineteenth century opened the doors to a flood of freeform painterly designs woven into the cloth. Regional differences became more marked than in the eighteenth century, and particular areas became known for distinctive types of kasuri (sanchimono). Kurume, for example, was well known for dramatic futon covers with a single composition filling the entire space. The compositions are bold and usually laterally balanced, if not bilaterally symmetrical. The image often appears to be made up of blocks of white on the dark indigo ground, almost like a child's building blocks. The depiction of Kotohira Shrine (cat. 59) is a fine example of this distinctive textile.

Although most other regions did not have such dramatic textiles as Kurume's nor ones as radically different from those of other areas, it is still possible to note certain local propensities. Weavers along the San'in coast, for example, fully exploited the curvilinear possibilities of the e-dai. They often played with a freeform motif, such as a flying crane, interspersing it with a geometric motif, such as a large well pattern. Cotton *zabuton* (sitting mats) and futon covers allowed ample space for painterly motifs of cranes, tortoises, and other flora and fauna. Farther north along the Japan Sea coast, the earliest extant kasuri fragments from Echigo convey the sense of spaciousness and tranquility of their Okinawan prototypes. Later textiles from the area are more crowded and complex. Motifs tend to be smaller there than on the San'in coast and fill the space in interesting ways. Some pieces have a lively interplay between allover plant, animal, or even Buddhist motifs, executed in weft kasuri, and unrelated vertical lines of warp kasuri which fall like rain over the fabric, now blending into the ground as a halftone, now jumping out as white warp unexpectedly crosses white weft. The child's kimono discussed above (cat. 53) is a good example of a particularly complex kasuri textile from Echigo. The "superimposed" pattern is a well-head, which means that the weft threads not only make the halftone patterns of pagodas, stylized clouds, and so forth, but at appropriate intervals must also depict the horizontal bars of the well pattern. The indigo of Echigo kasuri is often a clear sky blue, not the deep sea blue of the San'in coast and Kurume.

In Kyoto the dangawari tradition continued in noshime and shimekiri garments for samurai use, and in heavy silk costumes for the Noh theater. In the eighteenth century Kyoto weavers began to incorporate some ideas from the kasuri tradition into noshime (such as adding arrow patterns to a wide central thread-resist band) and other silk garments. Many of the patterns involved warp shifting, a more complex and difficult manipulation than weft shifting but one that achieves similar results. The invention and use of the *mokuhiki*, which allows minute adjustment of each of over one thousand warp ends, seems closely related to the Kyoto tradition, and it is still used there today.[33]

By the early twentieth century, the distinctions among these various sanchimono had become blurred as different geographical areas copied each other's work.[34] New technical inventions were designed to increase production and reduce costs. In 1909 in Kurume, for example, a foot-powered wrapping machine was invented that could change the length and frequency of the ties and could wrap several sections at once.[35]

In the two centuries since Satsuma invaded Ryūkyū, Japan had perhaps influenced Okinawa as much as Okinawa had influenced Japan. In the early seventeenth century, Satsuma had introduced cotton and encouraged sericulture. Cotton became very important at all levels of Okinawan society, while the ability of silk to take dyes clearly and subtly enabled Okinawan dyers and weavers to exploit fully the rich palette of the islands.[36]

Textiles were an important part of the "income" of the court at Shuri. They were used at court, sold for profit, and included in the annual tribute payments to Satsuma. The poll tax was a heavy burden on women in many

Cat. 58 (detail, top)
Bedding cover (futonji)
Meiji-Taishō period, late 19th-early 20th century, Kurume
Cotton cloth with double ikat (kasuri), 89.154

Cat. 53 (detail, above)
Child's kimono
Late Edo-early Meiji period, 19th century
Bast fiber (asa) cloth with weft ikat (yokogasuri or e-gasuri) and double ikat (kasuri), 89.108

Boy seated by a sugoroku board as a young woman teaches a dog to beg for a biscuit
Keisai Eisen
Edo period, 1826
Woodblock print
Spencer Museum of Art, 00.1499
The young woman is wearing a typical Kyoto-style warp-way thread-resist kimono.

parts of the country. Standards were high, specifications were exacting, and finished textiles were subjected to meticulous scrutiny by government officials before they were accepted. In time, artists attached to the king's procurement office in Shuri were assigned to paint design pages (*miezu*; see pp. 81, 87), which were full-color renditions of the designs to be copied in kasuri. Some extant leaves from the late eighteenth and the nineteenth centuries include the name of the island where the pattern was to be woven, probably indicating regional specialization.[37]

Okinawan court artists were sensitive to the demands of the kasuri technique and apparently also worked easily with the vocabulary of traditional design. As regulations became more stringent and exacting for the most highly prized textiles, there was a real danger that a desire for novelty might lead to the creation of designs inappropriate to the technique. Remarkably, the court artists at Shuri seem to have worked comfortably within the repertoire of existing motifs, or at least types of motifs, and to have had a good understanding of the kasuri process. This rather exceptional collaboration between village weavers and court artists produced a superb textile tradition with designs of an elegant simplicity that were neither truly naive nor overly sophisticated.[38]

When we look at Okinawan and Japanese kasuri textiles today, we are struck by their quiet beauty, by the lively interplay of motifs, and the sense of pattern emerging from and disappearing back into the ground. Unlike the sophisticated dangawari textiles of the Kyoto tradition, kasuri textiles were primarily rural in origin, nurtured by women weaving at home to clothe their families as well as to meet outside demands from people very different from themselves. In Okinawa these demands were the tribute requirements of the court at Shuri. In Japan, they were the opportunities of the urban markets.

Kasuri textiles are a rich repository of the rural and urban history of Japan in the seventeenth, eighteenth, nineteenth, and early twentieth centuries. They reflect the plants, animals, and colors of the islands and the everyday lives of their people, their hard work, ingenuity, and their boundless creativity.

Mary Dusenbury is Curatorial Associate at the Spencer Museum of Art, Lawrence, Kansas, and doctoral student in Japanese art, University of Kansas.

Acknowledgments:
I am greatly indebted to my teacher and mentor Takimoto Kazuko, a weaver of silk tsumugi kasuri, and to my friend and colleague Hiroi Nobuko for many shared field trips. I am also very grateful to Stephen Addiss, Jerry Dusenbury, and Karen Mack for their critical suggestions.

1. Cotton was not native to Japan. Brought from India, it was first cultivated in south China in the seventh century, in central China in the ninth, and in Korea in the latter half of the fourteenth. During the Ōnin War (1467-77), a large quantity of cotton cloth was imported from Korea for military purposes. Under the active sponsorship of the warlord Toyotomi Hideyoshi (1536-98), cotton was finally established in Japan. Cotton does not grow easily in Japan, but the fiber is so superior to asa in warmth, ease of dyeing, and speed of production that no efforts were spared to establish the plant, including such measures as the abduction of Korean cotton farmers. By the mid- to late eighteenth century, cotton cultivation had spread throughout the country except for the northern regions of Tohoku (northern Honshu) and Hokkaido, where the climate is too cold. The introduction of cotton radically altered the lives and dress of the common people and spurred rural textile production.

See Mary Dusenbury, "Kasuri: A Japanese Textile" *Textile Museum Journal* 17 (1978) and Hideo Oda, "Kasuri gijutsu no keifu" (The Development of Kasuri Techniques) *Senshoku to seikatsu* 6 (Summer 1974), p. 31.

2. The terms "dangawari" (rung-patterned) and "shimekiri" (cut stripes), for example, refer to the appearance of the textile, not to the thread-resist technique used to achieve that effect. Thread-resist effected shifts of background color were also often a crucial element in the overall design of karaori, atsuita, and noshime garments, although neither the thread-resist technique itself nor the visual effect it produced were reflected in the names of these textiles.

3. Kasuri was generally called *i'chiri* or *to'chiri* in Okinawa, although there were many other local names for particular types of kasuri cloth. Despite differences between Okinawan and Japanese kasuri, in both traditions the technique was used in a similar manner, and Japanese feel they are closely related. See Toshio Tanaka and Reiko Tanaka, *Okinawa orimono no kenkyū* (A Study of Okinawan Textiles), 2 vols., (Kyoto: Shikōsha, 1976), p. 39.

4. In the Okinawan language, the words for tribute, tax, and trade goods were the same. See Mitsugi Sakihara, *A Brief History of Early Okinawa Based on the Omoro Sōshi* (Tokyo: Honpo Shoseki Press, 1987), p. 174.

5. See Kichiemon Okamura, "Nihon no kasuri" (Kasuri of Japan) in *Nihon no kasuri, Senshoku no bi*, vol. 11 (Kyoto: Shikosha, 1981), p. 65 and Tanaka and Tanaka, *Okinawa orimono no kenkyū*, vol. 2, p. 40, no. 20. The *Rekidai hōan* is a Ryūkyūan record of tribute and trade from the fourteenth through the nineteenth centuries.

6. See Yoshitarō Kamakura, "Textiles," in *Craft Treasures of Okinawa* (Kyoto and Tokyo: The National Museum of Modern Art and Kodansha International, 1978), p. 261, and Sometoshi Akashi, *Kasuri no shiteki kosatsu* (Kasuri: A Historical Inquiry) as quoted in Oda, "Kasuri gijutsu no keifu," p. 31.

7. Members of aristocratic families often chose to wear dark patterns on a light ground, rather than the more common light patterns on a dark ground. The entire lighter area must be tied and reserved from the dye to produce a dark figure on a light ground, an extremely time-consuming process. Textiles thus produced were not only brighter and gayer in mood, but served to reveal the wearer's wealth and high social position. The finest kasuri garments, and those most difficult to produce, had colorful motifs woven into a clear yellow ground. These were reserved for the king and members of the royal family. See Kamakura, "Textiles," p. 261.

8. See Okamura, "Nihon no kasuri," p. 65. Kamakura has suggested that Ryūkyūans might also have been familiar with Indian warp-, weft-, and double-ikat textiles through the port of Palembang, which is described in the *Rekidai hōan*. See Kamakura, "Textiles," pp. 264-65.

9. See, for example, the complex warp ikats of Sumba and the imported eighth-century Taishi Kando fragments preserved in the Hōryūji Hōmotsukan, Tokyo National Museum, Japan.

10. See Tanaka and Tanaka, *Okinawa orimono no kenkyū*, vol. 2, pp. 41-46, for a catalogue of motifs.

11. In Japan, the inner bark of *kōzo*, a member of the mulberry family, was a common material used for binding off the sections of thread to be reserved from the dye. Kōzo is strong and shrinks when wet, gripping the fibers and preventing dye from seeping under the ties.

12. Some of the simplest and most common motifs resemble tatoo markings that can still be seen on the hands of elderly women from remote islands, motifs whose origins are unknown and meanings forgotten.

13. The yearly textile tribute consisted of 3000 *tan* of bashōfu (banana-fiber cloth), 6000 tan of Ryūkyū *jōfu* ("high cloth," or fine-quality hemp or ramie), and 10,000 tan of *kafu* ("low cloth," or rough hemp). One tan is enough fabric to make one full-length garment (kimono or kosode), or 36 ft. by 10 in. (ca. 11 m by ca. 37 cm).

14. See Okamura, "Nihon no kasuri," p. 67; and Amanda Mayer Stinchecum, "Textile Production under the Poll Tax System in Ryūkyū," *Textile Museum Journal* 27/28(1988/89).

15. The haori is now in the collection of the Tokugawa Art Museum, Nagoya. For a good discussion of this important textile in English see Amanda Mayer Stinchecum, "A Common Thread: Japanese Ikat Textiles," in *Asian Art* 3:1(Winter 1990). See also Kyoto National Museum, *Nihon no senshoku* (Japanese Textiles), (Kyoto: Shikōsha, 1987); and Sae Ogasawara, *Kasuri, Nihon no bijutsu*, 309 (February 1992), p. 2.

16. On at least one occasion "gifts" were brought directly to the Tokugawa rulers: "On the occasion of his visit of submission to the Tokugawa regime in the year Keicho 15 (1610), King Shō Nei called at Sumpu and presented Tokugawa Ieyasu with three hundred *tan* ... of *taihei* cloth and one hundred rolls of banana-fiber cloth. Shogun Tokugawa Hidetada in Edo received two hundred rolls of *taihei* cloth and one hundred rolls of banana-fiber cloth; a further one hundred rolls of *taihei* and fifty rolls of banana-fiber cloth were given to various dignitaries." See Kamakura, "Textiles," p. 261.

17. Although it would take more than one example to make definite statements about technique and aesthetic, this suggests that hikizurashi, "slide-pulling" the weft, was either a later development or one which was used for local textiles but not for the highest quality court or tribute textiles at this time.

18. References to *bashō nuno* (bashōfu), *terifu*, and *taiheifu* in the *Sumpu onwakemono-chō* (Register of the Legacy of Sumpu Castle) suggest that Ryūkyūan textiles were among the objects bequeathed by the shogun Tokugawa Ieyasu to his sons. The document was compiled between 1616 and 1618. See Stinchecum, "A Common Thread," pp. 45- 46; and Yoshinobu Tokugawa, translated and adapted by Louise Allison Cort and Monica Bethe, *The Tokugawa Collection of No Robes and Masks* (New York: Japan Society, 1977).

19. The great Asuka (552-645) and Nara (645-794) period temples, the Hōryūji and the Tōdaiji respectively, each own fragments of elaborate polychrome warp ikat banners that were used for Buddhist ceremonies in the seventh and eighth centuries. The motifs, technique, and traditional names of these textiles suggest that they entered Japan from the southern trade route, but their provenance is unknown. The Hōryūji textiles are now housed in the Hōryūji Hōmotsukan on the grounds of the Tokyo National Museum, and the Shōsō'in fragments are in the Shōsō'in Repository in Nara. See Mary Dusenbury, "Kasuri: A Japanese Textile", pp. 41-64; and Kaneo Matsumura, *Jōdaigire* (Seventh and Eighth Century Textiles from the Shōsō'in and Hōryūji), (Kyoto: Shikōsha, 1984).

20. The earliest extant hirao of which I am aware dates from the twelfth century and has been preserved in the Maeda family collection. It has sectionally dyed threads with a long purple central section fading to white at either end. For a reproduction and short discussion of this textile, see Sae Ogasawara, *Kasuri*, p. 2.

21. Both the merchant kosode and the Kenshin kosode have been reproduced in a number of publications. See Kyoto National Museum, *Nihon no senshoku*.

22. Most of the extant garments are Noh costumes and have been preserved within Noh theater. A few were given to a Noh actor as a reward for a particularly fine performance by a lordly sponsor. Such garments were highly treasured. The well-established Noh theaters, patronized by the ruling Tokugawa, were in a strong position to care for their costumes. They did this to preserve them for future generations and as a sign of their lineage. It is thanks to their care that so many fine seventeenth- and eighteenth-century silk garments have been preserved. For a description of these garments, see Tokugawa, *The Tokugawa Collection.*

23. See, for example, Jaap Langewis's pioneering study of Japanese *kasuri,* "Japanese Ikat Textiles," *Kultuurpatronen* 5/6(1963), pp. 40-83.

24. To control potential political rivals to the Tokugawa clan, the sankin kōtai system required that each local feudal lord or daimyo spend every other year in Edo, and that he establish his family in a permanent residence in the capital city. Families were, in effect, held hostage in Edo when the daimyo was in his home province. The maintenance in appropriate style of two residences seriously drained the provincial coffers, as did the biennial procession of the daimyo with full retinue between province and capital. Sometimes the Tokugawa government moved a daimyo from one fief to another in a further effort to corrode his power base. The system was enforced in different ways at different periods, but throughout the Edo period it provided an important channel of information from one part of the country to another. The daimyo traveled in style, sporting their finest apparel as they moved along the main thoroughfares from their provinces to the capital. Local people gathered to watch the great processions and to compare the lords' goods and attire. The daimyo's large retinues included artists and craftsmen, who were thus exposed to new fashions and techniques in the capital and who, in turn, brought new knowledge back to their own province or to the new province to which their lord had been assigned.

25. Oda, "Kasuri gijutsu no keifu," p. 33 (as in n.1); and "Kasuri," "Satsumagasuri," and "Satsumajōfu" in *Genshoku senshoku daijiten* (Fundamental Encyclopedia of Weaving and Dyeing), (Kyoto: Tankosha, 1977), pp. 229, 450.

26. Oda, "Kasuri gijutsu no keifu," p. 33, suggests a date between 1661-65, while Okamura, *"Nihon no kasuri,"* p. 71 suggests 1716-36 (as in n.14).

27. William Hauser has studied cotton production and marketing in the Kinai district near Osaka. Most of this cloth was plain, unpatterned white cotton which sold to katazome dyers: "Weaving skills became a marketable commodity in the Kinai region as evident from the 1793 wage scales for female agricultural laborers in the Tayasu domain of Izumi. One of the primary components of salary rankings among female laborers was weaving ability. Skilled laborers were expected to be capable of all kinds of agricultural work and able to weave one tan of cloth per day in the off- season. The lowest ranking female laborers were expected to weave one-half tan of cloth daily and do various kinds of labor service." See his article, "The Kinai Cotton Trade," *The Journal of Asiatic Studies* 4:33(August 1974), pp. 637-38.

28. Thomas C. Smith has studied the asa weaving industry in Echigo: "Such was the scale of production that marketing of the finished product was organized nationally. Peasant weavers, whose numbers in Uonuma county alone apparently ran to many thousands, sold their cloth in three local markets that drew buyers from as far away as Kyoto and Osaka. Toward the end of the eighteenth century certain wholesale merchants were given a monopoly of purchase in these markets by the local lord. This measure, as was intended by its authors, worked to depress the producer's price, and at length the peasant weavers began banding together into small companies (*nakama*) to circumvent the prescriptive monopoly and ship their cloth directly to Edo." See his book *The Agrarian Origins of Modern Japan* (Stanford: Stanford University Press, 1959), p. 77.

29. The Freer Gallery of Art in Washington, D.C., owns a fine impression of this print, which is part of the series *Thirty-Six Views of Mt. Fuji.*

30. See Okamura, "Nihon no kasuri," p. 68, for a chart and discussion of the tools and materials used in different parts of the country.

31. The itajime was first introduced from China in the Asuka (552-654) or Nara period (645-794) but was used at that time to dye finished fabric (*kyōkechi*). Some very fine examples of textiles dyed in this manner remain in the Shōsō'in. It gradually fell into disuse but was either revived or, more probably, reinvented in 1837 by Miura Tomoshichi in Yamato (the district around the old capital, Nara) as a method for resist-dyeing warps. The method is well suited to volume production, and the subsequent invention or introduction of the itajime in Omi (by Koroda Shinso of Takamiya in 1850) is said to have increased the daily production of one man by a factor of twenty. The initial cost of the ita and its carving was high, but, once made, it could be used any number of times and so was suited to the volume production desirable in an active market economy. Viscous dyes such as indigo do not run well through the grooves of the itajime, and yet if the apparatus remained too long in the dye bath, the edges were likely to fuzz to an undesirable extent (a characteristic of the itajime is its comparatively "hard" edges). As Yamato kasuri developed largely in accord with the use and development of the itajime, its patterns also developed in a way compatible with the itajime's peculiar characteristics, so that Yamato is now famous for its rather unusual white background kasuri with middle-sized indigo blue patterns.

After its initial development as a device for warp kasuri, the itajime was modified to produce weft kasuri. In 1839 Ohtsuka Taizo of Kurume is said to have started producing weft e-gasuri on the itajime. This perhaps marked the beginning of the rapid development of Kurume e-gasuri in the mid-nineteenth century, and before long the itajime was being used in many other kasuri producing areas of the country as well. See Oda, "Kasuri gijutsu no keifu," p. 34.

32. From information provided by the Ritto Historical Folk Museum and the Omi Jōfu Denryū Sangyō Kaikan in Shiga prefecture, Februrary 1992.

33. The mokuhiki allows for the minute adjustment of over a thousand individual warp threads as they are wound onto the back beam of the loom as it is being set up for weaving. The mokuhiki is a vertical frame that stands on the loom between the back beam and the harnesses or, as in Kyoto, on a separate stand devised for

this process. Thin wooden or metal slats are threaded horizontally through a series of closely spaced slots in the upright members of the frame. In Kyoto the warp is first put through an open-topped reed on the front of the stand, then through a series of rollers, then selectively let run straight to the back beam or put over one or another of the many horizontal bars. As the warp is wound on the back beam, the pattern slides into place. The back beam is then removed and placed in position on the loom and the warp set up as usual. The mokuhiki was used in Kyoto to shift blocks of warp and also to create vertical arrow patterns, a motif one often finds in silk thread-resist garments from Kyoto. Other areas adopted or invented the mokuhiki also. A simple version allowed women weaving work clothes to slide the warp a bit one way or the other to add visual interest to the cloth. Sometimes the mokuhiki was left on the loom and the patterned threads simply hung off the back and weighted.

34. See Kamon Yoshimoto, ed., *Kasuri moyo zukan* (*Traditional Ikat* [*Kasuri*]: *Design Collection*), (Tokyo: Gurafikusha, 1984) for reproductions of a collection owned by the Research Association for Old Textiles. The collection dates from the mid- nineteenth through the early twentieth centuries and is arranged by provenance.

35. See Oda, "Kasuri gijutsu no keifu," p. 36, for twentieth-century technical innovations.

36. Native and domesticated plants yielded the strong yellows of *fukugi* (*Garcinia spicata*) and *ukon* (*curcuma longa*, turmeric); reds of *sakishima suo* (*Heritiera littorali*, a species of sappanwood), *benibana* (*Carthamus tinctorius*, safflower), and *koro root* (*Droseorea rhipogonoides* Oliv.); the blues of the Ryūkyūan and Indian indigos; and browns from *momokawa* (*Myrica rubra*, a species of wild peach), *tekachi* (*Raphiolepis umbellata*), and other indigenous barks used in conjunction with the iron-rich mud of the islands.

37. We do not know when this system first started nor do we know much about the development of government control over textile production. The earliest extant copies of miezuchō leaves date from the late eighteenth century. See Stinchecum, "A Common Thread," p. 48.

38. Collaboration is perhaps not the right word. Although the textiles show the influence of both village weaving traditions and the design work of the court artists and standards they imposed, the collaboration was an enforced one, and all writers stress the hardships imposed on the weavers by the quantity and quality of the work demanded of them.

TEXTILES OF OKINAWA

AMANDA MAYER STINCHECUM

The women stand knee-deep in the aquamarine shallows of the sea, their figures casting long shadows through the water onto the white sandy bottom as early morning sunlight slants over the pines and scrubby trees crowding the edge of Sukuji beach. Each has unwrapped her furoshiki bundle, disclosing pristine rolls of crisp, ivory-colored Yaeyama jōfu. Taking the precious rolls of cloth, the product of weeks of painstaking work, they fling them one by one into the water, staking them at each end.

For hours, as the dazzling sun rises in the intensely blue sky, its rays refracting through the clear water, the ribbons of whitening fabric float. The seawater sets the dye to a rich, deep brown while the sun bleaches the nearly transparent ramie yarns ever whiter. For hundreds of years, the women of Yaeyama have taken their rolls of fine ramie cloth, patterned with starry ikat motifs, to the beach to soak them in the clear waters of the sea.

LYING BETWEEN THE PACIFIC AND THE EAST CHINA SEA AT THE crossroads of Japan, Korea, southern China, Taiwan, the Philippines, and Southeast Asia, the Ryūkyū Islands bear the imprint of all these cultures to varying degrees. But they also possess a distinctive tradition of their own — a social, religious, linguistic, and artistic heritage viable enough to have survived centuries of submission to China, subjugation to Japan, as well as annual devastation by typhoons and the near-total destruction of their material culture by both American and Japanese armed forces, followed by twenty-seven years of American military occupation between 1945 and 1972.

At the southern end of the Japanese archipelago, Okinawa is known to Americans primarily as the site of the most terrible battle of the Pacific theater of World War II. The name Okinawa (Ryū., Uchinaa) now refers to the largest island in the Ryūkyū (Ryū., Ouuchuu) chain — the dozens of islands stretching between Kyūshū and Taiwan — and to the prefecture that includes most of the islands since their involuntary annexation by Japan in 1879. (The Amami island group, Ryūkyūan in culture, was absorbed into Kagoshima prefecture.) In what follows the words "Ryūkyū" and "Ryūkyūan" refer to the period before annexation; Okinawa refers to the prefecture after annexation, as well as the main island. Now an integral part of Japan in terms of government, educational system, and official language, Okinawa and its people are bound to Japan by both ancient and recent cultural traits. Before its annexation, the kingdom was known as Ryūkyū, a Japanese name derived from the Chinese Liu Ch'iu.

Throughout the history of these islands, textiles have played a role that transcends their stunning beauty and practical utility. Their economic, social, and cultural importance is different historically from the role of textiles in mainland Japan; today textiles still embody the spirit of Ryūkyū and of Okinawans. Cloth woven from fibers raised on the subtropical coral islands and dyed with colors extracted from plants unknown on the mainland helped to shape the history and culture of Ryūkyū in a unique way. Textiles have been intimately bound up with the cultural and political identity of Okinawa and its people as trade goods, tribute to foreign governments, signifiers of court rank and social position, tax payments, products made by the common people for the use of the royal court, and eventually as goods produced for mainland markets.

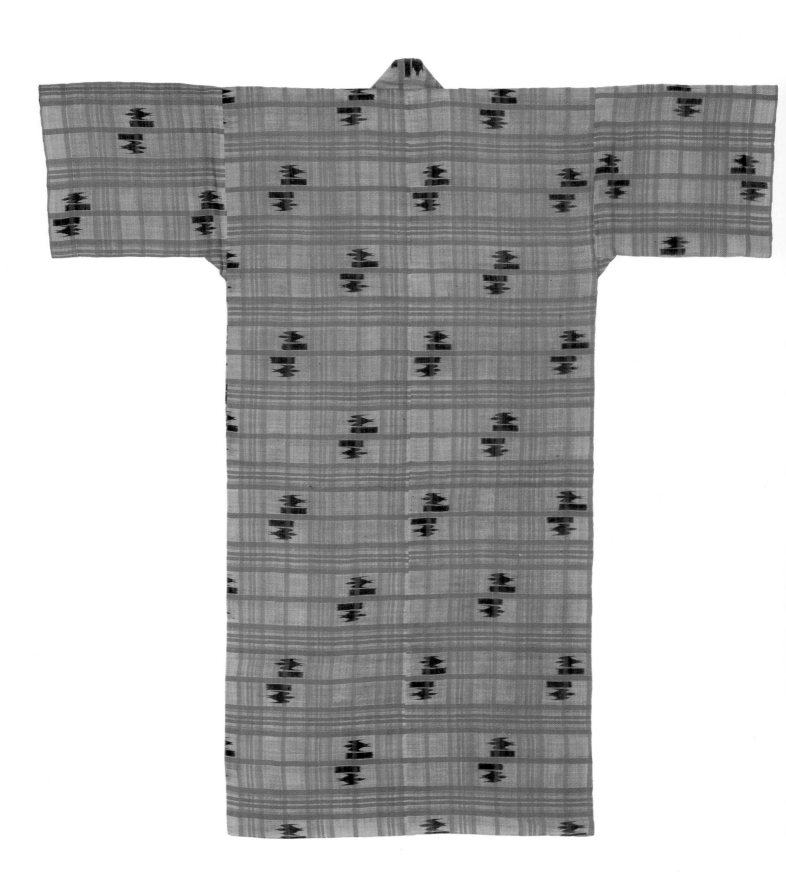

The massive destruction by the bombings of the war caused the loss not only of many precious textiles but also irreplaceable historical records and documents, books, and tools. Although textile history throughout the world deals with the most fragile artifacts of material culture, that of Okinawa has suffered more damage than most, and avoidable damage at that. Fortunately, outstanding examples of the islands' textile arts were collected before the war, mainly by Japanese members of the Mingei (folk craft) movement. Some of these artifacts have been returned to the people of Okinawa and preserved in the Okinawa Prefectural Museum; some are in the Japan Folk Art Museum in Tokyo. Objects belonging to the Shō family, the former royal family of Ryūkyū, are stored in the Tokyo National Museum, but are rarely on public view. In addition, some textiles and other objects, mainly lacquer and ceramics, were brought to America and to Europe. But in examining the history of Ryūkyūan textiles, one must remember that factual information beyond what can be determined from the textiles themselves is extremely scarce and must be teased out of obscure documents in which they are mentioned only in passing.

Although indications of human habitation in the Ryūkyū archipelago can be traced for many thousands of years, firm documentary evidence for the presence of woven textiles is no more ancient than the late fourteenth century, when Ryūkyū engaged in a flourishing maritime trade as an entrepôt between East and Southeast Asia. Ships not only transported goods from Siam, Palembang, Java, Sumatra, Malacca, Patani, Annam, Sunda, and Luzon to Japan, Korea, and China, but also exported cargoes of local products — sulphur, horses, cloth. In the mid-sixteenth century, competition from European ships began to erode Ryūkyū's lucrative trade. With the invasion of the kingdom and virtual subjugation of Ryūkyū by the Japanese feudal domain of Satsuma in 1609, commerce diminished greatly; what remained was closely controlled, and its profits taken by Satsuma. The first official tribute payment from Ryūkyū to the Ming court was made in 1372, according to a much later chronicle, but private trade must have existed previously. The 1372 tribute is said to have included — in addition to horses and sulphur — *seijuku kafu*, a type of cloth, presented by three kings of Okinawa Island.[1] *Kafu* (summer cloth) appears to refer to fabric made of ramie (*choma, karamushi*; Ryū., *maauu, buu*; *Boehmeria nivea* Hook & Arn.). It became an important item of foreign trade and tribute for the kingdom of Ryūkyū, which was united by King Shō Hashi in 1429.

Lively early accounts of indigenous cloth and clothing appear in reports of Koreans shipwrecked and cast ashore on islands of the Ryūkyū chain.

EARLY REPORTS FROM RYŪKYŪ

Lively early accounts of indigenous cloth and clothing appear in the reports of Koreans shipwrecked and cast ashore on various islands of the Ryūkyū chain, who were later escorted back to Korea by representatives of the court. These reports give us valuable first-hand information about many aspects of life in the islands. A Korean who drifted to the island of Gaja in 1452 and was taken to the Shuri court described the customs of the people on the main island of Okinawa.[2] He attested that they produced ramie but did not have cotton; while one in ten households raised silkworms, they had not yet managed to produce silk yarn or cloth. An account of Korean sailors cast ashore in 1456 on Kumejima, 100 kilometers west of Okinawa Island, noted that the people wove mats from rushes. They reported no mulberry, cotton, or

Unlined robe (detail)
Ramie with white weft ikat
Meiji period, second half 19th century, Yaeyama or Miyako
Collection of Nihon Mingeikan

Unlined robe
Meiji period, second half 19th century, Yaeyama or Miyako
Ramie with cotton warp and weft stripes and weft ikat
Collection of Nihon Mingeikan

asa (a vague term that probably refers here to hemp), but observed cultivated ramie.[3] Apparently on Kumejima, at least, efforts at sericulture had begun to bear fruit, for the account mentions that the people raised silkworms and wove some kind of multicolored cloth from silk.

The most extensive early account of both textiles and clothing was recorded by three Korean sailors cast ashore in 1477 on the small island of Yonaguni, at the southern end of the archipelago.[4] Rescued by the islanders, they were taken to seven other islands in the Yaeyama and Miyako island groups before reaching Naha in 1479. On returning to Korea that year, they made an extremely detailed report of their journey. It states that the people of Yonaguni had neither hemp nor cotton, nor did they raise silkworms. They wove cloth only from ramie — a fiber taken from the inner surface of the bark of the ramie plant, a member of the nettle family — wearing it undyed, or dyeing it with indigo.[5] Like Koreans, they used a loom equipped with a reed and shuttle (hence more complex than the simplest type of primitive loom), but in other respects their looms were different from Korean looms. They wove patterned cloth like that woven in Korea, and the density of warp yarns and the fineness or coarseness of the cloth were also similar to Korean textiles.[6] The people of Tarama used ramie cloth, which they dyed with indigo and then pounded to finish it. The castaways described the color "as like that of damask."[7]

The textiles and clothing the castaways observed at the capital of Shuri were much richer and more complicated than those of the outlying islands. Gifts of blue and red cotton cloth were given to their escorts; the king wore silk, and his retainers wore various types of multicolored fabrics as well as fine white ramie cloth. It may be that most of the formal clothing worn by the nobility at that time was made of textiles that entered Ryūkyū from China, Japan, or Southeast Asia in exchange for exported items, but the long robes of white ramie worn by the common people were probably produced locally.[8]

None of these accounts contains a mention of fiber-banana cloth (*bashōfu*; Ryū., *baasaa*; *Musa sapientum* L., var. *liukiuensis* Matsumura), which eventually became the clothing of kings and government officials as well as workclothes and even underwear for farmers and townspeople — men, women, and children. Bashōfu is unique to Okinawa, although a coarse cloth, *abaca*, is made in other Southeast Asian cultures from another species of banana tree (*Musa textilis* Nee). The fiber-banana tree (a tree closely related to the familiar fruit-bearing variety but lacking edible fruit; Jap., *ito bashō*) was not indigenous to the islands. Nevertheless, as ramie became increasingly important for trade and tribute, bashōfu replaced it as the textile most widely worn by the common people.

The first evidence of fiber-banana cloth in Ryūkyū appears in a 1546 account by another group of shipwrecked Koreans. The method described for making both fine and coarse cloth from fiber obtained from the stalk of the fiber-banana is uncannily close to the method used today in Kijoka, on the main island of Okinawa.[9] It is not mentioned in lists of tribute goods until 1587, suggesting that its production was refined during the sixteenth century and perhaps introduced not long before that. Even today in Okinawa, stands of fiber-banana trees grow only around houses and cultivated fields or near traces of ancient habitation, enforcing the notion that bashō trees were exotic, probably imported from islands to the south.

References to textiles as trade or tribute goods in early historical records and travel accounts give us some clues about the textiles and clothing produced and used by the people of the islands. But in light of our knowledge of Ryūkyū's thriving international trade and the elliptical nature of terms describing textiles in early records, it is often difficult to distinguish between local and imported goods. Lists of items presented by Ryūkyū in the fifteenth and sixteenth centuries to the Ming court, and to the courts of Korea, Siam, Malacca, Palembang, Java, and Sumatra include textiles clearly not Ryūkyūan in origin; items such as "lustrous green satin," "red cotton," "silk gauze in various colors," "color-patterned cotton cloth," "blue brocade with peacock feathers woven into it," must have entered Ryūkyū through the entrepôt trading activities of the kingdom. In addition, official sources list textile gifts received from other states: black, white, and red fine ramie or hemp cloth, "fine white cotton cloth," "red chain-patterned cloth," "red Western cloth," "yellow cotton kerchief [or sarong?] with colored silks woven into it," and many others described in strings of Chinese characters obscure in meaning.

The cultivation and spinning of cotton seems to have been introduced considerably later than that of silk or banana fiber. Xiao Chongye, a Ming emissary to the court of King Shō Ei in 1579, commented that cotton was neither cultivated nor woven in Okinawa, and that the only cloth woven was ramie.[10] Xia Ziyang, a slightly later envoy who came to Shuri in 1606, wrote that the climate of the islands was not suited to growing cotton. Unlike the technologies of fiber banana and silk, which probably came from islands to the south and from China respectively, cotton cultivation seems to have entered Ryūkyū from Japan. According to the Ryūkyūkoku yūraiki (Record of the Origins of Ryūkyū), published in 1713, a certain Gima Shinjō brought cotton seeds from Satsuma in 1611, planted them, and had the resulting cotton woven by two Japanese women living in Naha.[11]

During the period described in the early Korean accounts, the question whether the people of Ryūkyū were weaving or dyeing any cloth more complex than plain-weave cloth patterned with checks or perhaps simple indigo-dyed ikat must be examined in depth. It is more likely that the refined skills and decorative techniques characteristic of Ryūkyūan textiles from the sixteenth century on made their way gradually to the islands in the form of textiles (like those mentioned above) from China, Japan, Southeast Asia, and perhaps India, brought as tribute, gifts, or trade items. Besides transmission of sericulture and techniques of patterned weave structures, including gauze and float-weaves, which probably came to Ryūkyū from China, the most important Chinese legacy to the islands' textile arts was the complex system of regulating the colors and types of fabric for clothing worn at court by officials of every rank.[12] The skills and techniques — ikat in particular — transmitted from elsewhere in Asia were probably developed under the aegis of the Shuri court and the oppressive administration of local officials on the Outer Islands of Miyako, Yaeyama, and Kumejima during the period following the golden years of Ryūkyū's maritime trade.

In April 1609, three thousand armed men in the service of Shimazu Iehisa, feudal lord of the domain of Satsuma (present-day Kagoshima prefecture) in southern Kyūshū invaded the kingdom of Ryūkyū, ostensibly to punish Shuri for the king's failure to submit to the new Tokugawa shogunate.[13] King Shō Nei was captured and led triumphantly back to Edo by Shimazu, recently confirmed in a lapsed thirteenth-century title, Lord of the Twelve Southern Islands, by the first Tokugawa shogun, Ieyasu. The king, held prisoner for three years, as well as the officials who had accompanied him were forced to sign humiliating oaths not only declaring Ryūkyū's present and future submission to Satsuma but also stating falsely that the islands had been a Satsuma dependency since ancient times.

Although nominally it remained an independent kingdom until its forced annexation by Japan in 1879, Ryūkyū had in effect become a territory of Satsuma. Satsuma's interest in Ryūkyū was primarily financial: to use the kingdom's tributary and trade relations with the Ming court in order to bypass secretly the Tokugawa government's prohibition on foreign trade. In addition, Satsuma levied a tribute on Ryūkyū of 14,200 koku of rice, slightly less than 7 percent of the total revenues of the kingdom, plus an additional 8,000 koku from the king's private treasury.[14] In 1611 Satsuma also demanded from Shuri 6,000 rolls of fine ramie cloth (jōfu), 10,000 rolls of coarse ramie cloth, and 3,000 rolls of bashōfu.[15]

In order to pay Satsuma, the Shuri government levied taxes on its own people, which, on the islands of Kumejima, Miyako, and Yaeyama took the form of a poll tax. Every man and woman between the ages of fifteen and fifty had to pay a fixed amount each year, regardless of health or circumstances. The taxes were to be paid in rice, but soon a certain percentage of this levy was converted to cloth, easier to store and transport, and on which both Shuri and eventually Satsuma could make a much higher profit. In general, the cultivation of grain was allotted to men, the production of tax cloth to women.

In 1749, about half of the tax assessment on these islands was paid in cloth and half in gra[in] thus men and women bore equal financial responsibilities toward the government.

We know little about the textiles sent to foreign lands or those worn by the Shuri court before the Satsuma invasion. We might assume that women were given the job of making tax cloth because they were associated with the household dyeing and weaving of the kinds of fabrics observed by the Korean castaways. But after the instigation of the poll tax, the women of Kumejima, Miyako, and Yaeyama bore a significant part of the economic burden of each village and were officially recognized as sources of revenue. In 1749, about half of the entire tax assessment on these islands was paid in cloth and the other half in grain; thus men and women bore equal financial responsibilities toward the government. Even today the visitor to Okinawa cannot help noticing the prominent role played by women in supporting their families. Working outside the home is not only accepted, it is common.

On Kumejima, tax cloth took the form of silk pongee spun from silk batting, the cottony cocoon of the silkworm, and patterned with stripes, checks, or ikat. On the Outer Islands of Miyako and Yaeyama, ramie cloth, especially the finer grade known as jōfu, some of it ikat-patterned, filled the tax-cloth quotas. Although bashōfu was exported to China, Korea, and Japan and worn by the royal household and court officials in Shuri, there is no indication that its production was ever part of the poll tax system. Under this institution, not only was the quantity of cloth specified, but its type, quality, color, and pattern as well. Yarn-making, dyeing, and weaving were strictly supervised by officials appointed by Shuri in accordance with precise instructions dispatched from the court, either in written form or through books consisting of leaves of painted designs (*miezuchō*, "revered picture books").

The ultimate uses of tax cloth collected from the islands have yet to be investigated. Perhaps all of it was sent to Satsuma as tribute, but this is unlikely; some may have been sold directly by the Shuri government as trade goods, some sent to China or other governments as tribute or presents, or worn by the royal household. The vivid colorings and bold patterns of many of the extant *miezu* designs, even the term itself, point to their use by the nobility. We do know that both tax cloth (*kōnōfu*) and textiles made expressly for the court (*goyōfu*) were produced by the people of the Outer Islands under duress and strict supervision. Since Satsuma had taken over the spoils of Ryūkyū's maritime trade, the nobility could no longer rely on foreign goods for the luxury items they had come to treasure. Based on the skills already existing in the islands, the Shuri court built a system of craft production for its own use as well as for tribute to Satsuma.

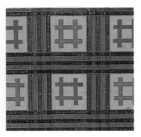

Design cartoons (*miezu*) Late Edo-early Meiji period, 19th century, Shuri, Okinawa Collection of Okinawa Prefecture Museum

The view that Satsuma singled out Ryūkyū for punitive assessment, and that the poll tax itself was a terrible burden on the islands' people, is still popular in both Okinawa and Japan. Nevertheless, studies have shown that Satsuma's demands were not unusually severe, and conditions on Ryūkyū were no worse than in some regions of the mainland. The injustice and cruelty of the poll tax appear to have resulted from the way in which it was administered by local officials, who took advantage of the people under their charge.[16]

Many of the textiles created during the Satsuma period were enlivened with ikat (*kasuri*; Ryū., *ichirii*, *to-tchirii*, *kashiirii*), as are many of the most beautiful traditional fabrics woven in Okinawa today. Textile-makers of Kijoka, Yuntanza, Shuri, Kumejima, Miyako, and Yaeyama each produced kasuri of abundant inventiveness and outstanding quality and design. Unlike mainland Japan, where the development and spread of ikat techniques has been associated (perhaps incorrectly) with textiles made by the common people for their own use, in Ryūkyū the use of kasuri garments was limited to the privileged classes. Refinement of techniques and aesthetic sensibility evident in the ikats of Ryūkyū was a direct result of court supervision. How and when ikat was first transmitted to the islands, and when Ryūkyūans first began to make their own ikat textiles, remains unclear; some of the patterned fabrics observed by the Korean castaways may have been locally produced ikat. They may also have been tie-dyed cloth resist, a form of *shibori*.

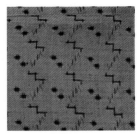

Unlined robe (detail) Meiji period, second half 19th century, Yaeyama or Miyako Ramie with weft and double ikat Collection of Nihon Mingeikan

Mainland Japanese and Okinawan historians point speculatively to possible roots for ikat in mainland China or India, despite the virtual absence of evidence for premodern ikat production in China. India, on the other hand, has a long and elaborate tradition of ikat production, at least as ancient as the seventh-century wall paintings of Ajanta, which depict unmistakably ikat-patterned garments. Archaeological finds dating to the early fifth century from Astana, in western Asia, push back the origins of ikat even earlier and suggest a source outside of India.[17] The means by which ikat textiles or techniques were transmitted to Ryūkyū, however, remain a persistent problem. Despite the absence of any convincing evidence, many Japanese scholars maintain that ikat technique entered Ryūkyū from Southeast Asia and was transmitted from there to Japan. The ikat fabrics of Southeast Asia are mainly warp-patterned, but weft ikats are made as well. Double ikat was (and still is) produced only in the Balinese village of Tenganan. This casts some doubt on the idea of a direct importation of techniques from the south. Inventive combinations of warp, weft and double ikats in an integrated design, however, appear to be characteristic of Ryūkyūan, and to a lesser extent, Japanese, textiles. In Japan, ikat was widely manufactured in a variety of fibers and styles and worn by people of virtually all social classes. The evolution of kasuri in Ryūkyū is probably closely tied to its development in Japan, but the transmission and history of ikat in Japan itself has yet to be unraveled. Extant examples of ikat in Japan date back to the fifteenth and sixteenth centuries. Japanese *emakimono* (handscrolls) dating to the fourteenth and fifteenth centuries unambiguously depicting ikat garments suggest the development of ikat in Japan considerably earlier than its documented appearance in Ryūkyū in the late seventeenth century.[18]

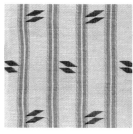

    The ikat of the islands encompasses most of the resist-dyeing techniques used in mainland Japan, but the most basic is that of binding off segments of yarn to be resisted (*kukuri*) with coarse yarns or ribbons of fiber. One method, known as weft-shifting (*hikizurashi*; Ryū., *mimigwaa yui*) is certainly more highly developed in Ryūkyūan textiles than any others, and may be unique. Sections of the weft yarns are bound off in simple blocks, and the yarns dyed. As the weaver incorporates these ikatted wefts into her web, she shifts each weft to right or left to form an oblique or curved motif. The example in this collection (cat. 62), woven with raw-silk warps and machine-spun ramie wefts, is patterned with almost black indigo-dyed stripes and pairs of weft-ikat motifs created by weft-shifting (the name of the motif, *mayu bichuu*, means "painted-on eyebrows"). Okinawan ikat motifs, even those which appear to be simple geometric or purely decorative forms, are derived from the everyday lives of the islanders — from domestic animals or agricultural implements, from parts of a house or of the human body, from elements in nature.

    In addition to the fine ramie cloth and silk pongee dyed and woven for tax cloth, other materials were made especially for the use of the court. Both jōfu from Miyako and Yaeyama, and Kumejima pongee were also dyed for the aristocracy in strong hues, including the yellow reserved for the use of the king and his household; blue and red with contrasting ikat motifs or bold stripes or checks; and pink, yellow, or pale blue-green jōfu with blue-black ikat motifs. Other textiles were produced in Shuri workshops for restricted use, including richly colored bashōfu, some in difficult gauze weaves; silks patterned with various float-weave structures, or combining float-weave with gauze; vivid silk checks with ikat motifs framed within each lattice; and *bingata* stencil designs printed on cotton, ramie, and silk.

CHARACTERISTICS OF BINGATA

    The word bingata literally means something like "scarlet patterns," but it refers to the gorgeously multicolored stencil-dyed cloth associated with the Ryūkyūan court. The early Ryūkyūan term for bingata is *katachiki* (Jap., *katatsuke*, stencil application). But scattered references in seventeenth- and eighteenth-century documents give us little idea of the techniques or designs of that time. Bingata has elements in common with both the stencil-dyeing and *yūzen* freehand paste-resist dyeing of Japan. How their history is interwoven with that of bingata remains a mystery, and earlier roots in the resist-dyeing techniques of China, India, and Southeast Asia are even more obscure.

The characteristic vivid colors of bingata textiles derive from the use of intensely colored mineral pigments in a medium of soybean liquid, built up in thinly applied layers, against a background of white, blazing yellow, deep pink, an aquamarine like the seas surrounding the islands, or a blue like the sky just before nightfall. Although most bingata designs make use of a repeated pattern unit, at its best the resulting design gives a sense of rhythmic movement, an illusory freedom completely different in feeling from the rigid stasis of Japanese stencil-dyed materials of the time. This rhythm overrides even the symmetry with which many of these designs are composed. Until the abolition of the royal court, the magnificently bold, large-scale designs — phoenixes and dragons, drooping wisteria blossoms, swooping swallows, and other motifs clearly Japanese (a few Chinese) in origin — were reserved for the highest aristocracy.

Bingata textiles were made to order in Shuri workshops and were never sold on the open market or used as trade goods. Although the use of bingata was no longer restricted after Ryūkyū became Okinawa prefecture, in fact only a small number of wealthy commoners and the remnants of the no-longer-official royal household and nobility still ordered it from the few dyers who continued to produce it. Everyone else used a kind of rough bingata dyed only with indigo.[19] Probably the examples in this collection (cat. 67 and 68) were made during this period. Until after Okinawa's reversion to Japan in 1972, few people in the islands could afford it, or, perhaps more difficult, bring themselves to wear the brilliant colors that had been the special prerogative of aristocracy.

The characteristic look of bingata results from the opaque pigment colors used for design motifs against a transparent background color of vegetable dyes or translucent color resulting from pigmentized dyes, called lakes. The specialized work of making bingata had been carried on within court workshops; after official court patronage disappeared, bingata was produced by individual families of dyers. The entire process, from cutting and preparing the stencils of Japanese paper to the final stages of dyeing and finishing, was carried on within one household workshop, as it is today. Usually the whole design unit would be dyed using only one stencil (for very large-scale patterns, more would be needed).

In the bingata technique, a single length of cloth (enough to make one garment) is laid on a long narrow board, and the stencil is placed on it. Resist paste made of glutinous rice, rice bran, salt, water, and lime is then spread over it with a spatula. The stencil is lifted, moved, and the process is repeated until the entire length of the cloth is covered. A sizing made of liquid extracted from ground soybeans is then brushed onto the fabric, sealing the paste; the protein in the liquid also binds the pigment colors to the cloth. Mineral pigments (now mostly synthetic) mixed with soybean liquid are applied with a stubby brush to the design areas not covered by the paste, in layers of increasing intensity. After the main color areas have been filled in,

Robe (detail, top)
Meiji period, second half 19th century, Shuri, Okinawa
Cotton with *bingata* stencil design of peonies, paulownia, and phoenixes
Collection of Nihon Mingeikan

Cat. 68 (detail, middle)
Lined robe, perhaps for dance
Meiji-Taishō period, 20th century, Shuri, Okinawa
Modern modified Ryūkyūan construction
Plain weave silk crepe with paste-resist stencil decoration (Oki., *bingata*), lined with modern replacement silk broadcloth, 89.155

Cat. 67 (detail, bottom)
Unlined robe
Late Edo-Meiji period, 19th century, Okinawa
Modified Ryūkyūan construction
Tombian-fiber cloth with paste-resist stencil decoration (Oki., *bingata*), 89.158

some are shaded with red, blue, or Chinese black ink, giving them depth and added definition. Alum solution is painted on the colored areas to help fix the pigments, and the paste is then washed off, leaving the white background. If the background is to be dyed in turn, the colored design areas are carefully covered with paste and the dye brushed on. The second coating of paste is then washed away.[20]

Color sensibility clearly distinguishes Ryūkyūan stencil-dyed textiles,

There can be no question that in Okinawa the blazing sunlight and clear colors of the landscape differ from the diffuse light and colors of Japan. 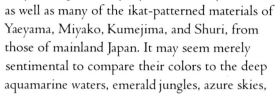 as well as many of the ikat-patterned materials of Yaeyama, Miyako, Kumejima, and Shuri, from those of mainland Japan. It may seem merely sentimental to compare their colors to the deep aquamarine waters, emerald jungles, azure skies, white sands, and profusion of crimson flowers that grace these islands. But for anyone who has visited Okinawa there can be no question that the blazing sunlight and clear colors of the landscape, the clarity of the air itself are different from the diffuse light and colors of mainland Japan.

The mineral pigments that gave bingata its special palette were vermillion (cinnabar, *shu*); red lead (*tan*), royal yellow or orpiment (*sekiō*), yellow ocher (*ōdo*), shell white (*gofun*), pigmentized indigo (*airō*), and Chinese ink (*sumi*). One of the most prominent elements of the bingata palette was lac (*enji*), a dye derived from an insect, *Coccus lacca,* imported into Ryūkyū through China, used in pigmented or lake form. Other colors were made by combining these pigments and layering them with vegetable dyes. Although the word bingata is written with the character *beni,* which means safflower, that plant was not used in bingata dyeing. The warm pink background color seen in many examples of old bingata may have been obtained from lac or madder. Some of these pigments and lakes are also used in various forms of Japanese dyeing, but extremely sparingly, and in these Japanese examples the pinks and reds thus dyed lack the intense hues of bingata.

With the exception of lac, the dyes used for background colors and for all of the ikat and pattern-weave textiles were (and still are) extracted from local flora, contributing to the unique character of the textiles. Yellows were obtained primarily from *fukugi* (Ryū., *fukuji; Garcinia spicata* Hook) and turmeric (*ukon,* Ryū., *uttchin; Alpinia curcuma longa* L.); browns from *sharinbai* (Ryū., *tekachi; Raphiolepis umbellata* Mak.); *kūru* (*Dioscorea rhipogonoides* Oliv.); and a kind of bramble, *hamasarutori-ibara* (Ryū., *guuru; Smilax sebeana* Miq.), used mainly for Kumejima pongee; and reds from safflower (*benibana;* Ryū., *hachimachi bana; Carthamus tinctorius* L.) and sappanwood (*suō;* Ryū., *shiiwaa; Caesalpinia sappan* L.).

Unlike the tax cloth of Yaeyama, Miyako, and Kumejima (discussed below), bingata was produced by male artisans. Women have learned bingata techniques only since the end of the war, although most of the larger workshops are still supervised by a (male) master craftsman.[21]

Tsutsugaki (*noribiki*; Ryū., *nuibichi*), a related type of paste-resist technique, is sometimes considered a subcategory of bingata. The resist paste is applied freehand by squeezing it through a paper tube fitted with a bamboo nozzle, like a pastry tube. The tsutsugaki technique was used to decorate wrapping cloths and backdrop curtains used at local festivals. These were dyed a deep indigo, with typical auspicious motifs of Chinese or Japanese origin, such as cranes and tortoises, pine, plum, and bamboo, irises, peonies, or plum blossoms reserved in white and colored with pigments. Sometimes the whole design was executed in varying tones of indigo and Chinese ink.

Although we know few specifics of color, patterning, or decorative techniques in Ryūkyū before the Satsuma invasion, correspondence dated 1690, from a local official in Yaeyama to Shuri complains that intricate double-ikat patterns are extremely time consuming.[22] Virtually all of the vibrantly beautiful Ryūkyūan textiles that have come down to us (most dating no further back than the later nineteenth century) are the result of an aesthetic sense and technical skills developed and refined under the oppressive poll tax system or the production of textiles for court use during this period of subjugation to Satsuma. They cannot in any sense be considered "folk art" or "folk craft." We know almost nothing of the cloth village women wove for their own or their families' use at that time, but common people (*heimin*) were not allowed to wear ikat.

RAMIE

The main textile fibers woven in Ryūkyū, then, were ramie, fiber banana, silk, and cotton. Ramie is indigenous to the islands and seems to have been widely cultivated and worn by the common people as well as the aristocracy, as described in the earliest accounts. From the later 1300s on, ramie was sent as tribute to the Ming court.[23] The islands of Miyako and Yaeyama became the focus of ramie cultivation and weaving in Ryūkyū. Of the vividly colored jōfu robes made for court use extant today (in collections such as that of the Okinawa Prefectural Museum in Naha and the Japan Folk Craft Museum in Tokyo), those with lighter background colors are usually attributed to Yaeyama origin, the darker ground examples to Miyako, but this questionable classification is based on twentieth-century production practice and, so far at least, not substantiated by earlier records or documentation. In 1883 the taxes levied on Miyako included white jōfu as well as two grades of coarser cloth, three grades of extra-fine dark blue jōfu, white crepe, and white cotton.[24] In 1739 ramie cloth produced in Yaeyama included both dark blue striped or ikat fine and extra-fine ramie cloth and white fine, medium, and coarse ramie cloth with dark brown ikat.

JŌFU TEXTILES AFTER ANNEXATION

During the transitional years of the Meiji period, after the abolition of the Ryūkyūan court and nobility, the former aristocracy and gentry could no longer support textile production. New textile styles developed that were more suited to mainland Japan's newly prosperous urban population. During this time, many of the flamboyant colorings and bold designs of earlier ages were abandoned in favor of the subdued colors and patterns preferred for the mainland fashions of the period. These textiles also incorporated new techniques — like *orijime* and *surikomi* in the ikats of Miyako and Ishigaki — that allowed the manufacture of greater and greater quantities of cloth. Orijime is a technique of resist dyeing, imported from Amami Ōshima into Miyako during the Taishō period (1912–25), in which the ramie yarns to be ikatted are tightly woven on a special wide floor-loom, with cotton warps grouped according to a selected pattern; the resulting web is dyed in indigo and then completely unraveled. The cotton warps will have left undyed white marks on the resulting dark blue ramie yarns, which are then rewoven to form patterns of fine white crosses on the dark blue ground. Surikomi is not, strictly

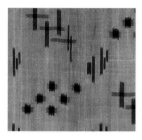

Unlined robe (detail)
Meiji period, second half 19th century, Yaeyama or Miyako
Ramie with weft and double ikat
Collection of Nihon Mingeikan

speaking, an ikat technique at all, because it is not a type of resist dyeing but a method of painting a pattern directly onto warp and weft yarns before they are woven, producing an ikatlike effect.

The processing of ramie in Yaeyama and Miyako today probably differs little from that of the Satsuma period, except that today's handmade yarn is considerably coarser than that once demanded by Shuri for its finest grades of tax cloth, and machine-spun ramie warps are widely used in Yaeyama. Miyako jōfu is one of two Okinawan textiles the making of which is designated by the Japanese government as an Important Intangible Cultural Property (the other is Kijoka bashōfu). Because of the conditions imposed by this designation, Miyako women still produce the finest handmade ramie yarn in Okinawa. Today the official version of Miyako jōfu is woven of yarns ikatted by means of the orijime woven-resist technique, dyed midnight blue with indigo, woven again into patterns made up of tiny white crosses on an indigo ground. The cloth is then starched and fulled with a wooden mallet to a highly glazed finish, washed off before the fabric is made into a kimono.

As in the days of the poll tax, this jōfu is not worn by the women and men who perform the highly specialized and painstaking tasks that go into its production. Officially designated Miyako jōfu is not marketed on the island, and with the increasing price of such labor-intensive products as well as the declining use of kimono, both production and market are dwindling.[25]

Yaeyama jōfu parallels the fine ramie cloth of Miyako in some ways, but there are significant differences. For years, probably since the early twentieth century, Yaeyama jōfu has been known by kimono merchants in Kyoto and Tokyo and by their customers as a dazzlingly white ramie cloth with an ikatlike pattern, harder in outline than real ikat because the characteristic bleeding of dyed color into white fiber has been replaced by the surface application (surikomi) of a thickened red-brown dye.[26]

BASHŌFU

The nature of the fiber-banana tree, in which both coarse and fine fibers are obtained from a single plant (as mentioned in the Korean account of 1546) suggests that from the beginning bashōfu may have been worn by the common people, gentry, and perhaps the nobility as well. Throughout the intervening years until the annexation of Ryūkyū by Japan and the abolition of the court nobility in 1879, bashōfu may have been the only fabric permitted to the poor farmers who made up the majority of Ryūkyū's population. Although an 1873 record of clothing restrictions states that common people (heimin) were permitted to wear cotton garments in winter and bashōfu in summer, cotton was considered a luxury material; and it is probable that the observation of Sasamori Gisuke (1845–1915), a former local official from Aomori, who traveled to Okinawa in 1893, that the wearing of cotton was prohibited to the common people, who wore bashōfu year round, was closer to actual circumstances.[27]

On the other hand, the finest quality of banana fiber went into robes (some brilliantly colored, of yellow with scarlet ikat, for example, or red with blue and yellow stripes, some in complicated gauze weaves) for the Shuri court and aristocracy. The bashōfu used for kurochō, a type of robe worn by court officials, dyed nearly black with indigo, is so fine it is difficult to distinguish from silk. Bashōfu clothed both the highest and lowest of Ryūkyūan society throughout much of its history.

In 1587, ten double rolls of extra-fine fiber-banana cloth were sent to the Ming court; forty double rolls in 1589; twenty double rolls in 1602; and twenty double rolls of extra-fine lustrous bashōfu in 1605.[28] This suggests that even before the Satsuma invasion, the skills of making fine fiber-banana cloth were highly developed. The cloth exported to China may have resembled the silky, shimmering black bashōfu of kurochō robes, like those in the National Museum for Natural History, Washington, D.C., and the Peabody-Essex Museum, Salem, Massachusetts. During the seventeenth century, red and yellow bashōfu and pattern-weave bashōfu are mentioned as tribute goods. These were the forerunners of the splendid garments preserved among the possessions (now in storage at the Tokyo National Museum) of the former kings of Ryūkyū, the Shō family.[29]

After the annexation of Ryūkyū, when textiles became a source of income for people in villages like Kijoka, ikat techniques were apparently introduced into bashōfu-producing areas that had previously woven only plain, striped, or checked cloth on undyed grounds. Kijoka, in the district of Ōgimi, is the only area today still producing a significant quantity of the cloth — 350 rolls a year. The fiber-banana garments in this collection (cat. 63-65) were probably made in the twentieth century for the mainland Japanese market or comparatively well-off townspeople in Okinawa.

COTTON AND SILK

Large-scale cultivation of cotton in Ryūkyū came to an end when the kingdom became part of Japan, and Japanese machine-spun cotton yarn became readily available. Until that time cotton was used for the clothing of the nobility and for small but precious items woven by the common people for their own use, such as the *tiisaji* scarves, often brocaded with supplementary wefts, and the *minsaa* sashes with ikat patterns. The exception seems to be the indigo-dyed cotton ikat garments embellished with supplementary warp or weft floats in white, red, or other colors known as Yuntanza *hanaui* (Jap., Yomitan *hanaori*). Short coats, long and short sleeveless jackets, and lined over-robes, said to have been worn for local celebrations, dances, and festivals, were woven in the village of Yuntanza (known as Yomitan since World War II), north of Naha. Textile historians, while claiming that they were worn by the common people of the village, are reticent as to their sources for this statement. When clothing restrictions were so severe elsewhere, it is difficult to believe that the common people of Yuntanza were allowed to wear garments intricately decorated with double ikat and sophisticated weaving techniques. The over-robe (cat. 66) lined with yellow cotton and stenciled with a small flower pattern is a good example of this genre.

Glossed, reeled silk was used for many of the fine fabrics worn by the Shuri court and gentry, including *tejima* (Ryū., *tiijima*), richly colored plaids combining marled yarns and ikat motifs, and *hanakura-ori*, a delicate fabric combining float and gauze weaves. The warmth of Kumejima *tsumugi* (silk pongee) derives from both the nature of the cottony floss silk from which it is spun and the earthy colors — often dark brown, gray, or yellow, with ikat,

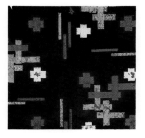
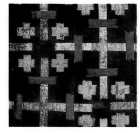

Design cartoons
(miezu)
Late Edo-early Meiji period, 19th century, Shuri, Okinawa Collection of Okinawa Prefecture Museum

checks or stripes of gray, beige, rust, and green, which have been mordanted by immersion in the iron-rich mud of the island's rice paddies or other marshy places. Today ikat-patterned Kumejima tsumugi is still woven and dyed by traditional methods in the hamlets of Nakazato district, although most of the silk floss used for the weft yarns and the reeled silk of the warps is imported from the Japanese mainland.

Two kimono include glossed or raw (i.e., unglossed silk, from which the sericin has not been scoured) silk yarns. One of them (cat. 65), of fine banana fiber, is striped with white silk as well as blue and brown cotton. The other (cat. 62) has warps of raw silk with machine-spun ramie wefts. The combination of different fibers, much more freely employed than in mainland Japan, adds texture and highlights to many Ryūkyūan textiles. A bashōfu kimono (cat. 63) includes cotton yarns and stripes and ikatted yarns.

In addition to cloth of ramie, fiber banana, silk, and cotton, woven throughout the islands, one other fiber appears in Ryūkyūan textiles (cat 67). Even its identification is enigmatic, and little is known of its history. Referred to in Okinawa as *tonbian*, or *tunbian* (Jap., *tombian*), it is of glassy transparency and luster, sparkling white in its undyed state, and has been described as a kind of agave fiber.[30] It was apparently imported as a luxury fiber, possibly from Fujian province in China, but not cultivated in Ryūkyū. Mentioned in *Ifuku sadame* (Clothing Regulations), issued in 1857, the wearing of tunbian was permitted to attendants and other servants of samurai.[31]

Between the fourteenth and late nineteenth centuries, the Ryūkyūan kingdom developed and refined a rich artistic tradition reflecting elements of other Asian states with which it had pursued trade

The vibrant beauty and technical virtuosity of Ryūkyūan textiles rank them among the great textile traditions of Asia.

relations. At the same time, the culture of Ryūkyū retained a vitality and spirit all its own, still evident in Okinawa today. The vibrant beauty and technical virtuosity of Ryūkyūan textiles rank them among the great textile traditions of Asia. Their appeal is irresistible: they draw our attention not only because of their compelling social and economic implications but because they are beautiful.

> *Amanda Mayer Stinchecum, a textile historian specializing in Japanese and Ryūkyūan textiles, is a research fellow at the Institute for Okinawan Studies, Hōsei University, Tokyo. She is the author of* Kosode: 16th-19th Century Textiles from the Nomura Collection *(Japan Society), 1984.*

1. Ōshiro Shizuko and Uezu Toshio, "Okinawan Woven Textiles," *Okinawa bijutsu zenshū kankō iinkai*, ed., Robin Thompson, trans. *Okinawa bijutsu zenshū* (The Art of Okinawa), (Naha: Okinawa Times, 1989), vol. III (*Senshoku*), pp. 218, 241.

2. Nihon Shiryō Shūsei Hensankai, ed., *Chūgoku, Chōsen no shiseki ni okeru Nihon shiryō shūsei: Richō jitsuroku no bu* (2), (Compilation of Japanese Historical Materials in the Annals of China and Korea: The Yi Annals, Part 2), (Tokyo: Kokusho Kankōkai, 1977), Tansō Daiō jitsuroku, vol. 6, pp. 574-76. See also Kobata Atsushi, "Richō jitsuroku: chūsei Ryūkyū shiryō" (Medieval Ryūkyūan Historical Records in the Yi Annals), *Nantō* 2 (1941), pp. 2-3, 11-13; and Higaonna Kanjun, *Reimeiki no kaigai kōtsūshi* (Early History of Foreign Relations), (Naha: Ryūkyū Shinpōsha, 1969), pp. 60, 63-64.

3. Nihon Shiryō Shūsei Hensankai, ed., *Chūgoku, Chōsen no shiseki ni okeru Nihon shiryō shūsei: Richō jitsuroku no bu* (3), (Compilation of Japanese Historical Materials in the Annals of China and Korea: The Yi Annals, Part 3), (Tokyo: Kokusho Kankōkai, 1978), Seisō Keisō Daiō jitsuroku, vol. 27, pp. 690-91, 693. Mulberry leaves provide food for silkworms; the statement of the absence of mulberry here is confusing, for there are clear references not only to the raising of silkworms but a few lines later to the use of mulberry wood to make bows, which were strung with ramie.

Although some scholars place the introduction of sericulture considerably later (Ōshiro and Uezu, "Okinawan Woven Textiles," pp. 220-21, 243-44), it is a subject Korean castaways took particular note of on a number of occasions, indeed inquired about, while in the islands, and there is to my knowledge no reason to doubt the veracity of these early accounts.

4. Nihon Shiryō Shūsei Hensankai, ed., *Chūgoku, Chōsen no shiseki ni okeru Nihon shiryō shūsei: Richō jitsuroku no bu (4)*, (Compilation of Japanese Historical Materials in the Annals of China and Korea: The Yi Annals, Part 4), Seisō Daiō jitsuroku, vol. 115 (Tokyo: Kokusho Kankōkai, 1979), pp. 961-68. See also Higaonna, ibid., pp. 133, 135, 137. Detailed interpretations of this account, which occurs in the Korean annals, *Yijo sillok* (Annals of the Yi Dynasty; Jap., *Richō jitsuroku*), appear in Ōshiro and Uezu, "Okinawan Woven Textiles," pp. 219-20, 241-43; and Tanaka Toshio and Tanaka Reiko, *Okinawa orimono no kenkyū* (Study of Okinawan Woven Textiles), (Kyoto: Shikōsha, 1976), pp. 4ff, 87ff.

5. The most common type of ramie cultivated in the islands is *Boehmeria nivea*, Hook & Arn., but related varieties are found in Yaeyama and Miyako (Tanaka and Tanaka, *Okinawa orimono*, p. 76).

6. Nihon Shiryō Shūsei Hensankai, ed., *Richō jitsuroku no bu (4)*, p. 962.

7. Ibid., p. 964.

8. Ibid., p. 965. Without corroborating accounts from other sources, it is impossible to guess the nature of the patterned textiles produced in Ryūkyū at that time.

9. Nihon Shiryō Shūsei Hensankai, ed., *Chūgoku, Chōsen no shiseki ni okeru Nihon shiryō shūsei: Richō jitsuroku no bu (7)*, (Compilation of Japanese Historical Materials in the Annals of China and Korea: The Yi Annals, Part 7), Meisō Daiō jitsuroku, vol. 3 (Tokyo: Kokusho Kankōkai, 1984), p. 2020. See Cort, "Bast Fibers," in this volume. With the members of her workshop, Taira Toshiko, whose art has been designated by the Japanese government an Important Intangible Cultural Property (Jūyō Mukei Bunkzai), still makes bashōfu using traditional materials and techniques.

10. Ōshiro and Uezu, "Okinawan Woven Textiles," pp. 221, 244, from the *Shih Liu-ch'iu-lu* (Records of Envoys to Ryūkyū). Clearly Xiao was not exposed to areas of the island where fiber-banana cloth was produced.

11. *Ryūkyūkoku yuraiki* (Records of the Origins of the Ryūkyū Kingdom, 1713), Iha Fuyū, Higaonna Kanjun and Yokoyama Shigeru, eds. (Naha: Fudokisha, 1988), vol. III, part 24, pp. 93-94. Since this account was written more than 100 years after the fact, yet mentions the names of the two weavers, it smacks of mythologizing, but there may be a germ of truth in it.

12. Tanaka and Tanaka, *Okinawa orimono*, pp. 226-43.

13. George H. Kerr, *Okinawa: The History of an Island People* (Rutland, Vermont, and Tokyo: Charles E. Tuttle Company, 1958), pp. 156ff.

14. Amanda Mayer Stinchecum, "Textile Production under the Poll Tax System in Ryūkyū," *The Textile Museum Journal*, 27/28 (1988/89), p. 60. One modern koku, based on the amount of rice necessary to feed one man — barely — for one year, equals 5.1 American bushels.

15. Ibid., p. 61. In modern terms, one roll of cloth, or *tan*, is the amount of cloth needed to make one kimono, about 12 m long and 40 cm wide.

16. The fact that these officials were members of the local gentry of the Outer Islands, whose descendants still flourish in Miyako and Yaeyama, may have dampened the zeal of Okinawan historians in their investigations. A recent important study by Kuroshima Tameichi, "Nintōzei," in Ryūkyū Shinposha, ed., *Shin Ryūkyū shi: Kinseihen ge* (New Ryūkyū History: Early Modern Period, 2), (Naha: Ryūkyū Shinpō, 1990), pp. 129-67, discusses many problematical aspects of the poll tax ignored by previous scholars.

Orthodox scholars in mainland Japan, on the other hand, would be forced to justify the Japanese government's decision to continue the poll tax system for its own profit until 1903, twenty-four years after the annexation of Ryūkyū. Araki Moriaki, an iconoclastic economic historian of Okinawan ancestry living in mainland Japan, suggests that the Meiji government chose this policy as the lesser of two evils in dealing with problems arising from annexation, particularly those relating to China's claim to sovereignty over Ryūkyū and the flight of members of the Ryūkyūan nobility to China. See his three essays on this period, "Ryūkyū shobun," "'Kyūkan onzonki' no hyōka," and "'Kyūkan onzonki' no hyō, sairon," in Araki, *Shin Okinawa shiron* (New Historical Essays on Okinawa), (Naha: Okinawa Times, 1980), pp. 174-331.

Many details of the administration of the poll tax and the textiles produced during this period await further study.

17. Amanda Mayer Stinchecum, "A Common Thread: Japanese Ikat Textiles," *Asian Art*, 3:1(Winter 1990), p. 38.

18. Ibid., pp. 45-51, 60 (n. 6).

19. Yomamine Ichiko and Isagawa Yōko, "Modern Bin-gata," in Okinawa Bijutsu Zenshū Kankō Iinkai, ed., *Okinawa bijutsu zenshū* (The Art of Okinawa), vol. 3, *Senshoku* (Naha: Okinawa Times, 1989), pp. 119-20.

20. This account and the following information on pigments follows Okamura Kichiemon, "Bin-gata: A Historical and Technical Study," in Okinawa Bijutsu Zenshū Kankō Iinkai, ed., *Okinawa bijutsu zenshū* (The Art of Okinawa), vol. 3, *Senshoku* (Naha: Okinawa Times, 1989), p. 109.

21. The late Shiroma Eiki was one of two bingata craftsmen who managed to hang on through the war and revive the art of bingata almost singlehandedly. Fujimura Reiko, once Shiroma's student, operates her own small workshop. Her delicate, rhythmic designs and subtle colorings, resulting from the use of ink washes layered over or under applications of pigment, exemplify the best of traditional bingata and contemporary sensibility.

22. Ōshiro and Uezu, "Okinawan Woven Textiles," pp. 226, 251. The document referred to, *Sankenjō*, exists only in an unpublished manuscript in the Kishaba collection.

23. Tanaka and Tanaka, *Okinawa orimono*, pp. 91-92.

24. Stinchecum, "Textile Production," pp. 61-62.

25. A few Miyako weavers, most notably Shinzato Reiko, have returned to older forms of Miyako jōfu for inspiration, employing the freer hand-tying method of ikatting and the broader palette available from other vegetable dyes in addition to indigo. They are also attempting to integrate, probably for the first time in its history, the actual use of Miyako jōfu into the lives of women on the island.

26. This cloth continues to be made by the Ishigaki City Cooperative for Textile Enterprise from machine-spun ramie warps and handmade ramie wefts. In addition, dyer/weaver Arakaki Sachiko has revived the old hand-tied ikat technique (much more exacting with white or light-ground cloth because the entire background area must be reserved), producing a true ikat Yaeyama jōfu in a subtle range of colors.

27. Uezu Toshio, "Senshoku shiryō sandai," (Three Textile-related Documents), *Shiryō Henshūshitsu kiyō*, 14:3(1989), p. 123.

28. Ōshiro and Uezu, "Okinawa no orimono," p. 220. The figures cited are said to come from the *Rekidai hōan*, a compilation of documents in Chinese concerning Ryūkyūan contacts with China, Korea, and Southeast Asian ports between the years 1424 and 1867, but no specific citations are given, nor are they in Tanaka and Tanaka, *Okinawa orimono*, p. 92, where some of the same sources are referred to.

29. See Kamakura Yoshitarō and Yamanobe Tomoyuki, *Ryūkyū ōke denrai ishō* (Costumes Handed Down in the Royal Family of Ryūkyū), (Tokyo: Kodansha, 1972).

30. Tanaka and Tanaka, *Okinawa no orimono: bessatsu (kireji no zuroku)* (Textiles of Okinawa: Supplementary Volume [Illustrations of Textile Samples]), (Kyoto: Shikōsha, 1976) n.p., identify tunbian as *Agave rigida* Mill., and suggest that tunbian was cultivated both on Okinawa and the Outer Islands, but later was imported from Fujian (*Okinawa no orimono*, p. 74). The species of agave, if tunbian is indeed a type of this leaf fiber, has yet to be identified precisely.

31. Uezu, "Senshoku shiryō," p. 126.

TRADITIONAL JAPANESE TEXTILES

in the collection of the

SEATTLE ART MUSEUM

AINU TEXTILES

MICHIYO MORIOKA

T HE AINU ONCE INHABITED NOT ONLY ALL THE ISLANDS COMPRISING present-day Japan from Kyūshū to Hokkaido, but the Kuriles and southern Sakhalin as well. Various theories existed concerning the identity of the Ainu people, who speak a language that is an isolate. Most scholars today believe that the Ainu originated in the Amur River region and represent the oldest population of that area.[1] In their own language "Ainu" means "the people." The Japanese referred to the Ainu people and their land as Ezo.

Contact between the Ainu and the Japanese began early. One of the earliest accounts of their relationship describes a skirmish that occurred in the year 658 in the Tohoku region in northern Honshu.[2] Ōu Ezo, as the Ainu who lived in Tohoku were called, fought often against the Japanese and interfered with the northward expansion of Japan until they ceased their rebellions in 878.[3] The Japanese continued to expand their territory, pushing the Ainu farther north until, in the twelfth century, Hokkaido became the last Ainu stronghold.

Hokkaido is the northernmost of Japan's four main islands. Separated from Honshu by the Tsugaru strait, it is also the second largest. The climate of Hokkaido is generally severe, with a long snow season. The island is well known for its natural beauty and includes several mountain ranges, volcanoes, rivers, and large lakes. The land is richly wooded and animals abound. The Ainu lived primarily by hunting, fishing, and gathering. In the mountains, the men hunted deer, bears, rabbits, foxes, and birds; they caught salmon and trout in the rivers. Some Ainu also went to sea to hunt whales and seals. Ainu women collected edible wild plants, berries, nuts, and roots. Although their dependence on natural sources of food required them to change the location of their settlement twice a year, the Ainu were not nomadic people. They practiced a migratory lifestyle, remaining in one place during the snow season and moving to another during the fishing season.[4]

In Ainu society, labor was divided between the sexes. Men hunted and fished, while women tended to all the domestic affairs. The family was the smallest unit of Ainu society. A group of families, numbering usually fewer than ten, formed a *kotan*, a village or settlement. One village or a group of villages constituted a local community, which was politically and economically self-sufficient. The solidarity of such Ainu communities was expressed by the acknowledgment of collective rights to specific fishing and hunting grounds. The village was the basis of Ainu life. Each village had a chief who presided over various ceremonies, settled disputes among members, and supervised

I.
Ainu robe *(attusi)*
Late Edo–early Meiji period,
19th century
Elm bark fiber *(ohyō)* cloth
with cotton cloth appliqué
and cotton thread embroi-
dery, 45½ x 46½ in. (113.8 x
116.3 cm) 89.136

hunting and fishing activities. The whole village cooperated in such enterprises as building a house, participated in rituals and ceremonies, and hunted and fished as a unit. In an Ainu village, cooperation was practiced not only in production but also in distribution:

> There was no borrowing and lending. . . . Food they obtained by themselves. It has been said that there are no Ezo who die of starvation, but if any do, the wealthy and poor perish together after the rich have exhausted their resources in supporting the poor. In daily life not even a glass of wine is enjoyed alone. They dined together and shared what they had to eat with everyone at the table. When there was very little food it was given to the old or to the children. For the old and feeble or those seriously ill who had no one to look after them, food was carried to them at each meal.[5]

The survival of the individual Ainu thus depended on the well-being of the whole village. Because the villages existed as separate economic and political entities, the Ainu never formed a nation or a large-scale political coalition. Ultimately this lack of cohesive union among the various Ainu groups allowed their conquest by the Japanese.[6]

Although living in the northernmost island, the Ainu did not remain isolated. In the north, they traded with the nomadic people and Manchurian tribes from the Sakhalin and the continent; in the south, they traded with the Japanese. Until the seventeenth century, the Ainu maintained a traditional lifestyle on Hokkaido without much disruption from the outside world. In 1599 the Japanese who had settled earlier in the southwestern area of Hokkaido were recognized as the Matsumae clan by Tokugawa Ieyasu. The Matsumae were given not only the ownership of the land in that area but also exclusive right to trade with the Ainu. Among other things, the Japanese traded rice, sake, tobacco, pans, lacquerware, and used clothes; the Ainu provided animal skins, fish, craft objects, and goods from mainland China, including Manchurian textiles. As trade flourished, the Japanese often took advantage of the trusting natives in order to increase profits; for example, they cheated in measuring and weighing trade commodities. In 1669 the Ainu rebelled against the unfair trade practices and oppressive treatment, but their revolt was quickly suppressed. Thereafter Japanese commercial activities on Hokkaido expanded rapidly. They invaded the Ainu fishing and hunting grounds, exploiting the natural resources of their territory. The Ainu were reduced to a labor force for the Japanese, who deprived them of their economic self-sufficiency. The worsening situation led to another Ainu revolt in 1789. As this incident coincided with the expansion of Russian mercantile activities in the north, the Tokugawa government sent an investigation committee to Hokkaido and in 1799 placed the Ainu under the direct control of the government. The government established military outposts in Hokkaido and concentrated on defense activities against the foreign invasion.

After the Meiji Restoration in 1868, the government encouraged the Japanese to emigrate and settle in Hokkaido, accelerating the colonization of the former Ainu territory and acculturation of its people. Education in the Japanese language became mandatory, and Japanese clothing and housing began to replace the native Ainu types. The Ainu were displaced, discriminated against, and forced to abandon their traditional way of life. By

1980 the population of pure-blood Ainu was believed to have dropped to only about 200,[7] and much of the unique Ainu culture seemed to be on the verge of disappearance.

The Ainu believed in the presence of spiritual beings in all elements of nature. They were a deeply religious people and their beliefs profoundly influenced their way of life. The Ainu religion is complex and difficult to classify. Perhaps it can be best understood as a type of animism with strong elements of totemism and shamanism. The Ainu had neither priests nor temples. The head of the family conducted the rituals, and they worshiped their gods in their own homes. In their language, the word *kamui* referred to gods or deities. The Ainu had an extensive pantheon of gods, from the most powerful to those of lesser importance. Some kamui were benevolent, others were malicious. Illness and disease were believed to be caused by evil gods, and men had a prosperous life when loved by good gods. Therefore the Ainu solicited favors from beneficent gods by gratifying them, while shunning the gods with ill intentions.

According to Ainu belief, gods had human forms and lived in their own land. When they visited the Ainu, they came in disguise. For example, the bear was in reality the mountain god; the owl was the village god. The most important among the Ainu rituals was *iomante*, the "bear-sending ceremony," in which a bear was killed not as sacrifice but to release the god-spirit from its body so that it could return to its home. For all their rituals and ceremonies, the Ainu made sacred objects called *inau*, a tree-branch ornamented with shavings which are part of and carved from the branch itself. Not simply offerings, the inau functioned as an intermediary between the people and the deities. Reflecting the complex nature of the Ainu religion, the shapes and forms of inau varied according to the deities to whom they were dedicated.

The Ainu believed that even inanimate objects could become gods. To form an object and give it a shape made it possible for a spirit to enter it.[8] Some Ainu children were forbidden to make dolls lest they become inhabited by harmful spirits, and until recent times certain Ainu tribes did not allow their children to make even a snowman.[9] This belief is nowhere more strongly manifested than in the breaking of personal possessions of the deceased at the funeral. Immediately before burial, objects which were to be buried with the corpse were broken so that their spirit powers would be released to accompany their owner to the afterworld. The very fact that their religious belief was integral to the objects they used in everyday life makes the Ainu's artifacts distinctive from those produced by the Japanese. Ainu textile objects were no exception.

Ainu textiles were made from the inner bark fibers of the trees such as *ohyō* (elm) and *shinanoki* (linden) as well as from the stems of a nettlelike plant called *irakusa*. It is not known exactly when and how the Ainu developed their textile techniques.[10] Prior to weaving, the Ainu fabricated garments from animal, fish, and bird skins, sewn together with tendons and plant fibers.

The fiber perhaps most readily identified with Ainu textile today is made from ohyō, found deep in the mountains not easily reached by people.[11] The Ainu were always reverential to the gods who protected and provided them with the necessities of life. Gathering ohyō bark involved some elements of danger. At the foot of the mountain, before entering the forest to collect the bark of ohyō, the Ainu offered a prayer to the mountain god. When they found an appropriate tree, they placed inau before it and thanked the tree for giving up the bark, or its "clothes." They were careful not to peel the bark from more than one side of the tree, so that the tree would remain partially clothed. When they finished peeling, they offered grains and tobacco to convey their gratitude and tied a piece of bark around the tree to prevent the rest of its "clothes" from being blown away by wind.

Preparation of ohyō fiber required a laborious process. John Batchelor, a British missionary, who lived among the Ainu for over sixty years starting in 1879, left the following account of the traditional method of preparing ohyō:

> The elm bark is peeled off the trees in the early spring, just when the sap commences to flow upward to the young shoots and newly forming buds. When sufficient bark has been taken, it is carried home and put into water to soak and get soft; and when sufficiently soaked it is taken out of the water, and the layers of bark separated, and the fibers divided into threads and wound up into balls for use. Sewing thread is made in the same way, only that is chewed until it becomes round and solid. When all the threads have been prepared, the women sit down and proceed with their weaving.[12]

The manufacture of textiles was exclusively women's domain. The Ainu women used a simple *izaribata* (back-strap loom, literally meaning "creep-

I.
Ainu robe (back)

along loom"). By the time they wove enough cloth to make one garment, more than two months would have passed since the initial gathering of ohyō bark.[13] The fabrics they produced were generally plain, showing the light ochre color of the bark fibers; sometimes, however, they were vertically striped. In order to create the stripes, the Ainu weavers colored their yarns with vegetable dyes. Later they began to apply imported blue or black cotton to create the striped weave. It is generally believed that the plain fabric predates the striped type.

Included here are two examples of *attusi* (cat. 1 and 2). "Attusi" is an Ainu word for the fabric made from ohyō fiber, or a robe made of such fabric, and is among the most representative type of Ainu garment. Worn with or without a belt,[14] the attusi is of below-the-knee or calf length and has no extra panels for overlapping in front. The striking ornamental designs seen on both attusi are distinctly Ainu. While decorative patterns for sculpture were handed down from father to son, the motifs for textile design were transmitted from mother to daughter, and children sometimes learned them by drawing in sand.[15]

The Ainu used two techniques to decorate their garments: appliqué and embroidery. They are the most basic of the textile techniques and apparently also reflect the patchwork techniques used to fabricate leather garments, which may predate woven fabrics by many centuries in Ainu culture.[16] Ainu appliqué technique is generally known as *kirifuse* (cut and lay

2.
Ainu robe *(attusi)*
Late Edo-early Meiji period,
19th century
Elm bark fiber *(ohyō)* cloth
with cotton cloth appliqué
and cotton thread embroidery, 50⅞ x 58 in. (127 x 145 cm) 89.140

down), in which small pieces of trade cloth from mainland Japan are sewn onto the garment. Some are created by stitching ribbonlike bands of fabric on the ground cloth in a predetermined design, as exemplified by the two attusi. Others show large sections of designs, which are first cut out of one piece of cloth in their entirety and then sewn onto the ground fabric. Embroidery complements the thick appliqué patterns by giving a more delicate and incisive effect. In general, the sleeves and the body of the garment were sewn together to create a finished garment only after they were manufactured and decorated separately.[17]

Batchelor discussed aspects of the design as he observed during the 1890s:

> The work of different villages presents different patterns; those of one are not necessarily the same as those of another. In fact, when an Ainu of one district goes into another clothed in an embroidered dress, the people he meets can with almost certainty tell where he comes from by the patterns of his coat! There are patterns suitable for men, and others for women. No man would think of wearing a coat with patterns on it which are recognised as belonging to women; nor would a woman put on a coat that had patterns appropriated by the men. The women's garments are not so highly decorated as those of the men. The wives take a pride in dressing up their husbands especially on the occasion of a bear feast; but they themselves prefer a good show of beads, earrings, finger rings, necklaces, and bracelets, set off with a tastefully tatooed mouth.[18]

Taking into account the importance of the village in the traditional Ainu life, it is tempting to believe Batchelor's comment that the garment design could be identified with a village to which the wearer belonged. Although a certain degree of regionality in the garment decoration must have existed, the matter is not as simple as Batchelor suggests. A large number of intervillage marriages involving a great distance occurred, resulting in the women incorporating designs from both areas and thus establishing a new tradition.[19] Today it is almost impossible to assign Ainu garments, particularly attusi, to specific regions on the basis of their decorative designs.[20] Although the difference in design elements between the sexes, as Batchelor mentioned, cannot be ascertained today either, his observation is accurate in that the decoration on women's garments tends to be plainer than on men's.

As noted by Batchelor, Ainu women tatooed their lips and the area around the mouth. The process of tatooing the mouth began at or before puberty and was completed over a long period of time, before the girl's marriage. The Japanese considered it barbaric and ugly, but for the Ainu woman it was symbolic of beauty and maturity. Not simply a social custom, religious significance was inherent in the practice of tatooing. It symbolized communion with the great spirit ancestress, who was also known as a deity of fire, and who was honored in the hearth of each household.[21] Her soot, which was used for tatooing, was believed to protect the Ainu woman against all evil spirits that might enter through mouth and nose.[22] The protective function exemplified by tatooing was also an important element of Ainu textile decoration.

3.
Ainu robe (ci-karkar-pe)
Late Edo-early Meiji period, 19th century
Cotton cloth with cotton cloth appliqué and cotton thread embroidery, 53¾ x 48¾ in. (134.4 x 121.9 cm)
89.161

Ainu textile designs are laid out symmetrically. This most prominent and consistent characteristic in Ainu design manifests their religious belief in that a design is added to a garment to safeguard all parts of the wearer's body evenly. The placement of the appliqué and embroidery motifs to the front opening, the upper back, the hem, and the cuffs, is to protect the vulnerable areas and apertures by magical designs that keep evil spirits from entering. The fact that men's garments are more elaborately decorated than women's may reflect the need and desire to secure more protection for men, who engage in dangerous outdoor activities, such as hunting.[23]

Although it is correct to describe most Ainu garment designs as symmetrical, a close observation reveals an element of asymmetry in some examples. The two attusi here present a case in point. Both display a symmetrical composition in the overall configuration of design. Yet one finds a subtle but distinct deviation from strict symmetry between the right and left in the embroidered design applied to the vertical hems of the front opening. Whether it is the personal signature of the maker or is symbolic of a hidden meaning is not clear.

Suggestions have been made in the past that many of the highly stylized Ainu patterns derive from animal representations.[24] It is likely, however, that patterns in themselves carry no representational meanings.[25] The two basic motifs in Ainu textile design are spirals and thornlike projections. On the back of one of these attusi (cat. 1), squared spirals are recognizable in the lower central portion of the appliqué. Thornlike motifs appear repeatedly in both attusi decorations in the corners of the appliqué, accentuated with definitive stitches as well as in brace-patterned embroidery superimposed over the appliquéd cloth. Rows of repeated brace patterns constitute an overall netlike design, as if ready to catch evil spirits and prevent them from entering the body.[26]

Of these two examples, the attusi with wide blue stripes (cat. 1) displays a more intricate, carefully executed design with attention to detail. A dark blue cotton strip is appliquéd in a symmetrical design over which is applied a chain-stitch embroidery of a repeating brace pattern in light blue cotton. On the back, the addition of the thin strip in the lower half of the design configuration enriches the larger, heavier pattern. The square corners of the strip are pulled in the directions of the thornlike stitches, making those projections seem alive with power. Such detail must have required careful execution to enhance the protective function of the ornament. Despite observing a general symmetry, the design on this attusi is not rigid or static. The bending and turning ribbons with corners gently rounded or sharply accentuated with projecting stitches seem full of movement and tension, while the freehand technique allows a pleasant unevenness in the final product. In other attusi (cat. 2) the weaver combined light and dark blue cotton with ohyō threads to create an attractive striped cloth. The appliqué and embroidery designs are relatively simple but cover all the strategic places. White cotton panels, which supplement the tapered sleeves under the arms, are placed in perfect symmetry and stitched neatly in light blue thread. They signify the decorative intention of the maker and not a miscalculation of the cloth.

This collection includes another type of Ainu robe generally known as *ci-karkar-pe* (cat. 3). Ci-karkar-pe (literally, our embroidered things) are made from cotton fabric imported from mainland Japan. Like this example, they often incorporate thick striped or plaid cotton or light *yukata* fabric. Ci-karkar-pe generally have no overlapping front panels, but those which are made from used Japanese kimono often retain the original form and have extra panels with diagonally extended collars.[27] This ci-karkar-pe displays an extensive decoration in kirifuse appliqué and chain-stitch embroidery. A relatively narrow strip of indigo cotton is affixed in a complex but typically symmetrical Ainu design. Juxtaposed with the turning and bending ribbons, embroidery in light blue cotton thread repeats brace patterns. The thornlike motif also occurs at the corners of the appliqué, accentuated with a projecting stitch. On the back, the upper and lower portions of the decoration extend toward the center, creating a powerful visual impact. The superimposition of the squared-ribbon appliqué and curvilinear embroidery patterns creates a captivating effect, as if to cast a magic spell.

4.
Ainu sword carrier *(emusi-at)*
Edo period, 19th century
Warp: possibly linden bark fiber *(shinanoki)* or celastrus plant bark fiber *(tsuru-umemodoki)*; weft: cotton thread; cotton pendants with cotton cloth appliqué and cotton thread embroidery, 34¼ x 2⅜ in. (85.6 x 5.9 cm) 89.137

A textile sword hanger (Ainu: *emusi-at*; cat.4) is illustrated here. Swords constituted personal treasures for Ainu men, who wore them proudly on formal and religious occasions when the weapons functioned as guardian gods to protect and enhance the wearer's fortune.[28] When not in use, they were displayed in the northeastern corner of the Ainu house, in the spot designated specifically as the storage area of treasures. Neil Gordon Munro, a British doctor who recorded valuable observation of Ainu life during the early twentieth century, wrote about such treasures:

> Among them...are iron swords, of which every man is supposed to possess at least one. The scabbards are often profusely decorated, some with Ainu and others with Japanese carving, and some have metal fittings. These swords are kept for ceremonial use. They are brandished in the processional dances to drive away evil spirits, which are held when there has been a death by drowning or other fatal

accident, or when a house has been burnt down. They are credited with great potency, and by some elders are regarded as kamui. Both they and the imitation swords usually have a broad sash attached wherewith they are hung over the shoulder.[29]

The "sash" mentioned by Munro is the emusi-at, which was slung over the right shoulder and ran diagonally toward the left hip, with a sword suspended through the loops above the square patches of fabric. No doubt the making of an emusi-at was a serious task for Ainu women. Often combining the shinanoki bark fiber and cotton threads in warp and weft, they created an intricate geometric design.[30] Described as an extremely difficult technique, very few Ainu today possess the skill to produce the strap.[31]

This emusi-at has a strap decorated in a black and brown zigzag pattern. Plain brown cotton is sewn onto it at each end, to make loops for suspending the sword. Hanging below the loops are two square cotton patches ornamented with characteristic Ainu designs. The motif of four spirals, cut out from a light brown cotton, is sewn onto the dark ground. Over the appliqué is the brace pattern embroidered in couching stitch. The same motif is repeated on the border which frames the spirals.

The four textile examples described here represent only a small portion of the unique Ainu textile tradition. Yet they open a door for us to an understanding of the rich culture in which they were produced. The life of the Ainu depended on the natural resources of the land they lived in. Their religious beliefs were inseparable from their subsistence lifestyle, for cooperation from good gods and avoidance of evil spirits was nothing less than a matter of survival for them. Furthermore, through dialogue with gods, the Ainu understood their place within the scheme of the universe and received graciously what was offered to them without ever destroying the nature which sustained them. The last decade in Japan has witnessed the resurgence of the Ainu cultural tradition: one hopes that through the effort of modern Ainu and others, the spirit of the Ainu people will continue to live on.

Michiyo Morioka is an independent scholar of Japanese art history.

1. W. Fitzhugh and A. Crowell, *Crossroads of the Continents* (Washington, D.C.: The Smithsonian Institution Press, 1988), p. 25.

2. Fred C. C. Peng and Peter Geiser, *The Ainu: The Past in the Present* (Tokyo: Bunka Hyōron Publishing Co., 1977), p. 10. Quoted from Basil Chamberlain, *The Language, Mythology, and Geographical Nomenclature of Japan Viewed in the Light of Ainu Studies* (Tokyo: Tokyo Imperial University, 1887), p. 45.

3. Shinichirō Takakura, "The Ainu of Northern Japan: A Study in Conquest and Acculturation," translated and annotated by John A. Harrison, *Transactions of the American Philosophical Society*, 50:4 (April 1960), p. 7.

4. Ibid., p. 17.

5. Quoted by Takakura, "The Ainu of Northern Japan," p. 15, from *Watarishima Hikki*, written by an anonymous author in 1808.

6. Takakura, "The Ainu of Northern Japan," p. 23.

7. *Encyclopedia of Japan*, vol. 1 (Tokyo: Kodansha, 1983), p. 35.

8. Ainu Bunka Hozon Taisaku Kyōgikai, ed., *Ainu minzokushi, jō* (Tokyo: Daiichi Hōki Shuppan Kabushikigaisha, 1969), p. 219.

9. Ibid.

10. Takakura suggests that the Ainu textile techniques were probably introduced from Japan, since those Ainu who lived in areas that had no contact with the Japanese lacked knowledge of textile techniques until fairly recent times. See Takakura, "The Ainu of Northern Japan," p. 13. Kichiemon Okakura believes that the weaving technique was introduced to the Ainu from the continent at a much earlier date: Kichiemon Okakura, "Kogeishi kenkyū nōto IV," *Tamagawa Daigaku bungakubu kiyō, Ronsō*, 25 (1984), p. 167.

11. The information in this paragraph comes from *Ainu minzokushi, jo*, pp. 3, 210, and 250; and Shigeru Kayano, *Ainu no mingu* (Tokyo: Suzusawa Shoten, 1978), p. 35.

12. John Batchelor, *The Ainu of Japan: The Religion, Superstitions, and General History of the Hairy Aborigines of Japan* (London: The Religious Tract Society, 1892), p. 45. A similar passage from *The Ainu and Their Folk-Lore* (London: The Religious Tract Society, 1901), p. 144, by the same author is quoted by Ann Pike Tay, "Ainu Artifacts," in Robert Moes, *Mingei: Japanese Folk Art from The Brooklyn Museum Collection* (New York: The Brooklyn Museum, 1985), p. 184.

13. Kayano, *Ainu no mingu*, p. 59.

14. *Ainu minzokushi, jō*, p. 210.

15. Mari Kodama, "Ainu moyō: sono tasai na sekai," *Me no me*, 104 (July 1985), pp. 30-31; and Ainu Bunka Hozon, Taisaku Kyōgikai, ed., *Ainu minzokushi, ge* (Tokyo: Daiichi Hoki Shuppan Kabushikigaisha, 1969), p. 716.

16. The Japan Textile Color Design Center, comp., *Textile Designs of Japan III: Okinawan, Ainu, and Foreign Designs* (Tokyo: Kodansha International, Ltd., 1980), p. 22.

17. *Ainu minzokushi, jo*, pp. 267-68.

18. Batchelor, *The Ainu of Japan*, pp. 47-48.

19. From an interview with Chisato Dubreuil, November 27, 1991. Dubreuil has conducted an extensive research on Ainu culture and generously made available to this author her paper "Culture and Its Effects on Ainu Art," Ed Potts Memorial Scholarship Research Paper, The Evergreen State College, Olympia, Washington, 1989.

20. Mari Kodama, "Ainu no ifuku to moyō," in *Ainu no moyō*, Ichirō Yotsuji, ed. (Tokyo: Sasakura Shuppansha, 1981), p. 154.

21. Neil Gordon Munro, *Ainu Creed and Cult* (London: Routledge and Kegan Paul, Ltd., 1962), p. 119.

22. Ibid.

23. Kichiemon Okamura, "Ainu kōgei no sōshoku," *Mingei*, 297 (September 1977), p. 20.

24. Frederick Starr, *The Ainu Group: At the St. Louis Exposition* (Chicago: The Open Court Publishing Co., 1904), p. 106. For example, the spiral motifs often affixed to the back of the Ainu garment have been interpreted by some to represent an owl, a protector-god of villages. See *Ainu minzokushi, jō*, p. 228.

25. Ainu patterns and motifs seem to express meanings which are very personal to the maker such as certain "feelings" and "messages from the ancestors." Hokkaido Bunkazai Hogo Kyōkai, ed., *Showa rokujūnen do Ainu ifuku chōsa hōkokusho I: Ainu josei ga denshō suru ibunka* (Hokkaido: Hokkaido Bunkazai Hogo Kyōkai, 1986), p. 43. This notion is supported by Chisato Dubreuil who believes that the making of the garment itself was an intensely personal and spiritual process inseparable from the magical function of the finished design.

26. It is known that the Ainu attempted to avoid epidemics such as smallpox by fleeing to the mountains after constructing a fence and spreading a net over the path; they also placed thorn bushes in the path to prevent the spirit of illness from approaching; *Ainu minzokushi, jō*, p. 221.

27. Ibid., p. 212.

28. Kyōsuke Kindaichi, *Ainu Life and Legends* (Tokyo: Japan Tourist Bureau, 1941), p. 50.

29. Munro, *Ainu Creed and Cult*, p. 29.

30. Kodama, *Ainu no moyō*, p. 157. Shinanoki bark, harder than ohyō, was an indispensable material for making ropes, straps, and bags. See Kayano, *Ainu no mingu*, p. 37. The Ainu also used the inner bark fibers of a vine called *tsuruumemodoki* (shrubs and vines, of *Celastrus orbiculatus*, Thunb.) for sword hangers. Tenri Daigaku Fuzoku Tenri Sanko-kan Minzoku Bunbutsu-bu, ed., *Ainu no fukushoku*, exhibition catalogue (Tokyo: Tenri Gallery, 1983), pp. 13-14.

31. Kayano, *Ainu no mingu*, pp. 75-76. They seem to reflect the Ainu mat-weaving technique, which is closer to braiding than weaving. *Textile Designs of Japan III*, p. 21.

SASHIKO, KOGIN, AND HISHIZASHI

MICHIYO MORIOKA

T OHOKU IS THE NORTHERNMOST REGION OF HONSHU, JAPAN'S LARGEST island. It is predominantly agricultural and far from the cultural center of the Kyoto-Osaka area. The sense of remoteness associated with the region was expressed in its old name, Michinoku, which originally meant "the farthermost reaches of the road." Throughout its history the area was often devastated by heavy snowfall and cold weather, which damaged or obliterated the rice crop, causing famine and starvation among the farmers.[1] For these reasons, to some Japanese even today, the words "Tohoku" and "Michinoku" evoke the image of a distant country that is culturally backward and economically impoverished.

During the Edo period (1615–1868), not only the elemental force of nature but also the man-made regulations of feudal society under the Tokugawa shogunate governed the lives of the farmers in Tohoku. The official policy toward the farmer class was often summed up as "letting them neither live nor die." The feudal lords regulated all aspects of the farmers' daily life in order to bind them to the earth and thus secure rice for their fiefs. Housing and clothing were almost matters of luxury for the farmers of Tohoku, who were forced to live in stringent conditions in which the provision of food for the family was always the primary concern.

Tohoku's cold climate required warm clothes for the winter but largely prevented the cultivation of cotton, the warmest fiber available at the time. Even after cotton production began in the southernmost part of Tohoku in the seventeenth century, this new fabric remained a commodity far too expensive for the farmers to acquire.[2] They used *asa* (bast fiber), made from plants which grew in the area, or purchased used cotton or fabric with out-of-fashion designs imported from the Kyoto-Osaka area. All textiles in Tohoku, whether home-spun asa or imported cotton, were precious commodities which the populace recycled for many generations.

Sashiko, a local term in Tohoku, refers to both the technique of stitching layers of cloth and the stitched product. It derives from the word *sashi* (to mend old garments or stitchwork used in mending clothes).[3] By improving a garment's warmth and strength, by prolonging the life of a fabric, or by creating a new piece of clothing out of an old one, through their stitchery technique the women of Tohoku contributed to the physical well-being and economic welfare of the family. Their needlework skill was as important as working in the field.

As sashiko originates from a need to stitch together multiple layers of old fabric, it is done with a running stitch method. A related but

5.
Kimono
Late Edo-early Meiji period,
19th century, Tsugaru
Yoke: bast fiber *(asa)* cloth
with counted stitch cotton
thread embroidery *(kogin)*
Body: bast fiber *(asa)* cloth,
51½ x 43⅛ in. (128.8 x
107.8 cm) 89.89

fundamentally different technique, also from Tohoku, is *kogin*, which creates specific designs achieved by counted stitch embroidery. It reinforces the asa fabric by densely and tightly filling the weave with stitches, as if to transform it into the closely woven texture of cotton.

Kogin, also called *sashikogin*, is a product of the Tsugaru area of Aomori prefecture. Located at the northern border of Honshu, the inhabitants had to endure long, severe winters. Yet the Frugality Act for Farmers, enacted in 1724, forbade them to wear cotton.[4] Forced to use home-grown asa, which is relatively strong but lacks warmth, Tsugaru farmers improved their garments through stitching, first with asa thread and later with cotton.

The term "kogin" derives from *koginu*, referring to the farmer's unlined work jacket made of asa. Although the exact historical origin of kogin, which we recognize today as elaborately stitched fabric, is unclear, the term appears in the Tsugaru clan diary as early as 1685.[5] It is likely that the stitchery art of kogin developed over the ensuing one hundred years. Furukawa Koshōken, a geographer from Edo, recorded a passage describing the Tsugaru people in his *Miscellaneous Records on the Trip to the East*, written in 1788:

> The farmers of below average means do not wear padded cotton garments. They stitch asa fabric and layer three such garments for warmth during the winter. Today it is the Bon festival…and eight women out of ten are dressed in white kimono embroidered with dark blue thread in various designs.[6]

In the same year Hirano Sadahiko, a vassal of the Tsugaru clan, wrote in his *Illustrated Records on the People of the Northern Provinces*:

> As for sashikogin, it is [used] to embroider a fabric in various designs and it is quite beautiful. Both men and women wear [such clothing]. Many are dark blue garments stitched with white thread.[7]

These two records indicate that by at least the late eighteenth century, kogin had become established as a distinct part of the Tsugaru culture and merited the attention of travelers from other areas. Koshōken's record notes that for the summer festival, Tsugaru women wore white kimono embroidered with blue thread, while Sadahiko's comment relates to indigo-dyed cloth stitched in white as the kogin example illustrated here (cat. 5). Beginning with the Meiji period (1868–1912), Tsugaru farmers were allowed to wear cotton garments, and kogin began to evolve into increasingly elaborate wear intended only for formal occasions.[8] The railroad established in the region in the early 1890s made available a wide variety of commodities, and thereafter the tradition of kogin began to decline rapidly.[9]

This blue kimono with an embroidered yoke is impressive in its refinement and sophistication. Its wide sleeves suggest that it was to be worn for a formal occasion. The coarse, indigo-dyed asa fabric of the yoke, decorated with elaborate stitchwork in white cotton thread, is much older than the rest of the kimono. Such embroidered cloth was used over and over, first in best clothing and eventually, when it became worn and old, as part of everyday wear. It was essential for Tsugaru women to master the kogin technique. They began their training in stitchwork before age ten. A skillful worker could complete a kogin garment in about five days in the winter season,[10] during which heavy snow confined people in Tsugaru to indoor activities.

The designs of Tsugaru kogin show specific regional characteristics. The examples from the western area, *nishi kogin* (west kogin), are distinguishable by a combination of diamond patterns with dense stripes over the shoulders. Those from the northern region are known as *mishima kogin* (three-striped kogin) and display patterns intersected by three wide horizontal bands on the chest and on the back. A third type, *higashi kogin* (east kogin), from the eastern region of Tsugaru (cat. 5) has an embroidered yoke with a relatively large overall design, continuing from the front to the back without interruption. The characteristic use of coarsely woven asa as a ground fabric for stitchery most faithfully reflects the tradition of kogin, which originated as work clothing rather than formal wear.[11]

Kogin embroidery designs are created by crossing the weft threads over and under odd numbers of warps. The various motifs, all based on a diamond-shaped unit, are achieved by a specific system of counting. This example displays in the center of the diamond unit a design called *sayagata*, a variation of interconnected swastika shapes. Around it, layers of diamonds constitute a consecutive pattern of *irekobishi* (enclosed small diamonds). The outermost borders extend and cross with others, achieving an X-shaped design called *tasuki*. It refers to the cloth rope used by the Japanese to hold up kimono sleeves during rigorous physical activities. Many individual patterns of kogin design are known by name in the local Tsugaru dialect, and they often refer to simple objects in the farmer's everyday life. Examples such as *beko no kura* (cow saddle), *mameko* (beans), and *neko no managu* (cat's eye) are based on visual association and reveal the refreshingly simple imagery that lies at the core of such magnificent stitchery art.

To the southeast of Tsugaru is the Nambu region in eastern Aomori and northern Iwate prefectures, where the colorful *hishizashi* apron (cat. 6) was produced. Hishizashi, too, incorporates the counted-stitch technique.

6.
Apron *(maekake)*
Meiji period, late 19th century
Quilted *(sashiko)* **cotton cloth and bast fiber** *(asa)* **cloth with counted stitch cotton thread embroidery** *(hishizashi)*, **23⅝ x 16½ in. (59.1 x 41.3 cm)**
89.131

7.
Farmer's coat
Meiji period, ca. 1900, Tsugaru
Quilted (sashiko) recycled
cotton cloth with thread-
resist decoration (shibori);
sleeves and trim of striped
cotton cloth, 41¾ x 45¼ in.
(104.4 x 113.1 cm) 89.147

However, in contrast to the Tsugaru kogin, Nambu hishizashi is created by systematically crossing the threads over and under even numbers of warps, resulting in a pattern of horizontal diamonds. Compared to kogin, hishizashi lacks diversity and freedom in larger design configurations because of its strict adherence to small diamond units. Allegiance to the diamond motif may be intentional on the part of the Nambu people, as it was a component of the family crest of the Nambu clan who ruled the region.[12]

Very little is known about the historical development of the Nambu hishizashi, which can be found decorating a variety of garments such as aprons, trousers, and coats. It is at least certain that it originated, like kogin, from the need to reinforce fabric for durability and warmth. The tradition is more recent than kogin as the earliest extant example of hishizashi is believed to date from 1856.[13] Originally hishizashi was applied to pale blue asa fabric with white and dark blue cotton threads. Each village had its own distinctive design, which was transmitted from generation to generation.[14] In the early twentieth century Nambu women began to incorporate brightly colored yarns creating a more striking and varied visual effect.

This apron is an excellent example of Nambu hishizashi. The use of colored threads contributes to a lovely flowerlike impression of its pattern, quite different from the elegant appearance of the Tsugaru kogin. Colors also expand the range of overall patterns by providing a larger framework of design. Like kogin, the individual motifs within the diamonds are named after common objects that surrounded the Nambu people's lives. The design motifs decorating this apron are *kiji no ashi* (pheasant foot) in each of the smallest unit of the blue diamonds in the central column, *hana no monko* (flower motif) in the columns of yellow diamonds flanking them, and *yanagi no ha* (willow leaf) in the outermost purple columns. Sashiko stitches of zigzag patterns on both borders complete the design. The beauty of such an apron easily convinces us that Nambu women wore hishizashi aprons not just for work but also adorned themselves with exceptionally beautiful pieces on special occasions such as the Bon festival.[15]

While kogin and hishizashi are characterized by structural uniformity of design due to the counted stitch technique, the sashiko running stitch results in greater diversity and variety in individual motifs as well as in overall organization of patterns. A delightful example of a Tsugaru farmer's sashiko work coat (cat. 7) has tapered sleeves, *tsutsusode* (tube sleeves), which allow the wearer active movement, while the front part becomes wider toward the hem for easy overlapping. The exterior fabric is decorated with tie-dyed floral and butterfly motifs, and the inner fabric displays a tie-dyed polka-dot design. Small stitches in white throughout the body of the garment bind the two layers of recycled fabric, demonstrating most faithfully the tradition of sashiko. The sleeves, which have no lining, are made of striped cloth, which is also used along the lapels. Although sashiko itself does not render a particular design, the combination of fabrics with contrasting designs achieves a wonderfully decorative result. Horizontal stitching meticulously applied over fabrics with stencil-dyed or tie-dyed patterns, as exemplified in this piece, is a characteristic frequently seen in sashiko from the Tsugaru region, where this type of work coat is known by many names, including *tsuzure*, *donja*, and *bodo*.[16]

A generously proportioned sashiko vest, called *sodenashi* (without sleeves), was usually worn over a coat or sometimes directly over an undergarment. The vest (cat. 8) is an example of true sashiko patchwork of

8.
Vest *(dōgi)*
Meiji-Taishō period, late 19th-early 20th century
Quilted *(sashiko)* **recycled cotton cloth with paste-resist stencil decoration** *(katazome)* **trimmed with cotton cloth with double ikat** *(kasuri)*, **32¾ x 13⅝ in. (81.9 x 34.1 cm)**
89.160

9.
Farmer's coat
Late Edo-early Meiji period,
19th century, perhaps Shōnai
Quilted *(sashiko)* recycled
cotton cloth and patchwork
cloth pieces with paste-
resist stencil decoration
(katazome), 44 x 45 in. (110 x
112.5 cm) 89.146

various fabric remnants. The main body of the vest consists of two layers of
stencil-dyed fabrics stitched together. Applied on cloth clearly made in the
city, the design shows peonies, butterflies, and leaf-shaped motifs filled with
diamonds, water patterns, and tortoise shells. As in the work coat (cat. 7),
small, horizontal stitchwork executed over stencil-dyed fabrics suggests that
this vest is from the Tsugaru region. The small *kasuri* panels on the bottom of
the front panels and the top of the side panels are also reinforced with
stitches. The maker of this vest has added lovely kasuri over the shoulders and
the upper back. Its woven designs, buoyant variations of rectangles and
triangles, complement the more rigidly defined, complex motifs of the stencil-
dyed fabrics. Another kasuri used for the lapels adds a strong, conclusive
accent to the vest. The juxtaposition of various motifs and different shades of
blue makes this vest an exceptionally handsome sashiko garment.

A magnificent example is a coat (cat. 9) from the northwestern area of
Tohoku. Stitchwork in white binds two layers of cotton, creating squared swirl
motifs, generally called *masuzashi* (*masu* stitch). Masu, a square wooden box
traditionally used to measure sake and grains, could symbolize one's assets and
was a propitious motif for farmers and merchants. Two rows of masu dissolve
on the front and back to compose different overall patterns. The maker of this
coat has modified the masuzashi motif by continuing some lines over the
shoulders to the front portion, achieving a dazzling effect on the upper back
of the garment, where the vertical and horizontal lines create a shape within a

shape that emerges independently from the original motifs. A straight, right-angle linear design is continued into the portion of the sleeves, where it meets with the curvilinear *shippō tsunagi* (overlapping circles) pattern on the cuffs, an auspicious design which means "seven treasures."[17] The sashiko design suggests its place of origin on the western side of Tohoku,[18] namely Akita, Yamagata, and Fukushima prefectures. In particular, sashiko from the Shōnai district in Yamagata are noted for abstract designs created by arrangements of straight lines.[19] The maker of this coat has added patches of light blue cotton with stencil-dyed designs, a fabric probably imported from the Kyoto-Osaka area. The motifs on the patched cotton on the sleeves show symbols of good fortune, such as the precious jewel and magic mallet, while the larger pieces on the back are patterned with pine needles, bamboo, and plum blossoms, or the "three friends of winter." The *shōchikubai* motif, a combination of these three plants, represented endurance in Chinese and Japanese art, and it carries particularly auspicious symbolism in Japan. By selecting such sashiko and stencil-dyed motifs that specifically express positive meanings, the maker of this coat conveys her fervent wish for a prosperous life. Seen as a whole, the large white sashiko patterns on the indigo ground juxtaposed with the patches of light blue cloth create a compelling and harmonious design.

Another coat (cat. 10) offers an entirely different visual experience. Two layers of blue and gold striped cotton are completely covered with large

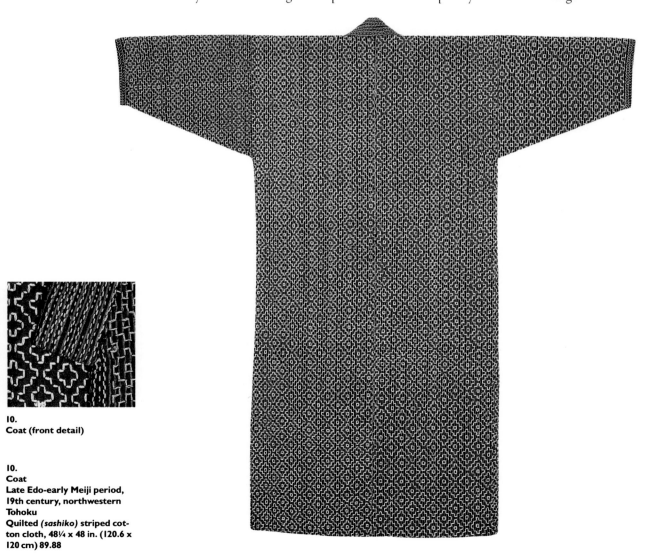

10.
Coat (front detail)

10.
Coat
Late Edo-early Meiji period,
19th century, northwestern
Tohoku
Quilted *(sashiko)* striped cotton cloth, 48¼ x 48 in. (120.6 x 120 cm) 89.88

white stitches repeating a motif called *kaki no hana* (persimmon flower).[20] The coat is notably long in proportion and has extra panels in front for overlapping, as in a standard kimono. In form and proportion, it resembles a *zubu* (fisherman's work jacket), a garment prevalent in the coastal region of Iwate and Miyagi prefectures in northeastern Tohoku. The long, thick zubu, often made of layers of striped cotton, protected fishermen from the elements, and when folded also functioned as a cushion to sit on.[21] Zubu generally feature plain sashiko, or the most basic straight stitches, without the decorative pattern seen in this coat. The persimmon-flower motif in sashiko is more commonly found in the Akita, Yamagata, and Fukushima prefectures on the northwestern side of Tohoku.[22] This coat may have been produced in one of the coastal villages in that area.

Two unusual examples of sleeveless sashiko coats demonstrate perfect integration of function, form, and aesthetic sensibility. One is a *sorihiki banten* (sled-hauling vest) from the Shōnai district in Yamagata, which features a band over one shoulder and across the front where the hauling rope was slung (cat. 11). For a Shōnai man, around the tenth day of January marked the first occasion of farm work in the new year; proudly wearing the vest that his wife had spent many months making, he pulled a sledfull of fertilizer to spread over the field.[23]

The body of the vest is made from indigo-dyed fabrics stitched meticulously with dark blue cotton thread forming rows of a stairlike pattern. The side panels are stitched in two different motifs: the persimmon-flower motif above and zigzag pattern below, which is generally known as *sugizashi* (cedar stitch). The taut stitchwork on the front and back panels is probably an example of *chirimenzashi* or *chijimizashi* (crepe stitch). By pulling the cloth tight, the stitches make the garment thicker and warmer while creating a crepelike, crinkly surface texture. Moreover, the vest's dark-on-dark technique, which makes the stitches not immediately noticeable, may reflect the tradition of

11.
Sled-hauling vest *(sorihiki banten)*
Late Edo–early Meiji period, 19th century, Shōnai
Quilted *(sashiko)* cotton cloth trimmed with cotton cloth with double ikat *(kasuri)*, 28½ x 13⅜ in. (71.3 x 33.4 cm) 89.127

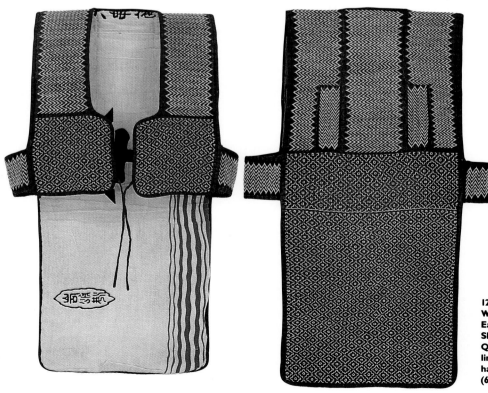

12.
Work vest *(nisuri)*
Early 20th century, perhaps Shōnai
Quilted *(sashiko)* cotton cloth lined with recycled cotton handtowel, 26½ x 12¾ in. (66.3 x 31.9 cm) 89.135

kakurezashi (hidden stitch). In this technique, an indigo cloth decorated with white cotton stitches was dipped in dye to conceal the patterns. As the garment was worn and washed, the indigo of the cotton thread faded, gradually revealing the designs of these "hidden stitches."[24]

In contrast to the subtle beauty of the vest's body, the band decorated with prominent white stitches visually dominates the garment. Among the three different sashiko designs reinforcing and adorning the band, the most prominent is the diamond motif reminiscent of kogin and hishizashi, which covers the entire surface of the band across the front and the lowest portion of the shoulder panel. While the possibility of contact with the Tsugaru region cannot be disregarded, Shōnai women may have independently arrived at the use of this motif because the dense diamond-shaped designs actually serve to reinforce the fabric against the tension that occurs from all directions when the vest is in use.[25] The bold diagonal orientation of the frontal band imbues the garment with a sense of motion and dynamism appropriate for its function.

Another vest with a peculiar shape is a type of back-pad called *nisuri* (cat. 12), probably from Shōnai, Yamagata. Generally women's garments, vests like this were worn with the front portion tied with the strings in the middle so as to function like a modern brassiere,[26] while the back formed a pad for carrying loads such as a shoulder-strap basket. As the wearer's body bends, stretches, and moves about, the upper portion of the nisuri around the shoulders and the back must endure the most friction and tension. Thus, the maker of this indigo cotton vest has reinforced its upper areas and the side bands with dense zigzag cedar stitches. The persimmon-flower motif covers the lower front area as well as the lower back, which extends toward the wearer's hip. The white cotton cloth casually used as a lining is a Japanese towel of the kind most likely given out as an advertisement by a local shop. The shop name is partly retained at the shoulders, and at the bottom are characters imitating a seal, which read "Iwafune Harbor."[27]

The farmers of Tohoku lovingly applied sashiko even to the humblest objects, such as socks. *Tabi* are traditional Japanese socks with divided toes, which allow one to slip into Japanese traditional footwear easily. Commonly made of cotton, they consist of three panels sewn together to fit the complex form of the human foot remarkably well. The metal clasps at the back opening, which hook over the loops of thick thread on the opposite panel, are used to adjust the fit. Tabi with sashiko are found throughout Tohoku, often showing straight stitches with no recognizable pattern. In particular, in Shōnai, Yamagata, where a pair of tabi was a valuable possession for ordinary farmers, skill in producing sashiko tabi was a prerequisite for a young woman who wished to marry: her sashiko skill, and therefore her desirability as a farmer's wife, was evaluated by the quality of the sashiko tabi she prepared.[28] A pair of blue tabi demonstrate a decorative flare (cat. 13). While the bottom is strengthened with straight running stitches, the back and sides are covered with neat layers of zigzag patterns in white stitching similar to the cedar stitch. The design culminates with larger zigzags around the toes, where both sides fuse to create a rich wavelike pattern.

13.
Footgear *(tabi)*
Meiji-Taishō period, late 19th-early 20th century
Quilted *(sashiko)* **cotton cloth, 12⅛ x 5½ in. (30.9 x 13.8 cm each) 89.90.1-.2**

14.
Wrapping cloth *(furoshiki)*
Taishō-Shōwa period, 20th century
Stitched *(sashiko)* **cotton cloth, 41⅜ x 39 in. (103.4 x 97.5 cm) 89.153**

If tabi represent an easily overlooked, mundane, yet uniquely three-dimensional construction in Japanese textile and clothing tradition, *furoshiki* (wrapping cloths) perhaps stand for the simplest but most versatile two-dimensional invention. The Japanese still use furoshiki today to carry gifts and various commodities. They vary from fine silk meant to be used in more formal and ceremonial occasions to large cotton and asa types used to transport heavy loads. This furoshiki (cat. 14) is relatively large and made from three panels of commercially dyed and woven cotton. Because the corners of furoshiki are repeatedly tied, untied, and picked up, they are the most vulnerable parts. The decorator of this furoshiki has reinforced its four corners with sashiko. The patterns include sayagata in one corner, a connected diamond motif in the opposing corner, and perhaps a variation of a folding fan in the other two corners. The unfolded fan stands for the idea of *suehirogari* (wider toward the end) which signals increasing prosperity in the future, while the swastika has been traditionally accepted as an auspicious symbol signifying long life. The straight, linear design which fans out from two corners makes a pleasant contrast with the smaller, denser designs of sayagata and diamonds.

The last two sashiko examples (cat. 15 and 16) and a related leather coat (cat. 17) transport us from the rural life in northern Japan to the heart of urban culture, which rose during the Edo period. The two sashiko firemen's coats (*hikeshi banten*) both belonged to *machi bikeshi* (townsmen firefighters); the leather coat belonged to a samurai firefighter. Unlike the farmers of Tohoku, who often both produced and used their sashiko garments, these city dwellers commissioned others to make and decorate their coats. The samurai's coat was no doubt produced at one of the nearby regional centers making these products, such as Kōfu.[29] These three coats represent the products

of a different socio-economic class and reflect a distinct taste associated with townsmen.

In old Japan, where wood architecture was predominant, fires occurred frequently. The capital city of Edo was often devastated by fire — one of the worst was the great fire of Meireki (1657), in which more than 170,000 people perished. Firefighting activities were first organized in the city of Edo in 1629 when the shogun Iemitsu decided to summon a group of daimyo to protect Edo Castle and other samurai estates from fire. During the next hundred years, the Tokugawa government continued to organize *daimyō bikeshi* (feudal lord firefighters) and other samurai firefighters to guard Edo Castle, mansions of the daimyo, and important religious structures against fire. It was not until 1720 that the system of machi bikeshi was finally established; its primary responsibility was the protection of ordinary citizens' properties. By 1730 Edo boasted 10,000 townsmen firefighters in well-organized groups.[30] And by the mid-eighteenth century, townsmen firefighters eclipsed the samurai firefighters both in effectiveness and popularity.[31]

Firefighting was an extremely hazardous occupation, as firemen resorted to the radical method of razing all structures in the fire's path as quickly as possible, to prevent the spread of flames. Before entering the scene of a fire, a firefighter wearing full gear, including a sashiko coat, hood, trousers, and gloves, soaked himself with water. The thick, water-drenched sashiko garment, which could weigh as much as eighty pounds,[32] provided the necessary protection from heat and falling objects. Using *tobiguchi*, a pole with a metal hook in the shape of a *tobi* bird beak, the fireman daringly attacked the burning building. Hence Edo firefighters were called tobi. (Tobi also referred to workers who erected tall buildings requiring scaffolding, a profession held by many firefighters.) For the hot-tempered Edo citizens, who boasted, "Fires and brawls are splendors of Edo," townsmen firefighters, known for their reckless action and audacity, held a special status. They were in fact immortalized in ukiyo-e prints as symbols of masculine glamour and ideals, just as courtesans were ideals of feminine beauty in late Edo-period Japan.

Firemen's cloth coats are made of several layers of thick cotton fabric quilted by sashiko. These coats are typically reversible. The more striking designs, paste-resisted and hand-painted, are found on the inner side of the coats and reflect the individual taste of the wearer. One of the coats is decorated with a painted ginkgo leaf motif (cat. 15). The fanlike ginkgo leaf has often been associated with a dancing crane, symbolizing longevity. The leaf shape is also related to the notion of suehirogari, or increasing prosperity in the future. In addition, ginkgo trees, difficult to burn, have been traditionally used in Japan to create fire barriers. A well-known story relates how a large ginkgo tree protected a house in a certain section of Tokyo from a fire following the great earthquake of 1923 by the moisture it exuded.[33] Above all, the blue-green leaves fluttering against the ochre background create a design at once dynamic and elegant. On the back the large blue Chinese character *ren* (connected) may relate to the linked-chain motif in blue on the other side of the coat, which was usually worn on the outside.

The owner of the other coat chose an entirely different design, an image of a man riding on a tiger in the style of ukiyo-e (cat. 16). Wearing a billowy coat and trousers, the figure strikes a dramatic posture. The scroll in his mouth and his hand gesture indicate that he is endowed with magical

15.
Commoner's firefighting coat (hikeshi banten)
Late Edo-early Meiji period, mid-19th century
Quilted (*sashiko*) cotton cloth with freehand paste-resist decoration (*tsutsugaki*), 34⅜ x 46⅞ in. (85.9 x 117.2 cm) 89.81

Coat illustrated at right with fireman's hat (*zukin*)

16. (overleaf)
Commoner's firefighting coat (hikeshi banten)
Late Edo-early Meiji period, mid-19th century
Quilted (*sashiko*) cotton cloth with freehand paste-resist decoration (*tsutsugaki*), 35⅛ x 47¾ in. (89.7 x 119.4 cm) 89.82

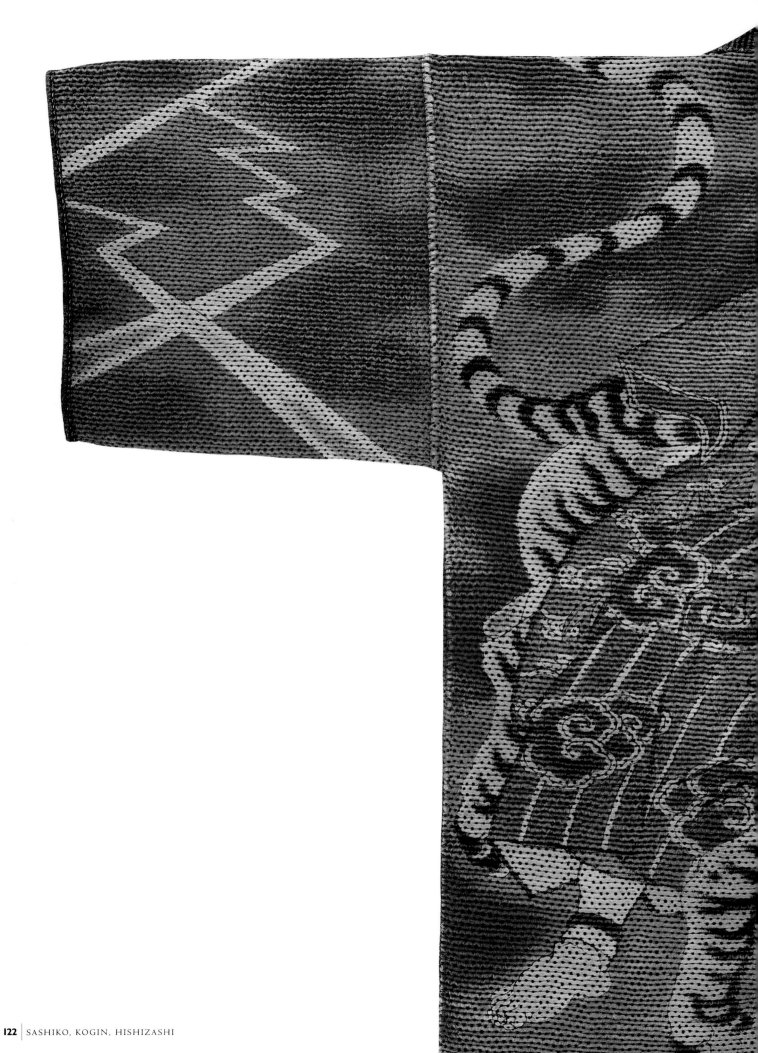

power. Looking upward to the sky, he seems to be calling forth the rain. The lightning patterns on the coat sleeves and the clouds which surround the figure suggest the approaching storm. In Chinese and Japanese tradition, a tiger has been paired with a dragon who brings a storm as he descends from the heavens. The ferocious expression of the tiger, whose sinuous tail contrasts with the sharp angularity of the thunderbolts, implies the imminent presence of the dragon.[34] In his appearance, the figure strongly evokes the image of Jiraiya, a Robin Hood-type Kabuki hero who rides on a giant toad and combats villains. This figure is likely an imaginary personage whose heroic and gallant appearance echoes the pride and self-image of the wearer. The reverse of the coat is plain indigo blue, and on its back is the large white Japanese phonetic symbol *te*, enclosed in a white circle. On the lapels both inside and

outside are the characters *Nakamura Kichi*, probably identifying the owner. The exterior of the coat, by its plainness, must have intensified the dazzling effect of the interior when it was reversed for display after its owner had battled a fire, or on holidays when the acrobatic antics of the firemen entertained the neighborhood and decorated coats added color to the festivities[35].

    Leather garments were sometimes fashioned and decorated in the same way woven fabrics were treated, or as the coat here (cat. 17), decorated with special techniques. The *kawabaori* is a samurai's fire brigade coat made

17.
Samurai leather firefighting coat (kawabaori)
Edo period, late 18th century
Leather with paste-resist stencil decoration, smoke-induced color *(fusube-gawa or inden)*, 37 x 52⅛ in. (92.5 x 130.3 cm) 89.93

from that leather which has been smoked and dyed to create the overall decoration of linked diamonds. The smoking process (*inden*) exposes the leather to the smoke of smoldering materials such as pine needles or rice straw, which imparts color to it.[36] Before smoking, a paste-resist pattern was added by means of a stencil, and these resisted areas were not affected by the smoke. The exterior and one face of this coat's lapel were also dyed with indigo. The linked-diamond pattern was apparently popular for a fireman's attire in the latter part of the Edo period.

Ordinary citizen firefighters wore cotton sashiko garments with fanciful tsutsugaki designs, while the samurai brigade leaders wore a variety of garments, including *haori* made of *rasha* (wool) or inden-decorated leather. The exact nature of the leather, however, is nowhere well explained. The leather of this coat, though supple, seems too thick to be deerskin, which is the usual identification given. Perhaps hides, like the rasha fabric (cat. 34), were imported through Nagasaki. Such importation might partially explain the reference to India in the term "inden," and, if the hides were of water buffalo, that would perhaps explain their thickness.

Like the sashiko hanten, the leather coats were reversible. The linked-diamond pattern is on the inner face of this coat; it was not exposed during the firefighting action. The brown-and-white pattern is accented with indigo lines that cut vertically through the diamond shapes. On this face, the collar is brown. The coat's decorated interior was reversed and exhibited only upon the fireman's triumphal return after the blaze.

The coat's normal exterior face is dyed blue with indigo, with a *mon* showing in very dark blue and white within a white circle. The mon shows an upright leaf of a type of oak tree. The lapels and collar have been dyed with indigo on this side, so that the plain blue coat exterior is trimmed with a sweeping blue collar and lapels.[37]

As we have seen, the sashiko technique can be found on garments transcending class distinction between farmers and merchants, as well as the regional difference between country and city. For the farmers of Tohoku, who often sustained themselves at the barest material level, to recycle old fabrics was an economic necessity that could be equated to producing rice. The act of stitching, moreover, had moral overtones in that it nurtured in women the perseverance and patience essential to live as a farmer's wife.[38] For them, sashiko was both a technique and a discipline with which they learned to overcome physically and psychologically their adverse living conditions. Year after year, diligently stitching throughout the winter, they gave new life to an old garment, just as the spring revitalized the earth beneath the snow. Over the generations, the women of Tohoku developed what originated as a basic mending technique into a unique textile tradition, vernacular in form and expression but universal in appeal.

If the farmer's sashiko can stand for rejuvenation of life, the fireman's coat perhaps symbolizes celebration of life here and now. During the Edo period, the popular culture of the townsman class became firmly established, reflecting their newly gained economic power. Ukiyo-e, the pictures of the floating world, often depict boisterous scenes of pleasure as townspeople spent their energy on frivolous pastimes, as if to make up for the transience of human life. In the fireman's coat, the focus of decorative design is the painted imagery, which relegates sashiko to its basic, utilitarian function. Unlike the tenacious and humble beauty of the farmer's sashiko, the painted designs seen on these coats are as assertive and dramatic as the fireworks which blossomed in the sky over the city of Edo at times of festival. They echo a strong sense of individualism and worldly confidence felt by the townsmen.

1. For example, during the Edo period, the farmers of Nambu in present Aomori and Iwate prefectures suffered lean harvests every three to four years, poor harvests (50 percent of the average year) every five years, and complete crop failure every eighteen years. Kiku Tokunaga, *Sashiko no kenkyū* (Tokyo: Iseikatsu Kenkyūkai, 1989), p. 42.

2. Ibid., pp. 57-58

3. Ibid., p. 80.

4. *Tsugaru kogin to Nambu hishizashi*, (Sapporo: Hokkaido Kaitaku Kinenkan, 1985), p. 32.

5. *Sashikogin to hishizashi* (Aomori: Aomori Kenritsu Kyōdokan, 1976), p. 54.

6. *Tsugaru kogin to Nambu hishizashi*, pp. 33-34.

7. Ibid., p. 34.

8. Ibid., p. 36.

9. Ibid.

10. Victor and Takako Hauge, *Folk Traditions in Japanese Art* (Washington, D.C.: International Exhibitions Foundation, 1978), p. 249.

11. *Tsugaru kogin to Nambu hishizashi*, p. 36.

12. *Sashikogin to hishizashi*, p. 58.

13. Ibid.

14. *Iwate no shigotogi-ten* (Morioka: Iwate Kenritsu Hakubutsukan, 1985), p. 46.

15. Ibid., p. 60.

16. Satoshi Narita at Aomori Kenritsu Kyōdokan, personal correspondence, March 28, 1991.

17. The design is an abstraction from an overall pattern of overlapping circles, the overlap being equal on four sides. Its name seems to derive from a Japanese pun on *shiho*, or "four directions" in this case. John W. Dower, *The Elements of Japanese Design* (New York: Weatherhill, 1971), p. 134.

18. Narita, personal correspondence, March 28, 1991.

19. Tomoyuki Yamanobe, *Nihon no senshoku*, (Tokyo: Chūō Kōronsha, 1981) vol. 6, *Shomin/Kindai*, p. 252.

20. This motif is also known as *hanazashi* (flower stitch) and *zenizashi* (money stitch). Tokunaga, *Sashiko no kenkyū*, p. 156.

21. See *Iwate no shigotogi-ten*, p. 27.

22. Narita, personal correspondence, March 28, 1991.

23. Tokunaga, *Sashiko no kenkyū*, p. 239.

24. The technique is believed to have been invented by the farmers of Shōnai during the Edo period, who by official order were allowed to wear only blue or gray colors decorated with patterns no larger than a grain of rice or with stripes no wider than the thickness of a straw. Since no regulation forbade the farmers from wearing clothes on which patterns gradually emerged, kakurezashi provided them a means to wear larger decorative designs. Tokunaga, *Sashiko no kenkyū*, pp. 87, 227-28. Whether this vest is an example of true kakurezashi, i.e., dipped in dye after stitching, is difficult to determine at this point.

25. Tokunaga, *Sashiko no kenkyū*, p. 240.

26. Ibid., p. 218.

27. It may come from the Iwafune district near present-day Murakami in Niigata, close to the neighboring Fukushima prefecture. Narita, personal correspondence, March 28, 1991.

28. Tokunaga, *Sashiko no kenkyū*, pp. 71-72.

29. Junichi Sasaki, "Kawabaori, Fusubegawa ni tsuite," *Mingei*, 373 (Jan. 1984), p. 45.

30. Tōgo Fujiguchi, *Edo bikeshi nendaiki* (Tokyo: Sōshisha, 1962), p. 155.

31. Ibid., p. 223.

32. Jinichi Suzuki, Tsugio Miya, and Tokyo Rengō Bōka Kyōkai, *Hikeshi fūzoku datesugata* (Tokyo: Haga Shoten, 1985), p. 128.

33. Jullie Piggot, *Japanese Mythology* (London: Paul Hamly, 1969), p. 127.

34. An almost identical figure on a tiger is juxtaposed with another on a dragon in a design that decorates a hikeshi banten in the collection of Peabody Museum of Salem, Massachusetts. See Money Hickman and Peter Fetchko, *Japan Day by Day: An Exhibition in Honor of Edward Sylvester Morse* (Salem: Peabody Museum of Salem, 1977), p. 82. This was brought to my attention by David Hogge, a graduate student in art history at the University of Washington, Seattle.

35. See Hickman and Fetchko, *Japan Day by Day*, pp. 69ff., ills. 65, 86-87. Photography of 1880 shows acrobatics of the firemen. Cf. discussion of sashiko coats (cat. 15 and 16); see M. Chaplin Ayrton, *Child-life in Japan* (London: Griffith and Farran, 1879), pp. 39-40, ill. p. 39 for a Meiji-period description of how fire brigades made acrobatic displays during the New Year celebration.

36. The term "inden" is an abbreviation of *indo-denrai* which means "transmitted from India." The process is also known as *fusube-gawa* (literally, smoked leather). It is believed that the current inden technique was introduced to Japan in the sixteenth century from India. There is, however, a leather sutra-wrapper dating to the eighth century in the Todaiji Temple collection which has decoration some believe was created through a smoking process like inden. See Katsumi Nakae, ed., *Senshoku jiten* (Dictionary of Weaving and Dyeing), (Tokyo: Tairyūsha, 1981), p. 58; also Kaneo Matsumoto, *Jōdai-gire* (Ancient Cloth Fragments), (Kyoto: Shikōsha, 1984), ills. 119, p. 240.

For a description of the process see Junichi Sasaki, "Kawabaori," p. 45, ills. 2, 4, 5, 9, 11, 13, 15, and cover. Sasaki says that the color, its intensity and shading, could be controlled by the choice of material set to smoldering, the length of time of exposure, and the heat.

37. Suzuki, et. al., *Hikeshi fūzoku datesugata*, ills. 12-14, 26-29, 41, and 51-52, pp. 97ff. Many woodblock prints illustrate the fireman's experience and appearance; see also Naoko Iwasaki, *Nihon no ishō jiten* (Dictionary of Japanese Clothing), (Tokyo: Iwasaki Bijutsusha, 1984), p. 18. The diamond pattern also was done in dark blue alone.

38. Tokunaga, *Sashiko no kenkyū*, p. 72.

M ETHODS OF DECORATING FABRIC SURFACES BY RESISTING certain areas through various means were known as early as the seventh and eighth centuries. It is possible that resist techniques were applied to make patterns on early, now-lost clothing and articles of daily use, and that the practice was more widespread than is suggested by the few remnants found today among temple treasures.

By the eighteenth century, a repertoire of techniques for making resist patterns had developed, creating a rich legacy of graphic design. Once established in use, these techniques, which employ in common an inexpensive rice-paste resist, proved to be exceedingly popular and enduring methods of decorating garments and fabrics that were worn and used by all classes of Japanese society. The most frequently employed of these rice-paste resist techniques were the freehand *tsutsugaki* and the stencil-patterned *katazome*. *Yūzenzome*, a unique set of resist dyeing and patterning techniques, is technically allied with tsutsugaki techniques, but through extreme delicacy of resisted line and hand-applied colors, becomes a separate aesthetic. While the delicate lines of uniform thinness are a hallmark of yūzenzome, often now yūzen pattern outlines and coloring result from the use of stencils, creating *katayūzen*. No matter how adept the technique, the ultimate source of novelty was the artist's invention and creativity. In each of these paste-resist techniques, Japanese dyers achieved unique expressions and established their preeminent place in the history of textile decoration.[1]

Among examples featuring the tsutsugaki technique, the *yogi*, or kimono-form comforters, are among the visually most arresting and, in regard to their ambiguous nature, are highly enigmatic icons of comfort and security.[2] Yogi (literally, night garment) are kimono-shaped bed coverings stuffed with raw cotton. Generally made with *hirosode* (wide sleeves, in which the wrist opening is as large as the length of the sleeve), yogi often have triangular gussets where the sleeves meet the body to provide more width. An extra panel inserted in the center back also makes the yogi considerably wider than regular kimono.

The use of yogi is believed to have become common at the beginning of the Edo period (1615–1868).[3] Before this time, most Japanese simply used kimono as bed covers. The *futon*, a rectangular bed stuffed with raw cotton, came into use, first in the Kyoto and Osaka areas around the end of the seventeenth century, about a hundred years later than yogi.[4] The comfort of warm yogi and futon became available to the ordinary Japanese populace only.

19.
Coverlet in kimono form
(yogi)
Meiji period, 19th century
Cotton cloth with freehand
paste-resist decoration (tsutsugaki), 61 x 55½ in. (152.5 x
138.8 cm) 89.145

18.
**Coverlet in kimono form
(yogi)
Late Edo-early Meiji period,
19th century
Cotton cloth with freehand
paste-resist decoration (tsutsugaki),** 59 x 61 in. (147.5 x
152.5 cm) 89.91

after cultivation of cotton became established in Japan. Even then, it was not a commodity affordable to all Japanese; well into modern times, poor townsmen and farmers continued to sleep wrapped in straw, paper, and old rags.

Thus it is easy to understand that yogi and futon were valuable assets for those who possessed them. The illustrated examples are decorated beautifully with auspicious designs, for these objects were once a part of wedding trousseau in rural Japan. The bride's parents were expected to provide valuable gifts such as chests and bureaus filled with kimono and bedding; a lavish trousseau was a way to demonstrate their status to society and publicly celebrate their daughter's new life.

Tsutsugaki-decorated cotton in the forms of yogi, futon, *yutan* (chest cover), *furoshiki* (wrapping cloth), and other textile items played an important part in the rural wedding. When the marriage was agreed upon, the bride and other women of her family spun cotton, wove it into cloth, and took it to the local indigo dyer to have it decorated with auspicious patterns and family crests. The choice of design from the large repertoire of traditionally accepted motifs depended on the taste as well as the financial resources of the family. After the cloth was dyed, the final sewing of the textile items was carried out by the bride and her family. Tsutsugaki bedding produced in this manner was valued and handled with great care at the bride's new home.[5]

Two yogi illustrated here (cat. 18 and 19) present a delightful motif of a hare on waves (*nami usagi*), one of the most endearing themes in Japanese decorative arts. The hare motif appears in ancient Chinese bronzes. In Japan the earliest known examples are preserved in the embroidered mandala dedicated to Prince Shōtoku (574–622) and known as *Tenjukoku shūchō*, and in a painting on the so-called Beetle-wing Shrine (*Tamamushi no zushi*) in the Hōryūji. Both date to the seventh century. The hare motif gained popularity, however, during the Momoyama (1568–1615) and early Edo periods.[6]

Legends and old fables abound concerning this creature. The association of a hare and the moon is well known in Far Eastern art. Chinese

132 | TSUTSUGAKI AND KATAZOME

legend relates how a hare and a frog produced the elixir of immortality on the moon. In Japan the hare remained associated with the moon, but as a lovable creature who pounds special rice to make *mochi* (rice cake), possibly reflecting concerns of an agricultural society.[7] A Buddhist legend tells how a hare was given the privilege of living in the moon for its act of self-sacrifice for Taishakuten (Indra).

The specific motif of the hare on the waves cannot be explained by any single source. According to Japanese legend, a female hare conceives by running on the waves on the eighteenth day of the eighth moon, or by licking the fur of the male during the same period.[8] Perhaps the best-known story is of the white hare of Inaba (*Inaba no shiro usagi*), which derives from a Japanese mythology preserved in the *Kojiki* (Record of Ancient Matters), written in the eighth century. It tells of a cunning hare that crossed the ocean from one island to another by tricking sharks into lining up in the water to form a bridge. Upon reaching the other island, the hare ungratefully ridiculed the sharks, prompting them to flay the hare. When a kind-hearted god passed by the suffering hare, he advised the animal to roll in cattail pollen. The hare did so, was quickly healed, and prophesied to the god that he would be chosen from among his many brothers by a princess as her husband.

Another possible source for this motif comes from an entirely different tradition, a Noh play titled *Chikubushima* (The Island of Chikubu). In this play, a Zen monk, Jikyū, boards a boat to visit Chikubu Island on Lake Biwa. While sailing, he admires the reflections on the water and imagines the hare running on the waves.[9] The island enshrines Benzaiten (Sarasvati), one of the Seven Lucky Gods. Benzaiten is the goddess who not only promotes music and languages but ensures longevity and fortune.

Among frequently published objects adorned with the hare-on-the-waves motif are a ship captain's leather coat, horse trappings, war helmets, a lacquered inkstone case, a lacquered cosmetic box, and various ceramic wares. On such items, the motif may signify different meanings or simply be a charming design. A wish for speedy travel or a prayer for Benzaiten's protection is a likely message when the motif is used in decorating horse trappings, war helmets, or a ship captain's coat. On an inkstone box, it may refer to Benzaiten as the patron of arts.[10] In yogi, one cannot help but read the motif as having multiple associations: the *Chikubushima* Benzaiten who brings good fortune, the Inaba hare who foretells the conjugal union, and the old legend about a hare begetting children by running on the waves.

Of the two illustrated examples, the yogi with a single hare (cat. 18) has the more dynamic effect. On the upper back of this yogi is a crest of three sedge hats (*ichimegasa*) arranged within a circle. The dominant use of light blue highlighted with indigo and natural white gives a sophisticated appearance to these everyday objects while enhancing the whiteness of the hare below. Directly beneath the crest a magnificent white hare leaps fearlessly above the waves. Suspended in mid-air, feet kicking high, the image is the embodiment of speed and motion. Its tense body, alert expression, and large, strong feet convey the animal's cunning and speed, like the Inaba hare, which one should never underestimate.

The hare's body was first defined in paste outline and its entire silhouette paste-resisted before being dipped in indigo dye. The artist later added ink brushlines to depict the form and the details of its body. On its torso, where the ink outline is omitted, short parallel lines describe the texture of the fur. The wave behind the hare rises dramatically, echoing its leaping posture. The beautifully stylized patterns of the waves are achieved with steady, smooth tsutsugaki lines. The white hare is the focal point of this decoration, set apart from the light blue color of the waves and the crest as well as the indigo background.

The same theme is approached in a different manner by the artist of the other hare-motif yogi (cat. 19). Nine hares in diverse poses appear among the swirling and rippling waves. Unlike their more ferocious counterpart, these animals have rounder faces and smaller feet, conveying a milder impression. Seven of the hares relate to each other either by their action or by the direction of their eyes: they seem to be keenly aware of the others' presence.

Seemingly indifferent and oblivious to the commotion around them, a whimsical pair quietly sits in one corner, at the lower left hem. One is viewed from behind and the other frontally. With feet tucked under its furry body, the latter stares at us curiously with buttonlike eyes. As in the first hare-motif yogi, the artist has brushed in lines to delineate the anatomy of the animals. In certain areas, extremely fine brushlines represent the fur texture, and modulating lines define musculature. Furthermore, three hares display extensive ink shading, indicating the artist's interest in showing the three-dimensional form. The large white crest above the animals is composed of three mandarin orange blossoms (tachibana) forming a circle. Its crisp, geometric design enhances the naturalistic representation of the hares below, and its circular shape evokes the presence of the full moon above the horizon.

The crane is an ubiquitous motif on tsutsugaki bedding. In Chinese legend, this bird inhabits Mount Hōrai, Land of the Immortals. Believed to

20.
Coverlet in kimono form
(yogi)
Late Edo-early Meiji period,
mid-19th century
Cotton cloth with freehand
paste-resist decoration (tsu-
tsugaki), 57¾ x 56⅝ in. (144.4
x 141.6 cm) 89.92

live for a thousand years, the crane symbolizes longevity and is often paired with a tortoise. The Japanese love the crane for its graceful profile and consider it the symbol of beauty and nobility. One yogi (cat. 20) is decorated with a picturesque composition of two large cranes spreading their wings. The faint suggestion of red on their heads indicates that they are *tanchō zuru* (*Grus japonensis*), the most magnificent of the cranes. Varying their poses slightly, the artist has skillfully achieved a unifying, well-balanced composition. Although it is unclear whether the birds' closed and open mouths have any symbolic meaning, paired cranes on yogi appear this way frequently.[11] The gray areas of their beaks, heads, necks, and feathers are brushed in with ink, while the dark blue lines are added to outline the leaves of the white bamboo as well as the white feathers of the birds. The artist has reversed the color scheme of the wings and tail feathers of the two birds in order to achieve a harmonious and elegant effect. The bamboo that ornaments the hem of the yogi is a traditional symbol of perseverance and resilience, as it does not break under the weight of snow.

A fourth yogi (cat. 21) has a multicolored tsutsugaki design. Although it lacks a lining and has the appearance of a standard kimono with sleeves with narrow wrist openings (*kosode*), an extra piece inserted in the back indicates its origin as a yogi. A large crest of an encircled oak branch in white dominates the back of this yogi. Around the crest other tsutsugaki designs are placed seemingly at random, but nonetheless strategically, on the sleeves and the lower area of the garment. Although all the plant motifs cannot be identified with certainty, a maple branch seems to decorate the yogi's front left sleeve; on the right is either a cherry, judging from the indented form of its petal, or a camellia, as suggested by its sturdy-looking leaves. The juxtaposition of cherry and maple appears frequently in Japanese art, each representing the beauty of

21.
Coverlet in kimono form (*yogi*)
Late Edo-early Meiji period, 19th century
Cotton cloth with freehand paste-resist decoration (*tsutsugaki*), 58 x 53½ in. (145 x 133.8 cm) 89.143

its own season. But a camellia, with its thick, evergreen leaves, was believed to have a magical power to expel the evil spirits.

On the sleeve backs are a flaming magic jewel (*hōju*) on the right and a plum (or perhaps a camellia) with a Chinese vine (*karakusa*) on the left. The plum, which blossoms when the snow still lies on the ground, symbolizes bravery and nobility. The flaming magic jewel, which could produce anything one desired, appears in larger size below the crest and again on the front of the yogi. Other motifs are a magic mallet (*uchide no kozuchi*) that can hammer

out a good fortune, a war fan (*gumbai*), a pine branch, and a paulownia leaf. The war fan, its shape originally introduced from China, was used by Japanese military leaders to command their armies at the scene of battle. Thus it can stand for wisdom and power. It also carries an auspicious meaning through its association with one of the eight Daoist Immortals. The pine is a commonly seen symbol of longevity, and the paulownia is also an auspicious tree, the only place where the fabled phoenix alights. The relatively understated design scheme of this yogi is echoed by the restrained colors in muted reds, greens, golds, and browns.

Two examples of *futonji* (cat. 22 and 23), or futon covers, are each made from four panels of cloth which measure about 13 inches in width. The futonji were originally bordered and lined so that when finished they would be approximately 65 inches in width and 75 inches in length. One futonji (cat. 22) is decorated with a rhythmical overall pattern of a ship's anchor (*ikari*) with a rope,[12] an interesting but not an unusual motif in tsutsugaki textiles. The emphatic clarity of the flat white shape set apart from the indigo background seems in perfect harmony with the practical nature of the object it represents. Symbolically, the ship anchor motif is said to give stability to a young bride in her new life.[13] More specifically, perhaps, it expresses society's expectation that the bride will remain securely in one place, her new home, and will not return to her parents.[14]

The second futonji (cat. 23) contrasts with this one in subject matter and the manner of representation. It is decorated with a mythical bird in vibrant colors, a majestic phoenix (*hōō*) perched on a paulownia tree, which is a popular wedding motif. According to Chinese legend, a phoenix is seen only in times of peace and prosperity, signaling the appearance of a great ruler. The mythical bird, a hybrid of many animals, is said to perch only on the paulownia tree and eat only the seeds of bamboo and drink sweet water. Furthermore, the phoenix is considered to be the product of the sun or fire. This association with *yang*, the active principle, is believed to cause the phoenix to influence the conception of children.[15] The word hōō, written in two Chinese characters, is also used as an allusion to sexual pairing in poetry.[16] These symbolic meanings associated with a phoenix make this motif particularly appropriate for a wedding.

On this futonji, a magnificent phoenix with outstretched legs has just flown down to perch on a paulownia tree. Its own cascading tail-feathers frame it. With its head turned back and its body curved in a C-shape, a part of its right wing and the underside of its left wing are visible. This particular pose appears frequently among the tsutsugaki phoenix and crane. Its five colors —

22.
Bedding cover (futonji)
Taishō-Shōwa period, first
half 20th century
Cotton cloth with freehand
paste-resist decoration (tsu-
tsugaki), 61¾ x 52 in. (154.4 x
130 cm) 89.148

23.
Bedding cover (futonji)
Meiji period, 19th century
Cotton cloth with freehand
paste-resist decoration (tsu-
tsugaki), 60½ x 51 in. (151.3 x
127.5 cm) 89.144

orange, green, blue, ochre, and gray-black — are echoed in the representation of the paulownia tree and bamboos growing by the stream. The naturalism of the rugged tree trunk, its knots and twisted or broken branches depicted with detailed surface texturing (with paste-resisted white lines), contrasts with the decorative color scheme and more conventional rendering of its foliage and flowers.

The themes represented in tsutsugaki textiles, whether simply decorative or emphatically auspicious, are numerous and varied in treatment, reflecting the individual touch of the dye artist. The dynamism of bold designs, the clarity of images defined by white outline, and the beauty of different shades of indigo are only a few of the visual pleasures of tsutsugaki textiles.

Kazuki, or *katsugi*, as it was known later, was also a kimono-style garment; however, unlike the yogi comforter, kazuki were worn like a veil draped over the head to conceal the woman's face during excursions and traveling. The custom is generally traced to the Heian period (794–1185), when women wore a plain white kimono, with hirosode, over the head. A hat with a long veil hanging from the brim was also used for the same purpose. Not only providing protection from the sun and rain, to wear this concealing garment was also regarded as proper etiquette for upper-class women. Kazuki took on the kosode form after the latter became established as a basic garment during the late Muromachi period (1392–1568).[17] Around the end of the seventeenth century, kazuki assumed a characteristic cut in which the neck-opening was lowered in front by about 8 inches, making extra room for the head, to accommodate more easily the newly fashionable three-dimensional coiffure of Japanese women.[18]

In the city of Edo, the use of kazuki was banned after the mid-seventeenth century, following an incident in 1652 in which an unemployed young samurai disguised himself under a kazuki and attempted to assassinate a high-ranking adviser to the shogun. In Kyoto and other areas, however, the use of kazuki seems to have continued until much later.[19] In some rural areas, the kazuki tradition remained alive into modern times, serving a primarily ceremonial function at weddings and funerals.[20]

Several classifications of kazuki existed during the Edo period. *Gosho kazuki* (Imperial Palace kazuki) were generally made from dark blue silk gauze decorated with a striped pattern in the midsection. As the term indicates, it was worn by women of Kyoto who were associated with aristocratic families. Women among the commoners seem to have had more freedom in their choice of color and decoration: the *machi kazuki* (town kazuki) they wore was also made from silk but came in a variety of colors and designs. There was also an *asa* type, the *daimon kazuki* (large-crest kazuki), which began to circulate in the late seventeenth century.[21]

24.
Veil kimono (kazuki)
Edo period, late 18th century
Bast fiber (asa) cloth with freehand paste-resist decoration (tsutsugaki) and paste-resist stencil decoration (katazome), 54⅛ x 47⅛ in. (135.9 x 117.8 cm) 89.95

Two kazuki illustrated here (cat. 24 and 25) are both made from asa. The large crests on their backs indicate that they may exemplify the daimon type. Neither shows the lowered neckline. The kazuki in two shades of blue (cat. 24) is from the Shōnai district in Yamagata prefecture. The standard kimono cut, the use of asa fabric, the horizontally divided areas of decoration in which the large motifs are achieved by both the tsutsugaki and katazome techniques, and the prominent crest on the back are common features of Shōnai kazuki.[22] The fashion of silk kazuki worn by Kyoto women is believed initially to have influenced Shōnai dye artists, but gradually they developed an entirely different set of design motifs and schemes, which then became the hallmark of locally produced kazuki.[23]

The enormous chrysanthemum motif, outlined in white and dyed in deep indigo blue, is centered on the neck-opening, its petals radiating over the back and shoulders and continuing to the front. When the garment was worn, this design would encircle the wearer's head. In China, the chrysanthemum is traditionally associated with longevity. Drinking chrysanthemum wine was believed to ensure long life; the story "Kikujidō" (Chrysanthemum Immortal) relates that a young boy attained immortality by drinking dew drops from a chrysanthemum leaf. The shape of this flower also evokes the sun: its petals project outward suggesting the sun's rays. Thus it is an auspicious design symbolic of both longevity and growth.

Below the chrysanthemum are three horizontal bands of different motifs. The top band depicts sailboats and pines. The combination of sailboat and pine suggests the theme of a Noh song, "Takasago," which celebrates the longevity of a happily married couple.[24] The sails of the four upper boats are patterned with cherry blossoms; the two below them have plum blossoms. Beneath the boats is a band of kōhone (candock) combined with a swirling stream. The bottom band, set apart by a dark indigo background and scalloped edge defined by parallel white lines, shows plovers (chidori) flying over the waves. The outlines of the chrysanthemum and the scalloped lines of the bottom band were created by using the tsutsugaki paste-resist technique, while the artist used stencils for all the other motifs. The dramatic contrast between the dark and light blue and the large size of the individual design elements make this kazuki especially striking.

In contrast to the eye-catching appearance of the first kazuki, the second example (cat. 25) displays more modest, restrained designs on the muted blue background. Even the chrysanthemum motif on the back is small, neatly stylized and confined to the center of the back. The garment is divided into four horizontal sections, each decorated with a different motif. A multitude of maple leaves covers the top portion, followed by zones of open fans and tiny flowers.[25] Below a white line that creates cloudlike shapes are well-drawn sawarabi (bracken fern sprouts) growing on the ground.

The chrysanthemum, the cloudlike white line, and the bracken sprouts are produced by tsutsugaki, while the small, delicate patterns of leaves, fans, and flowers are stencil-resisted. The gentle, flowing lines of bracken sprouts provide a welcome contrast to the density of komon stenciled patterns above. It is tempting to associate the design motifs on this kazuki with the four seasons: brackens with the spring, fans with the summer, maples with the fall, and flowers — perhaps representing snowflakes, since they are six-petaled — with the winter. The collar's orange silk lining was doubtlessly once much brighter. Not only the difference in decorative motifs but also the choice of color for such a lining reflects the individual taste of the wearer.

25.
Veil kimono (kazuki)
Late Edo-early Meiji period,
19th century
Bast fiber (asa) cloth with paste-resist stencil decoration (katazome) and freehand paste-resist decoration (tsutsugaki), 51½ x 47⅞ in. (128.8 x 119.7 cm) 89.138

26.
**Kyogen theater vest
(kataginu)
Edo period, early 19th
century
Bast fiber (asa) cloth with
freehand paste-resist decoration (tsutsugaki), 25½ x
26¾ in. (63.8 x 65.9 cm) 89.86**

Tsutsugaki-decorated examples relating to traditional theater and festivals grandly convey their messages. *Kataginu*, one of the most frequently used garments in the Kyogen theater, is a kind of vest with broad shoulders and "lapels" in front. This kataginu (cat. 26) is made of asa fabric dyed light blue and decorated with the tsutsugaki technique. If sumptuously decorated woven brocade can best represent Noh theater, which was patronized by the ruling warrior class, the use of more humble material and dyeing techniques exemplified by this vest perhaps reflects the essence of the popular Kyogen theater patronized by commoners.

On the back of this kataginu and partially visible on the front lapels are a pair of turnips (*kabura*). Large and bulbous, with crinkly green leaves, they take up almost the entire back area. Kyogen kataginu typically display large, bold designs.[26] The naturalistic details — worm-eaten holes on the leaves, the fine, whiskerlike roots, and ink-shading added to the neck — contribute to the unpretentious nature of the object. Represented on a heroic scale, this ordinary vegetable image relates to the earthy Kyogen humor that appealed to the common folk.

The three crests — one on the center of the back and two on the front lapels — represent a weed called *nazuna* within a snowflake (*yukiwa ni nazuna*).[27] The crest is always marked not only on Kyogen vests, but also on costumes of matching asa jacket (*suō*) and trousers (*hakama*). Its white shape was paste-resisted before dyeing; then the green and yellow plant motif was directly printed onto the cloth with the use of a stencil. Nazuna is medicinal; it is one of the "seven plants of the spring," which have been traditionally eaten mixed with rice gruel on the seventh day of the first month of the year as a symbolic gesture to invite good fortune and to guard against disasters. Although it is tempting to associate its commonness and vitality with the nature of Kyogen theater, the same crest also appears on the costumes used in Noh plays.[28]

Another theater garment authentically illustrates the shape, if not the pattern, of a much earlier garment. The *hitatare* (cat. 27) with wide and open

sleeves and loose-fitting jacket originally was worn daily by common people in the late Heian period. After the garment was adopted by samurai and aristocrats in the Kamakura period (1185–1333), it was customarily combined with long, flowing hakama. By the end of the Muromachi period in the sixteenth century, the combination of jacket and hakama was standardized.[29] The small yellow appliqués of tied cord are termed *kikutoji* (chrysanthemum binding). They are vestiges of original loops for fastening cords to hold the upper garment closed or out of the way. Kikutoji took their name from their resemblance to a chrysanthemum flower head.[30]

Originally a humble garment woven of asa, once the hitatare was adopted by the upper classes, it was made from expensive and gorgeous materials. Typical of Kyogen costumes, this example is woven from asa; its handsome *uroko* (fish scale) pattern clearly indicates its theatrical use as a costume for an actor portraying a commoner. The fabric was resisted freehand with a tube of paste; the blue pigment was also added by hand. Blue and white triangles make ever-enlarging patterns that overlap and intersect in a fascinating rhythm. The triangular forms, moreover, are not entirely uniform, nor are they colored with complete accuracy. The occurrence of lapses in a mechanical repetition of dyed and undyed triangles suggests the dyer was working with great speed.

Another example from the stage, with very ancient origins, is the long, loose-fitting garment called a *kariginu* (literally, hunting clothes; cat. 28). Most familiar today as the robe of Shinto priests, the name of the garment tells of its origins as an aristocrat's hunting jacket of the Heian period. Later it was adopted by courtiers for informal wear indoors and consequently was cut from costly silks and gauzes. The robe is worn with *sashinuki*, short hakama which are gathered at the ankles. A distinctively large, round neck-opening is circled with stiff material, which is fastened with a looped cord and knotted cord button, one of the few instances of button fastenings on traditional Japanese costumes. The strings (*kukuri-no-o*) that are threaded at the cuff of the wide sleeves relate to the origin of the garment as a hunting jacket, when it was useful to close the sleeves for active movement.

27.
Theatrical or festival robe (*hitatare*)
Late Meiji-Taishō-Shōwa period, 20th century
Bast fiber (*asa*) cloth with freehand paste-resist decoration (*tsutsugaki*), 31⅛ x 74⅜ in. (77.8 x 185.9 cm)
89.118

The sleeves are attached only at the shoulders, and the sides of the body are left open; the rear panel often is made long enough to trail on the floor. When worn, the front panel is bloused over a sash or belt. Given the flowing character of the panels and the wide, full dimensions of the sleeves with billowing hakama below, courtiers appear elegantly majestic in the handscrolls of the Kamakura and Muromachi periods. Kariginu are either lined (*awase*) or, like this one, unlined (*hitoe*), and are worn by actors portraying aristocrats.

Aristocratic garments were typically decorated with subtle woven patterns and dyed solid colors. This example was first dipped into a vat of indigo dye and then into yellow to create a sumptuous green. Vat-dyeing normally occurs while the fabric is still uncut; however, in this instance, stitches sewing the sleeves to the body are also dyed green, indicating the piece was constructed and then dyed.

Among several pieces specifically for festival or ritual use, the *uma-no-haragake* (literally, horse belly covering) is one of the most unusual. Generally made from plain homespun asa, a haragake was often used to protect the horse from mosquito and other insect bites as well to prevent it from being coated with dirt and mud. This example (cat. 29) is made from indigo-dyded cotton fabric bordered with *sarasa*, a printed cotton fabric inspired by imported Indian chintz. At both ends are three loops for cords that were tied across the horse's back. Large crossed falcon-feather crests in bright red, flanked by vermillion carp, decorate the haragake at each end. Falcon feathers stand for a combative spirit, and the carp swimming up the river symbolize strength and determination: a carp was believed to transform into a magnificent dragon by leaping up a waterfall at the end of its journey. The abstract design of the falcon feathers in a circle is effectively juxtaposed with the more naturalistic style of the carp and the water. The rhythmic treatment of the waves enhances the liveliness of the carp, whose bodies bend with tense energy. Skillfully executed in tsutsugaki technique, the design is particularly satisfying in the use of bold colors and balanced composition. The sarasa border framing the indigo cloth, is a cotton fabric of multicolored printed floral patterns. This type of Indian chintz was imported to Japan by the early seventeenth century, perhaps earlier. Its vivid colors and exotic patterns greatly appealed to samurai and wealthy merchants, who coveted it as a rare fabric. Both the auspicious designs and the application of sarasa on this haragake suggest that it was used for special occasions when the owner proudly displayed his horse.

A very decorative type of haragake is the *yuiage* (literally, tied up). This example (cat. 30), made of asa fabric, has a central portion which covered the belly of the horse, and long panels divided in two at both ends, which were tied on its back and left hanging along its flanks. Yuiage-type haragake appear in the images of horses on various *ema*, or painted votive tablets offered at shrines.[31] The long, cascading side panels of this piece, however, are extremely unusual.

The central rectangle of the yuiage is tsutsugaki-decorated and framed with two borders. It shows two encircled crests of *sasarindō* (gentian) in light blue. Peeking from the four corners of the inner border are quarter-chrysanthemums in yellow. Chrysanthemums with leaves decorate the ends of the outer border, and vines extend to both sides from the flowers. The

28.
Theatrical or festival robe
(kariginu)
Meiji period, 19th century
Bast fiber *(asa)* cloth with
double-dyed color, 59½ x
64⅛ in. (148.8 x 160.3 cm)
89.129

combination of chrysanthemum and vine motifs, although in much more abstract form, is repeated on the stencil-dyed panels where the linked diamonds frame multicolored flowers. The chrysanthemum is a traditional symbol of longevity. The vine, with its steadfast growth habit, symbolizes longevity and prosperity. The portions of the divided panels are also decorated with stripes in yellow, white, and red. Beauty of colors and layers of contrasting designs make this haragake an outstanding work, and it is easy to imagine how superbly it must have adorned a magnificent horse.

This yuiage is believed to come from the Nambu region (presently the southern area in Aomori and the northern area in Iwate prefectures), an area traditionally known for breeding excellent horses.[32] For several centuries, the city of Morioka in Iwate has held an annual procession of horses. Popularly known as Chagu Chagu Umakko,[33] the festival originated from the custom of taking horses to the local shrine where the guardian god of horses was worshiped. This type of yuiage with long end-pieces is still seen on Nambu horses in this procession today, and it is believed that originally it was used to decorate horses owned by samurai.[34]

Traditional festivals and public entertainments featured flags (*hata*) and banners (*noboribata*) which were hung on tall poles or mounted on bamboo frames. These flags and banners might carry only the name of the shrine deity in big characters. Often, however, they were colorfully decorated, heightening the impact of the message, which was further sharpened by flapping and fluttering sounds. A vertical banner, the *nobori* (cat. 31) was probably used for the Boy's Day Festival, which is still celebrated on the fifth day of May, a date made official in the Edo period. (The Doll Festival for girls was held on the third day of March.) On Boy's Day, families set out a tall banner on a bamboo pole and displayed armor, and boys were encouraged to engage in war games and martial contests using *shōbu* (sweet flag) leaves as swords. This festival has antecedents in the customs of ancient Japan. It was customary then for people to pick medicinal herbs, place shōbu on the house roof, and take a bath into

29. (left)
Horse trapping (*uma no haragake*)
Late Edo-early Meiji period, 19th century
Cotton cloth with freehand paste-resist decoration (*tsutsugaki*) and trimmed with cotton cloth with stencil decoration (*sarasa*), 51¾ x 27¾ in. (129.4 x 69.4 cm) 89.119

30.
Horse trapping (*uma no haragake*)
Meiji period, 19th century
Bast fiber (*asa*) cloth with freehand paste-resist decoration (*tsutsugaki*) and paste-resist stencil decoration (*katazome*), 182½ x 25¼ in. (456.3 x 63.1 cm) 89.120

which shōbu had been placed, to drive away evil and purify themselves on the fifth day of the fifth lunar month. The origin of this custom was ultimately traced to the Chinese belief that the fifth lunar month was unlucky.

At the same time, native Japanese tradition had designated the fifth month as the first occasion of rice-planting, an activity considered sacred. In the countryside, the May festival included the day when women rice-planters gathered to seclude themselves for abstinence and purification. The shōbu plant (as well as others) was essential in the May festival, initially because it was believed to possess the power to dispel evil spirits. The word "shōbu" written in different characters could also mean "competition" or "to honor the martial spirit." With the emergence of a samurai-ruled society, the May festival came to be identified as a celebration for boys.

Tall banners marked with family crests were originally used by samurai on battlegrounds in medieval Japan. The custom of hoisting banners decorated with family crests on Boy's Day is believed to have begun among samurai families.[35] Appropriate for the festival, the themes that decorate the banners were mostly warrior figures, as the example illustrated here. This type of banner was ceremoniously given to the child by his maternal grandparents on the occasion of his first Boy's Day Festival. A long, flowing banner aloft in the breeze signaled the presence of a male child upon whom rested the responsibility of carrying on the family name and obligations; it represented the family's pride and wish that he grow up to be strong and healthy.

Executed in the combination of tsutsugaki and hand-painting technique, this cotton banner displays a wide range of brilliantly colored motifs. The upper portion of the banner shows two large family crests: an encircled peony (botan) above and halved mandarin orange blossoms (tachibana) arranged in a circle below. In general, the topmost crest represents the child's paternal family and the second one his maternal family.[36] The painting in the lower half of the banner shows a group of warriors on horseback in a landscape near the ocean. The subject derives from a scene in the Genji-Heike clan wars, representing the warriors who served Minamoto no Yoshitsune (1159–89). Yoshitsune, the younger brother of Minamoto no Yoritomo (1148–99), who established the Kamakura government after defeating the Heike clan, was eventually destroyed by his own brother. Yoshitsune's tragic and dramatic life has fascinated the Japanese, and he has been immortalized as a popular hero in literature and drama.

The scene depicted in this banner probably relates to the battle at Yashima (1185) on the Inland Sea, a battle well known for the archery contest between the Genji and Heike clans. Accepting a challenge from the Heike, Nasu no Yoichi, a young warrior who fought for the Genji clan, rode his horse into the sea and successfully shot off a fan placed by a Heike lady at the top of a pole on a boat. The youthful figure on horseback in the water most likely represents Yoichi, the archer. Also present among the armored warriors is Benkei, Yoshitsune's monk-warrior retainer, who eventually perished with his master. Benkei's loyalty and bravery were legendary, and he, like Yoshitsune, was idolized in literature and drama. Here he is depicted wearing a monk's cap and carrying on his back the seven types of unusual weapons with which he subdued his enemies. The white curtain in front of Benkei is marked with the gentian, family crest of the Genji clan.

31.
Festival banner (nobori)
Meiji-Taishō period, late 19th-
early 20th century
Cotton cloth with freehand
paste-resist decoration (tsutsugaki) and hand-painted
pigments and ink decoration,
24 x 300 in. (60 x 750 cm)
89.162

31.
Festival banner (detail
opposite)

Within an extremely elongated format, the artist has achieved a dynamic and unified composition. The zigzag arrangement, emphasized by the leaning tree trunk in the foreground, the diagonal direction of the rope suspending the curtain in the middle, and the long branch cutting across the picture plane above, is reinforced by the gestures and glances of the figures as well as by their placement. The large pine tree frames the warriors on the ground with its rooted trunk below and diagonally stretching branch above. The pine branches also separate the figure of Yoichi in the ocean, who is backed with the auspicious image of the sun filled with cherry blossoms. The vivid blue ocean is marked by the rhythmic pattern of the waves, while the large area of the ground, defined by black ink wash, gives a sense of gravity. The bright coloring with red, green, blue, and yellow makes this banner appropriately festive for the occasion.

The fragment of a nobori (cat. 32) is also decorated with a military theme. The figure is probably that of Benkei carrying a *naginata*, or halberd, and holding a horse closely by the reins. Without the whole composition, it is impossible to determine which incident from the Genji-Heike wars is represented by this scene. The heroic pose, the tight grip on the horse, and the determined look on his face, however, all convey the sense of strength and bravery associated with Benkei, which boys were traditionally encouraged to emulate. Within a red seal seen above the rock is the date, the thirteenth year of Tempō (1842), and the name Daishōya.

Clothing styles and customs flowed from the samurai and daimyo classes to the commoners, as seen in the travel cape, the uma-no-haragake, and the nobori. Several examples of clothing for the military class, however, illustrate how techniques available to both classes were given special treatment for samurai or daimyo use. One is a daimyo's campaign jacket or *jimbaori* (cat. 33). Jimbaori were adapted from European prototypes introduced through the Portuguese, and in their early forms were completely functional. Constructed to withstand the rigors of life in the field, jimbaori were often made of asa or heavy cotton, and were made both with and without sleeves. By the latter part of the sixteenth century, during the Momoyama period, taste in jimbaori had changed, and military leaders such as Toyotomi Hideyoshi regarded them as personal adornment. Hideyoshi indulged his flair for ostentation with elaborate and fanciful examples of these garments.

Jimbaori remained in favor among daimyo throughout the Edo period and over time underwent changes in appearance. This example relates in style to the earlier ones of the sleeveless type. The high collar, flaring profile, and wide lapels (*eri*) turned back and faced with elegant brocade were typical of the style current into the eighteenth century.[37] The body of the jacket is dyed in two different colors, divided by resisting the two portions, with the upper part a sensuous orange-brown and the lower part dyed a deep indigo. The lower portion carries a thunder pattern (*raimon*) created, like the rest of the decoration, by freehand tsutsugaki technique. The upper part carries a large mon of resisted white. The eri which turn back at the front opening and the collar are faced with a pale green silk gauze termed *monsha*. The pattern is of clouds with occasional groups of supplementary gold wefts

32.
Banner fragment (nobori)
Late Edo period, dated 1842
(Tempō 13)
Cotton cloth with freehand paste-resist decoration (tsutsugaki) and hand-painted pigments and ink decoration, 69 x 25⅜ in. (172.5 x 63.4 cm)
89.122

33.
Samurai vest (jimbaori)
Edo period, late 18th century
Bast fiber (asa) cloth with freehand paste-resist decoration (tsutsugaki) trimmed with colored silk gauze (monsha) with supplementary gold weft threads, 35¼ x 16¾ in. (88.1 x 41.9 cm) 89.96

affording the glint of metallic highlight. The lapels turn back over the thunder pattern, neatly revealing through the sheer fabric the thunder and lightning motifs among the clouds.

As a type of imported garment, a second jimbaori (cat. 34) reveals in a related example a more extreme taste for the exotic by using imported fabrics. With its big epaulets (*tachi-uke*) and squarish cut, this jimbaori reflects a type popular from about 1800 through the end of the Edo period. In contrast to their original purpose, a garment to be worn in camp when in the field, jimbaori became purely ceremonial and the decorative aspects prevailed as the daimyo's role grew increasingly administrative under the peaceful rule of the Tokugawa shogunate.[38] Made from imported European red wool fabric (*rasha* in Japanese), this example would have been for cold-weather wear.[39] Rasha derives from the Portuguese word *raxa* which indicates a thick woolen cloth; the blazing scarlet color (*shōjō-hi*)[40] was probably dyed with cochineal, a color source used in Europe at that time which imparted to the hue a brightness and stable character not possible with native Japanese dye stuffs.

The silk brocade for the lining is probably imported from China. The lining is continuous with full-length, wide lapels that turn back and are held in place by metal buttons and ornamental knots of Chinese black silk braid. Brightly colored jimbaori like this were usually decorated with patterns executed in couched gold thread (*koma-nui*), as seen in the embroidered mon on the back.[41]

A pair of trousers (cat. 35) is decorated with a stenciled komon style paste-resist motif combining stylized peonies and stiff-legged lions. A lighthearted rendition of the traditional grouping of peonies and lion (*botan ni shishi*), the lions resemble versions of Pekinese dogs.[42] The playful and innocent form given the lion in the motif suggests the spiritual distance that the samurai class of the late Edo period had strayed from the fierce warrior lifestyle on which their military traditions were based.

The construction of the trousers, which are pleated front and back along the top, clearly indicates they were customized to fit smoothly about the waist. Further, tapered legs and the wide, curving cut of the cloth seem intentionally designed to accommodate a mounted rider.[43] These details of tailoring, along with the komon pattern, relate the trousers to the world of the samurai and contrast them with the fireman's *sashiko* tight-fitting trousers (cat. 15) which are more like "sleeves for legs" attached to an amorphous wrap-around top.

A coat for a samurai attendant (cat. 36), the *happi* is a short, unlined cotton fabric coat with wide sleeves, a tall collar, and a pair of strings that tie in the front.[44] Made of hand-spun cotton fabric dyed light brown, the happi is decorated with three white stripes in tsutsugaki paste-resist technique. The slit at the center back of the coat generally marks its wearer as a samurai, for this opening provided extra room for carrying swords around the waist. This particular happi, however, was worn by a late Edo-period samurai's attendant of the rank of *chūgen*.[45] Chūgen worked as gatekeepers, carried luggage, delivered messages, and ran errands. Not members of the samurai class, chūgen were not allowed to wear swords, but sometimes they carried a wooden sword.

35.
Trousers
Edo period, late 18th century
Bast fiber *(asa)* cloth with small-pattern paste-resist stencil decoration *(komon katazome)*, 35¼ x 16¾ in. (88.1 x 41.9 cm) 89.169

35.
Trousers (detail)

34.
Samurai vest *(jimbaori)*
Edo period, late 18th century
Wool cloth imported from Europe, with metallic wrapped thread couching and lined with Chinese colored silk cloth with weft patterning, 41½ x 27 in. (103.8 x 67.5 cm) 89.156

After the mid-Edo period, groups of *watari chūgen*, those who moved from one master to another under a temporary service contract, became common in Edo. Typically during the late Edo period, watari chūgen wore a brown happi marked with white stripes, like this one. The origin of the three-stripe motif is uncertain; however, it is sometimes suggested the motif originated from a specific family crest. During the late Edo, it seems to have identified the chūgen rank — such a coat, in effect, was their uniform.[46] This happi's notable simplicity proclaims the humble status of the wearer within the strict military hierarchy and contrasts with the penchant for dramatic colors and fancy materials that characterize the samurai jimbaori.

A group of children's pieces illustrates the range of delicacy and lively interpretation possible with the use of katazome and tsutsugaki techniques. In imaginative interpretations, dyers might incorporate details and in some instances large portions of decoration, brushed by hand with ink or pigments as a type of painterly yūzenzome (*tegakiyūzen*). While children's clothing tends to display a greater variety in pattern and design than does that of adults, even for a child's world, traditional cultures like Edo-period Japan established ritual and standardized motifs for clothing.

Formal attire for samurai in the Edo period, the *kamishimo* was frequently illustrated in the art of the time. It has since become the accepted attire for performers of traditional music and dance, and long ago became a standard costume for samurai roles in the Kabuki theater. Generally made from asa, a kamishimo consists of a vest (kataginu) with prominent, angular shoulders and pleated hakama. Worn over a kimono, the bottom of the vest is tucked into the trousers at the waist. During the Edo period, kamishimo with a matching vest and trousers constituted an important part of the samurai's formal clothing, and by the late Edo period, it was also worn by townsmen on special occasions.[47] Initially there was no regulation of colors or fabrics used for kamishimo, but after the mid-Edo period, subdued colors such as black,

36.
Samurai attendant's jacket (*happi*)
Edo period, early 19th century
Cotton cloth with freehand paste-resist decoration (*tsutsugaki*), 35 x 51¾ in. (87.5 x 129.4 cm) 89.126

blue, and brown were encouraged. Such kamishimo were usually decorated with komon.[48]

The child's kamishimo (cat. 37) is modern, probably from the Taishō period (1911–26). By the twentieth century, the tradition of kamishimo as official wear had virtually disappeared except for some rural areas and in the specialized field of traditional performing arts. This example was worn by a child, probably in relation to a performance, such as *gidayū*, the art of reciting ballad-drama.

The light blue cotton fabric is covered with fine stenciled *sayagata* patterns of connected swastika motifs. The shoulders and the upper back portion of the vest are lined with starched paper or other stiffening, such as a baleenlike material on thin metal rods, to achieve the appropriate ritual sharpness of profile. As customary with kamishimo, a mon — possibly the crest of the particular gidayū school — is seen on the front and the back of the vest. It also appears on the waist panel of the trousers at the back. The crest is composed of three partial views of the wood sorrel (*katabami*), a common plant, which is enclosed in a roundel with a scalloped edge representing a snowflake.

An example of stencil-decorated textiles for children far removed in feeling from the formality of kamishimo is seen in the lengths of asa kimono fabric (cat. 38), dyed light blue with a pattern of the child's balancing toy called *yajirobei*. The name comes from a tiny figure of the doll known as Yajirobei, who holds across his shoulders, as though carrying a heavy load, long curving rods which have weights at the tips. Balancing on the child's fingertip, the doll, tipping and turning this way and that, much to the delight of children, is kept upright by its low center of gravity.

The finely woven asa fabric has been decorated with an allover pattern of a series of yajirobei toys, almost like serial imagery, showing the toy in different positions as it swings and turns. The stencil was designed to emulate the effect of freehand work of the tsutsugaki technique. The fineness of execution is reflected in the delicate fabric and in the fact that both sides of the fabric were resisted, the patterns falling identically on both sides of the cloth, a technique that assured the clarity of the resisted pattern. These panels capture the summer fun of childhood and evoke the sensation of coolness through the sheer asa fabric.

Some of the most intriguing of these garments are designed for tiny infants' first visit to the family shrine, the *miya-mairi*[49]. As the practice has come down to the present, in the miya-mairi, the child is carried draped with a kimono sized for an older child, like those illustrated here. This set of two kimono and a bib (cat. 39) was designed for the first shrine visit of an infant boy.[50]

37.
Child's formal vest (katiginu) and trousers (hakama)
Taishō-Shōwa period, 20th century
Cotton cloth with small-pattern paste-resist stencil decoration (komon katazome) lined with paper, 19¼ x 14 in. (48.1 x 35 cm) and 23 x 18½ in. (57.5 x 46.3 cm) 89.124

38.
Child's kimono fabric
Meiji period, late 19th-early 20th century
Bast fiber (asa) cloth with paste-resist stencil decoration (katazome), 63½ x 13⅛ in. (158.8 x 32.8 cm) 89.157

39. (overleaf and page 154)
Three-piece child's cere-monial kimono (miya-mairi)
Shōwa period, early 20th century
Silk gauze (rō) with paste-resist stencil decoration (katazome); bib of silk crepe (chirimen), 46½ x 33¼ in. (116.3 x 83.1 cm) and 46½ x 34 in. (116.3 x 85 cm) and 9 x 13½ in. (22.5 x 33.8 cm) 89.165

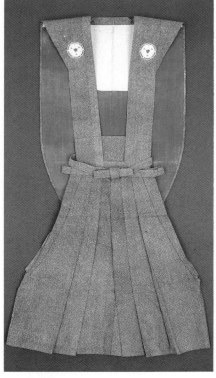

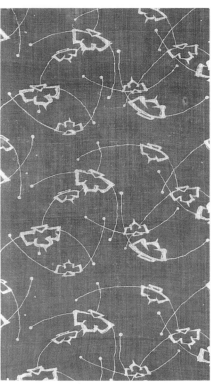

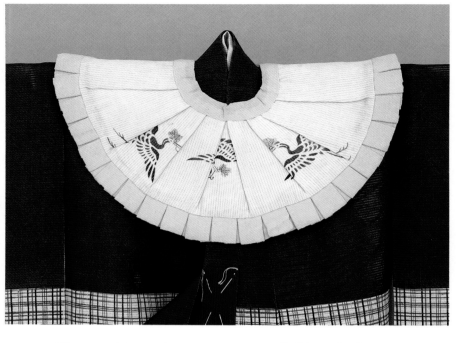

39.
Bib

The outer kimono is *ro*, a gauze-weave silk fabric, that has been dyed blue across the shoulders and at the lower part of the body of the garment, with five mon reserved in white. Across the center, including the lower portion of the wide sleeves, is a band of *kōshi*, or lattice pattern. Kōshi patterns are normally woven;[51] however, in this kimono, the dyer has imitated the woven kōshi pattern with a stenciled line pattern dyed in golden yellow, dark blue, and gray to create a plaid effect. The plaid-pattern band is found on both the back and front of the garment as well as at the lower part of the long ties attached to the front.

Reflecting Shinto ritual purity, the under-robe of creamy white ro is marked only with small blue-dyed mon. Long ties at the front opening are of the same fabric, and the sleeves are left open, though hemmed at the edges. The bib (*yodare-kake*) is also made from ro fabric, with peach-colored *chirimen* (silk crepe) forming the ties and bordering the neck. At the outer edge is a pleated frill. On one face the bib is white, and on the other the fabric is dyed blue. Auspicious motifs have been stenciled on each face of the bib: the white ro face has blue flying cranes bearing pine boughs in their beaks, and the blue ro face has stylized pine boughs, plum blossoms, and bamboo resisted in white.

The adult model of a silk kimono with a band of woven plaid decoration slicing through the center is called *noshime kosode*, or simply *noshime*. In the Edo period it was worn by samurai beneath their formal kamishimo. The garment is found today among costumes for certain roles in the Noh and Kyogen theater. Used for a child's miya-mairi and coming from recent time, the noshime styling was no doubt intended to proclaim a strong masculine image, perhaps even militant spirit, the parents wished for their son.

A child's ceremonial kimono in asa fabric shows a typical Meiji-period (1868–1912) use of the newly introduced analine dyes, and although new patterns and motifs were also introduced at that time, a tendency to employ classical Chinese motifs has persisted. This kimono (cat. 40) offers a Japanese interpretation of the traditional motif of cranes in flight, a symbol of longevity. Perhaps an allusion to Mount Hōrai of Chinese Daoist legend,[52]

40.
Child's ceremonial kimono
Meiji period, late 19th century
Bast fiber (*asa*) cloth with
freehand paste-resist decora-
tion (*tsutsugaki*) and hand-
painted pigments and ink
decoration, 45 x 40 in.
(112.5 x 100 cm) 89.103

the motif includes only the basic thematic elements of cranes, pines, and waves. Wave patterns form swells that emphasize the flowing nature of the cloth, while pine trees forming the top border of the motif make a stage for the flight of the cranes. The pines appear as a darkened silhouette, foliage made clear with an outline of carefully applied resist.

Placement of color also creates interesting contrasts. The light turquoise color came from an aniline dye commonly used during the Meiji period. The simple contrast set up between subtle background color and the brightly colored cranes, brings a new intensity to a traditional motif. The cranes' bodies, resisted, then outlined in sumi, capture the supple grace of the birds by delicate lines, calligraphic in their simplicity.

A second child's asa kimono is boldly patterned with dragons and hares in blue, gray, and white (cat. 41). From the late Edo period, this *furisode*

(literally, swinging sleeves) again incorporates different techniques, such as freehand painting and the meticulous use of rice-paste resist.

The resisted areas of cloth, which remain uncolored, highlight the blue features of the dragons winding their way across the kimono as well as the stylized clouds that are created with varying shades of sumi ink. These classically stylized dragons (*amaryū*), with their spoon-shaped snouts, flourishing eyebrows, and beardlike whiskers well defined by a line of white resisted cloth, dissolve into S-curves and wavelike stylizations.[53] Blue hares, ears highlighted by fine white lines, and hares whose light color forms a silhouette in paste-resist frolic in waves simulated by diagonal lines of dragons and clouds. Riding the crests of the waves are mortars and occasionally a pestle, making striking displays of white against dark blue. At the bottom center on both front and back, the blue areas bordering the motif highlight a foot here, a tail there, a set of long pointed ears somewhere else.[54] The design

41.
Child's kimono
Late Edo period, 19th century
Bast fiber *(asa)* cloth with freehand paste-resist decoration *(tsutsugaki)* and hand-painted pigments and ink decoration, 39¾ x 30⅛ in. (99.4 x 75.3 cm) 89.109

42.
Child's kimono
Late Edo-early Meiji period, 19th century
Cotton cloth with freehand paste-resist decoration *(tsutsugaki)* and hand-painted pigments and ink decoration, 30½ x 24⅛ in. (76.3 x 60.3 cm) 89.130

is boisterous and whimsical, related by motif but quite different from the treatment of the theme in the two yogi (cat. 18 and 19). These motifs, like many Shinto and Buddhist festivals, celebrate the creation of life,[55] and this kimono bears a strong wish for the child's long and healthy life.

An example of a provincial garment is the child's kimono made from hand-spun cotton and dyed blue, with tsutsugaki decoration of a caparisoned samurai horse rearing in front of a blossoming cherry tree (cat. 42). The design is a combination of paste-resisted patterns (*shiroage*), hand-painted coloring, and details in ink. Colored details on the horse and the tree include a strong orange, pale yellow, and turquoise. The mon are simple, resisted patches with line patterns rendered in sumi. On the front are branches of cherry blossoms and a riding crop crossing the handle of a water dipper (*shaku*).

The samurai horse and the associated cherry blossom motif would be sufficient to indicate the kimono was for a little boy. This is confirmed, however, by the talisman to dispel evil spirits and illness that is stitched up the back of the kimono. These *semamori*, or *se-mori* (literally, back-protecting), are stitched by the child's mother in the belief the amulet will avert illness and misfortune. For boys, these threads angle from the top in a downward direction to the left, and for little girls, to the right. Two long strands of thread are allowed to hang down the back and are knotted together with a third, which issues from a divided diamond stitched at the base of the vertical line of the semamori. The thread colors are yellow, red, light blue, and golden brown.

The tsutsugaki freehand technique, employed here with rather broad handling, is sometimes termed *inakayūzen* (country yūzen) in contrast to the elegant, hand-painted, paste-resisted decoration made famous by studios in Kyoto and Kanazawa during the eighteenth and nineteenth centuries.

43.
Child's kimono
Meiji period, 19th century
Bast fiber (*asa*) cloth with freehand paste-resist decoration (*tsutsugaki*) and hand-painted pigments, 35⅞ x 30¾ in. (89.7 x 76.9 cm) 89.106

44.
Child's kimono
Meiji period, 19th century
Bast fiber *(asa)* cloth with freehand paste-resist decoration *(tsutsugaki)* and hand-painting, 39⅛ x 39⅜ in. (97.8 x 98.4 cm) 89.111

Traditional motifs continued to abound during the Meiji period; however, the location of the design on garments continued to move toward the hemline. This change in placement on furisode offered exciting new possibilities, including new variations on old themes. Two other children's furisode (cat. 43 and 44) exhibit many typical qualities of Meiji kimono decoration, particularly the more elaborate types for wealthier urban customers. In the first of these, more complex techniques are employed, imparting a highly pictorial character to the design, which encompasses the entire garment, from the mon on the shoulder downward to the bottoms of the sleeves and to the hemline. The design wells up from the hemline and the sleeve-bottoms to meet graduated shades of gray suggesting the sky,[56] which was painted after the rice-paste resist had been applied to the reserved areas of the design. Painted designs were covered with another layer of resist to assure that they were impermeable and the background color was brushed on.

This kimono has three distinct bands of shading, with gradual shading from blue (water) to gray (sky) in an example of *akebonozome* (literally, twilight dyeing), a technique involving the gradual shading of one color into another.[57] This lends another level of depth to the design as the background colors highlight different areas of the foreground. The creation of an appearance of background and foreground with the subtle positioning of shading is evidence of the designer's great skill; it offers a contrast with the effect of the furisode with dragons and hares.

Seasonal change, a favorite Japanese motif, was treated anew in Meiji textile design. This kimono uses typical motifs of autumn grasses *(akikusa)*: miscanthus *(susuki)*, with its long graceful blades and the fernlike shoots that once held blooms, and bush clover *(hagi)*, which has small, smooth leaves in sets of threes with faded blooms on the tips.[58] The graceful curves of the susuki together with the abstract floating pattern of the leaves of both susuki and hagi complement the sway of the asa fabric.

Overlaying the autumn grasses motif are elements of *bugaku*, a traditional Japanese dance form. Bugaku, performed at the imperial court with much ceremony and ritual, is recalled by a series of instruments and dance properties used in a performance. These include the traditional musical accompaniment — the panpipe (*shō*), on the right sleeve; a small hand-held drum (*furitsuzumi*) on the left sleeve; and another sort of panpipe on the lower left front. On the back of the garment appear objects from a child's butterfly dance, which are mixed with a depiction of a butterfly, a dance helmet, and a court fan.

A purple asa furisode from the early to mid-Meiji period (cat. 44) recalls the gray kimono with autumn grasses and bugaku-related objects (cat. 43). Even though this too is an autumn setting, the scope of decoration is much compressed over that of the gray kimono, with a quiet stream, its flow checked here and there by large rocks and gracefully arcing susuki, still-blossoming hagi, and *kikyō*, the Chinese bellflower.

The tranquil stream wanders among these flowers and around large rocks in serpentine curves. The green shading bordering it suggests a lush, verdant setting. The shaded purple backdrop coloring the upper reaches of the kimono drops its hazy billowing border to just above the motif. Its deep purple tones, together with the stillness of the water, create a mood of solitude and serenity.

No chance for a splash of color goes unexplored however; even the stitches that reinforce the seams between the sleeves and body of the garment are a bright orange-red, which stands out prominently against the purple. They, too, make a small contribution to the floral motif with their leaflike patterns. The attraction of this kimono lies in the interaction of a great amount of intricate and varied brushwork with a creative selection of background colors.

A group of four coats effectively demonstrates the wide scope of decorative effects that could be achieved by weavers and dyers of Japan using

45.
Work coat (*noragi*)
Shōwa period, 20th century
Bast fiber (*asa*) cloth with paste-resist stencil decoration (*katazome*), 33¾ x 52 in. (84.4 x 130 cm) 89.159

techniques ranging from minimal technology and the most basic materials to an effete reproducing of a painting by a well-known artist on an elegant silk garment. The work coat (*shiboto*) of heavy asa cloth with katazome decoration (cat. 45) comes from the countryside, and is a rare instance of decorating rough fabric with paste-resisted stencil patterns. The stencil-cutter created a motif that defies positive identification.[59] Inept piecing of the material on one side has resulted in a gap in the pattern at the back, compounding this problem. Nevertheless, extra material was devoted to the triangular gussets (*machi*) connecting the sleeves to the body of the coat. The stenciled, allover pattern, so unexpected on this type of garment with its extremely rough fabric and the unskilled tailoring generate a folkish charm.

Two other related country coats show a more typical appearance for rural garments, with their plain, natural colors and simple edging of cotton cloth. Termed *noragi* (literally, field wear), both are woven from bast fibers derived from the mountain wisteria (*yamafuji*). This fabric, called *fujifu* or sometimes *fujinuno*, was never made commercially and was strictly for home use. It is extremely tough, and was used to make storage bags and heavy-duty work clothes. Among work clothes, the most frequently encountered items are noragi.

The darker coat (cat. 46) exhibits the natural appearance of fujifu; the light-colored noragi (cat. 47) is fujifu that has been bleached, probably with wood-ash lye.[60] The rough and prickly fuji fibers soften only after prolonged use and many washings; consequently weavers seek to ameliorate this "hairshirt" aspect of wearing fujifu garments by incorporating other materials, such as paper wefts, in strategic areas like that across the shoulders.

The inclusion of these paper threads to produce this softening is clearly evident where the weaver calculated the distances in order to have the paper wefts occur across the shoulders of the garment. The tiny black and gray dots that appear mixed into the body of the garment result from the calligraphy or printing which existed on the paper when it was shredded and spun for weaving.[61]

At the other end of the technical and socioeconomic spectrum stands the gentleman's *hanten*, a short coat, like a jacket, (cat. 48).[62] Beginning in the Meiji period, townspeople, becoming more affluent, pursued increasingly refined clothing not only for ceremonial occasions but also for everyday use, and this hanten demonstrates the heights of refinement to which techniques of paste resist and hand-applied pigments could rise. Dating probably from the early Shōwa period (ca. 1930–40), its brilliant, exuberant design is evidence of the proud status of the wealthy merchant in modern Japanese society.

The motif of a pair of mandarin ducks (*oshidori*) at a wintery pond descends directly from a well-known hanging scroll-painting by Itō Jakuchū (1716–1800), an artist of the late Edo period. The similarity between the two works indicates that the dyer and probably the owner of the garment, too, were familiar with the Jakuchū painting. The dyer has followed the Jakuchū painting faithfully, altering the composition somewhat to accommodate the shift of format; yet the Jakuchū composition, two-dimensional in its original form, envelops the whole garment with awesome grace, and at the same time produces a unique showcase of the finest yūzenzome techniques.

46. (opposite, top)
Work coat (noragi)
Meiji-Taishō period, early 20th century
Mountain wisteria fiber (fuji) cloth, 36¾ x 44½ in. (91.9 x 111.3 cm) 89.166

47.
Work coat (noragi)
Meiji period, ca. 1900
Mountain wisteria fiber (fuji) cloth with some paper wefts (shifu) and stitching (sashiko) over shoulder, 39 x 49½ in. (99 x 126 cm) 89.168

48. (overleaf)
Coat (hanten)
Shōwa period, ca. 1930-40
Silk cloth with freehand paste-resist decoration (yūzenzome), 36⅛ x 50⅜ in. (91.6 x 125.9 cm) 89.163

The back of the garment displays a creative mix of techniques of rice-paste resist and artist's pigments. The most dramatic effect is the falling snow in the central scene, created by scattering particles of dried rice paste over the fabric while it was wet, a technique called *makinori*. The dyer has invoked texture strokes basic to scroll-painting techniques, as in the tree-trunk and rock forms which are especially well captured. The delicate coloring of the birds and the blossoms accents the snow-filled twilight of the scene.

We conclude on a flowery note with the gentleman's silk hanten and its reprise of a painting by a renowned artist executed in yūzenzome technique. Yet the paste-resist decorative techniques of katazome and tsutsugaki, employed over the centuries, filled a range of textile decoration reaching from the complicated designs on kazuki (cat. 24), jimbaori (cat. 33), yogi (cat. 19), and children's miya-mairi kimono (cat. 39) to the simple provincial child's kimono (cat. 42) and the primitive stenciling of the hemp-cloth work coat (cat. 45). Unlike paste-resist stenciled decoration, tsutsugaki-decorated textiles allowed more directness and freer range of imagination, permitting large-scale motifs and more dynamic imagery. Though occasionally a tsutsugaki piece might consciously emulate the effect of a stenciled piece, the influence seems predominantly in the other direction, and the enduring popularity of the tsutsugaki technique clearly left it a favorite champion.

The preeminence of freehand paste resist, especially in regard to yūzenzome, pressed katazome dyers to create ever-more complex patterns, some using dozens, even scores, of stencil patterns to capture the elaboration possible with the freehand technique. The immense popularity of tsutsugaki techniques perhaps can also be seen in kasuri weaving which ultimately produced motifs with a more freehand appearance than is usual in loom-generated patterns. Clearly, once established during the Edo period, paste-resist techniques proved amazingly resilient to changes in fashion, the economy, and the government, serving humble and elite alike; and they remain the basis for a continuing textile industry today.

1. Julia Sapin-Yenne, graduate assistant, provided research regarding yūzenzome.

Yūzenzome was first developed for fabric in Kyoto, around the time of the Genroku period. Developments in yūzenzome during the Edo and Meiji periods through the early years of modern Japan represent the manner in which technological innovations associated with modernization were assimilated into traditional Japanese culture.

Meiji-period leaders were eager to incorporate modern technology into Japan's textile industry; the first plant that produced chemical dyes was founded in 1875, in Kyoto. As was true of many of the modernization efforts of this period in Japan, students were sent to Europe to study; in the case of the textile industry, they went to learn dye production.

Stencils were frequently used to create the fine-lined and gorgeously colored designs that typify earlier yūzenzome. Efficiency was the key; stencils were better tools for production. Kyoto, site of the factories and residence of those trained in these new techniques, became the center of this new movement to modernize textile production. Makers of yūzen in Kyoto at this time began to incorporate the new chemical dyes into their designs, undoubtedly to simplify production but also to increase their artistic range.

2. Michyo Morioka provided research and prepared draft entries for yogi, futonji, kazuki, uma-no-haragake, noboribata, happi, and kamishimo.

3. Haruhiko Asakura, Kikuji Andō, Hideo Higuchi, and Makoto Maruyama, *Jibutsu kigen jiten: I shoku jū hen* (Tokyo: Tokyodō, 1979), p 61.

4. Ibid.

5. For example, a merchant family in Sanuki (present-day Kagawa prefecture in Shikoku), preserved tsutsugaki bedding for guests; family members used patterned kasuri and their servants used striped cotton for their futon material. See Hitoshi Nakaya, "Tsutsugaki no furusato Sanuki," in *Tsutsugaki zome, Nippon no senshoku* 14, by Katsumi Nakae, ed., (Tokyo: Tairyūsha, 1977), p. 85.

6. Haruko Iwasaki, *Nippon no ishū jiten* (Dictionary of Japanese Clothing), (Tokyo: Iwasaki Bijutsusha, 1984), p. 89.

7. Ibid.

8. Henri Joly, *Legends in Japanese Art* (London and New York: John Lane The Bodley Head, John Lane Company, 1908), p. 112.

9. In this Noh play the speech which relates to this motif can be roughly translated: "The reflections of the green trees on the water sink deep to the bottom. The fish swimming in the water appear to be climbing up those trees. When the moon casts its reflection on the lake, the hare on the moon may run on the waves. What an amusing sight this island offers!" Japanese scholars invariably explain the hare-on-the-wave motif as deriving from this Noh play. See Mitsukuni Yoshida, Shigenobu Kimura, Kazuo Yagi, and Kazuo Tanaka, *Nippon no monyō fūgetsu* (Kyoto: Tankōsha, 1969), p. 166; and Iwasaki, *Nippon no ishō jiten*, p. 86.

10. Yoshida, et al., *Nippon no monyō fūgetsu*, p. 225.

11. In Izumo (in present-day Shimane prefecture), there is an association of an opened-mouth crane with a female and closed-mouth crane with a male. Takatoshi Ishizuka, ed., *Izumo Oki no mingu* (Tokyo: Keiyūsha, 1971), p. 207.

12. In ancient Japan, they simply used a rock tied to a rope to anchor a boat. The iron anchor with four hooks (called *yotsume ikari*, or four-hooked anchor), depicted on this futonji, was in common usage in Japan after the Edo period. Nippon Daijiten Kankōkai, ed., *Nippon kokugo daijiten*, vol. 1 (Tokyo: Shōgakukan, 1972), p. 648.

13. Reiko Mochinaga Brandon, *Country Textiles of Japan: The Art of Tsutsugaki* (New York and Tokyo: Weatherhill, Inc., 1986), p. 25.

14. This motif is common in the Izumo area on the tsutsugaki baby diaper, which was part of a ceremonial gift prepared by the baby's maternal grandparents. In this case it was symbolic of "anchoring one's life," i.e., longevity. See Ishizuka, ed., *Izumo Oki no mingu*, p. 208.

15. C. A. S. Williams, *Outlines of Chinese Symbolism and Art Motives* (Rutland, Vermont, and Tokyo: Charles E. Tuttle Co., 1974), p. 325.

16. Ibid.

17. Kosode (literally, small sleeve) is similar in its cut to the modern kimono. Its wrist opening is small compared to the wide-sleeved hirosode.

18. To minimize the direct friction with a kazuki and protect the arranged coiffure, women wrapped a cotton band (*watabōshi*) around the upper part of their hair and placed a long, wooden hairpin (*kazuki kōgai*) at the center of their coiffure before wearing kazuki. See Kampō Yoshikawa and Sadao Ueda, eds., *Nippon josō hensenshi* (Tokyo: Sōdo Shuppankyoku, 1980), pp. 126-131.

19. In Kyoto, common-class women were forbidden to wear kazuki after the 1770s. Yasutaka Kanazawa, *Edo fukushokushi* (Tokyo: Seiabō, 1962), p. 264. He argues also that the increasingly elaborate hairstyle of Japanese women after the mid-eighteenth century made kazuki-wearing custom impractical and unfashionable.

20. See Kiku Tokunaga, *Sashiko no kenkyū* (Tokyo: Iseikatsu Kenkyūkai, 1989), p. 278; and Keisen Motoyama, *Seikatsu minzoku zusetsu* (Tokyo: Yatsuhiro Shoten, 1942), pp. 30-35.

21. Yoshikawa and Ueda, *Nippon josō hensenshi*, p. 121.

22. Tokunaga, *Sashiko no kenkyū*, pp. 279-85. According to Tokunaga, most of Shōnai kazuki show the standard kimono cut. If they lower the neckline, it is only four inches or so. Silk kazuki was also called Kyō-kazuki as the Kyoto women favored this material.

23. *An Exhibition Presented by the Museum of Folk-Crafts* (Tokyo: The Museum of FolkCrafts, 1955), n.p. The Edo-period merchants of Yamagata prefecture exported rice, asa, and safflower to Kyoto while bringing back various commodities from Kyoto such as textiles and ceramics. See Tokunaga, *Sashiko no kenkyū*, p. 278.

24. Tetsurō Kitamura, *Zoku Nippon no monyō* (Tokyo: Genryūsha, 1988), p. 84.

25. We are grateful to American textile artist John Marshall for pointing out that the central stencil pattern on this kazuki, which shows an open fan motif has had a layer of yellow dye added to create a greenish cast to the section. The yellow was probably added by hand after the piece had been dipped in the vat of indigo dye.

26. Kataginu with matching trousers (kamishimo), was a garment of official attire of Edo-period samurai, which was generally decorated with restrained komon (small-scale patterns).

27. The weed could be a dandelion (*tampopo*). Shōzō Masuda, "Kyogen no shōzoku to funsō" in *Senshoku no bi*, 14 (1981), p. 72.

28. Ibid.

29. Tarō Sakamoto, *Fūzoku jiten* (Tokyo: Tokyodō, 1983), p. 607.

30. Katsumi Nakae, ed., *Senshoku jiten*, (Tokyo: Tairyūsha, 1981), p.142, 342. Some kikutoji are more directly reminiscent in form of the chrysanthemum blossom than the ones on this hitatare.

31. For example, ema, dated 1721, in the Seattle Art Museum collection acc. no. 58.93.

32. Shichizō Nakamura, owner of Shōtokukan in Morioka where he exhibits old documents on horses and traditional horse equipment, believes that this yuiage most likely comes from the Nambu region. Personal correspondence with Michiyo Morioka, March 26, 1991.

33. *Chagu chagu* is onomatopoeia for the sound of the small bells which hang on the horse's body. *Umakko* is *uma* (horse) in the local dialect.

34. See Moriokashi Kyōiku Iinkai, "Chagu Chagu Umakko chōsa hōkokusho," *Moriokashi bunkazai chōsa hōkuku*, vol. 22, (1981), p. 19.

35. Brandon, *Country Textiles of Japan*, p. 17.

36. Ishizuka. *Izumo Oki no mingu*, p. 204.

37. For additional examples see *The Shogun Age Exhibition from the Tokugawa Art Museum, Japan* (Tokyo: Tokugawa Art Museum, 1983), p.52.

38. Toyotomi Hideyoshi, military leader of the late sixteenth century, who was also the leader in opulent display, set a standard for lavish jimbaori by having one made from a Near Eastern carpet. See: *Nihon no Senshoku* (Kyoto: Kyoto National Museum, 1985), p.104.

Jimbaori were also made with wide sleeves. For additional woolen examples see Yoshiaki Shimizu, ed., *Japan: The Shaping of Daimyo Culture* (Washington, D.C.: National Gallery of Art, 1988), nos. 265-66.

39. All rasha was imported through European traders at Nagasaki. A mark of the popularity of this fabric is the story that in 1800 Ienari, the eleventh Tokugawa shogun, tried to get a factory to weave rasha at Nagasaki. The proposal did not appeal to the Dutch traders who sensed a loss of profit and the project never really got off the ground. Subsequent efforts to develop sources in China also failed. Woolen textiles were first produced in Japan in 1877: see Hyōbu Nishimura, "Orimono," *Nihon no bijutso*, no. 12, (April 1967), p. 90, ill. 121, and Nakae, *Senshoku jiten*, p. 421.

Like many other articles of clothing jimbaori were classified seasonally. The lightweight example (cat. 33) is typical of jimbaori for summer weather.

40. *Shōjō-hi* conveys an appropriately exotic tone, as *shōjō* is the term for orangutan, known for its reddish color; it is also a term for a heavy drinker, presumably because of flushed or florid appearance; there are also mythical creatures called *Shōjō* very fond of alcoholic drinks, who have long, straight, bright red hair, which is said to produce red dye. *Hi* by itself means scarlet. See Joly, *Legends in Japanese Art*, p.321.

41. This *mon*, or crest, is called *kuginuki* ("nailpuller") within a circle. Kuginuki is a pincerlike tool; when two kuginuki are crossed, the paired handles create a square which seems eventually to have symbolized them in a stylized representation. This very popular mon, adopted by commoners for its powerful associations, is frequently encountered on textiles.

42. The Pekinese dog (*chin*) was introduced from China through Korea in the reign of Emperor Shomu (r. 724-49). Kept as amusing pets, they were purely lap dogs. Pekinese dogs appear as motifs in embroidery and lacquer.

43. The leg openings have been shortened slightly and bound with modern fabric.

44. The happi is similar to the *haori*, a short coat worn over kimono. It was originally different from hanten, a cotton coat with a low collar and no string, which was used by townsmen during the Edo period. During the late eighteenth and early nineteenth centuries, happi and hanten became close in form and virtually undistinguishable. See Sumio Itakura et al, *Genshoku senshoku daijiten* (Kyoto: Tankōsha, 1977), p. 826; and Tomoyuki Yamanobe, *Nippon no senshoku*, vol. 6, *Shomin/kindai* (Tokyo: Chūō Kōronsha, 1981), p. 254.

45. As written in characters, *chūgen* literally means "between" or "middle." The term is believed to derive from the fact that the rank was between that of samurai and *komono*, another class of attendant. Masamoto Kitajima, "Buke no hōkōnin," *Edo jidai bushi no seikatsu*, Yoshiki Shinshi, ed., Seikatsushi sōshō, vol. 1, 8th ed. (Tokyo: Yūzankaku, 1974), p. 126.

46. Tokusaburo Ikeda and the research staff at Seikatsu Shiryōkan at Tokyo Kasei University Junior College identified this coat as a "chūgen uniform," particularly as that of watari chūgen, and supplied general information on chūgen. Personal correspondence with Michiyo Morioka, April 15, 1991.

47. During the early part of the eighteenth century, it became acceptable for samurai to wear kamishimo with an unmatched vest and trousers as part of daily work clothes. Sanehide Kawabata, ed., *Nippon fukushoku jiten* (Tokyo: Tokyodō, 1969), pp. 59-60,

48. Nakae, *Senshoku jiten*, p.129. These patterns were cut by a technique called *kiribori*. The *kiri* is a tool with a crescent-shaped blade that is pressed into the stencil paper and with a half-turn will remove a tiny dot of paper. The scale can be so fine that hundreds of holes can be counted in a square inch of the stencil. See Suzanna Kuo, *Katagami: Japanese Textile Stencils in the Collection of the Seattle Art Museum* (Seattle: Seattle Art Museum), 1985.

49. The first shrine visit is on the thirtieth day after birth for girls and on the thirty-first day for boys. This is now called miya-mairi, shrine visiting, and is often a lighthearted celebration. As at an earlier time, however, the visit seems to be to give thanks for the child's safely reaching the first full month of life, and for the purpose of giving the child its name.

Dr. Philipp Franz von Siebold, a German physician employed by the Dutch at Dejima in the nineteenth century, has left a description of the name-day visit to a shrine in his account of his stay from 1823 to 1829. See Dr. Philipp Franz von Siebold, *Manners and Customs of the Japanese in the Nineteenth Century* (New York: Harper and Brothers, 1st ed., 1841, Rutland, Vermont, and Tokyo: Charles E. Tuttle Company, 3rd printing, 1981), p. 124.

50. It is possible that the examples here are older than now assumed, that they were made merely for the procession and left stored elsewhere.

A term frequently used for celebration kimono is *iwaigi*. This term today is ambiguous in its meaning, and people think first of the miya-mairi and the fancy kimono in which the infant is swaddled. It is possible the term iwaigi once referred to specific ritual garments, and today refers to a broader range of clothing for celebrations, one of which is the miya-mairi. Kimono used today for the miya-mairi, even as these examples, are sized for a much older child, and the long ties, as also seen on the examples here, are fastened about the mother's neck and shoulder. The account of von Siebold would indicate a different procedure at the time of his stay in Japan.

51. See the kimono from Hachijō-jima (cat. 61).

52. This motif has been more fully suggested in other works, which confirm the location with a descriptive rendition of Mount Hōrai, and visions of cranes transporting immortal spirits to the island. See *A Thousand Cranes: Treasures of Japanese Art in the Collection of the Seattle Art Museum* (San Francisco and Seattle: Chronicle Books and Seattle Art Museum, 1987), pp. 195-96, pl. 69. This painting by Hine Taizan (1814-69), who was known to study and employ Chinese motifs, is further evidence of the variety of ways in which Chinese motifs were interpreted by Japanese artists. Another way of referring to the myth of Mount Hōrai is to render cranes with boughs of pine in their beaks; see the katazome baby's bib (cat. 39).

53. This type of dragon is often used in Japanese design to give the impression of choppy water. See Sadaharu Okanobori, *Moyō no jiten,* 4th ed., (Tokyo: Tokyodō Shuppan, 1973), p. 12. For different stylizations of *amaryū,* see Sadaharu Okanobori, *Nihon moyō zukan* (Tokyo: Tokyodō Shuppan, 1969), p. 258.

54. One small area among the clouds on the back of the kimono looks as if the cloud cover were going to break — the resist didn't hold, and the area had to be painted in by hand.

55. For introductory details on Japanese festivals, see Helen Bauer and Sherwin Carlquist, *Japanese Festivals* (Garden City, New York: Doubleday and Co., 1965).

56. Tomoyuki Yamanobe, ed., "Meiji jidai igo no senshoku," *"Nihon no bijutsu, Some,* p. 116. This somber, conservative color was usually worn by adolescent girls. It was especially popular during the second decade of the Meiji period.

57. Helen C. Gunsaulus, *Japanese Textiles* (New York: Japan Society of New York, 1941), p. 68.

58. Autumn grasses had been mentioned in Japanese poetry for centuries, but from the mid-Edo period on *akikusa* became popular in textile designs. A group of seven *akikusa (aki no nanakusa)* are frequently depicted including the two pictured here. There are: arrowroot (*kuzu*), *patrinia scabiosaefolia* (*ominaeshi*), Chinese agrimony (*fujibakama*), wild pink (*nadeshiko*), and Chinese bellflower (*kikyō*). See The Japan Textile and Color Design Center, *Textile Designs of Japan,* vol. 1, *Free-style Designs* (Tokyo: Kodansha International, 1980), p. 33.

59. One possibility for the motif is the *fundō* or scale weight, which was a circular disk of metal with areas cut out to achieve the specified weight. The cut-outs were stylized as half-moon "bites."

60. Louise Cort describes bast fibers in her essay in this volume.

61. *Kamiko* and *shifu* are two techniques for turning paper into garments. See the travel coat (cat. 51) for a description of the *kamiko* technique. *Shifu* (literally, paper cloth) is made from threads made of paper which are usually woven as wefts, but sometimes are used for both warp and weft. See Sukey Hughes, *Washi: The World of Japanese Paper* (Tokyo, New York, and San Francisco: Kodansha International, 1978), pp. 56-57.

62. Julie Sapin-Yenne provided research and draft entries for this garment.

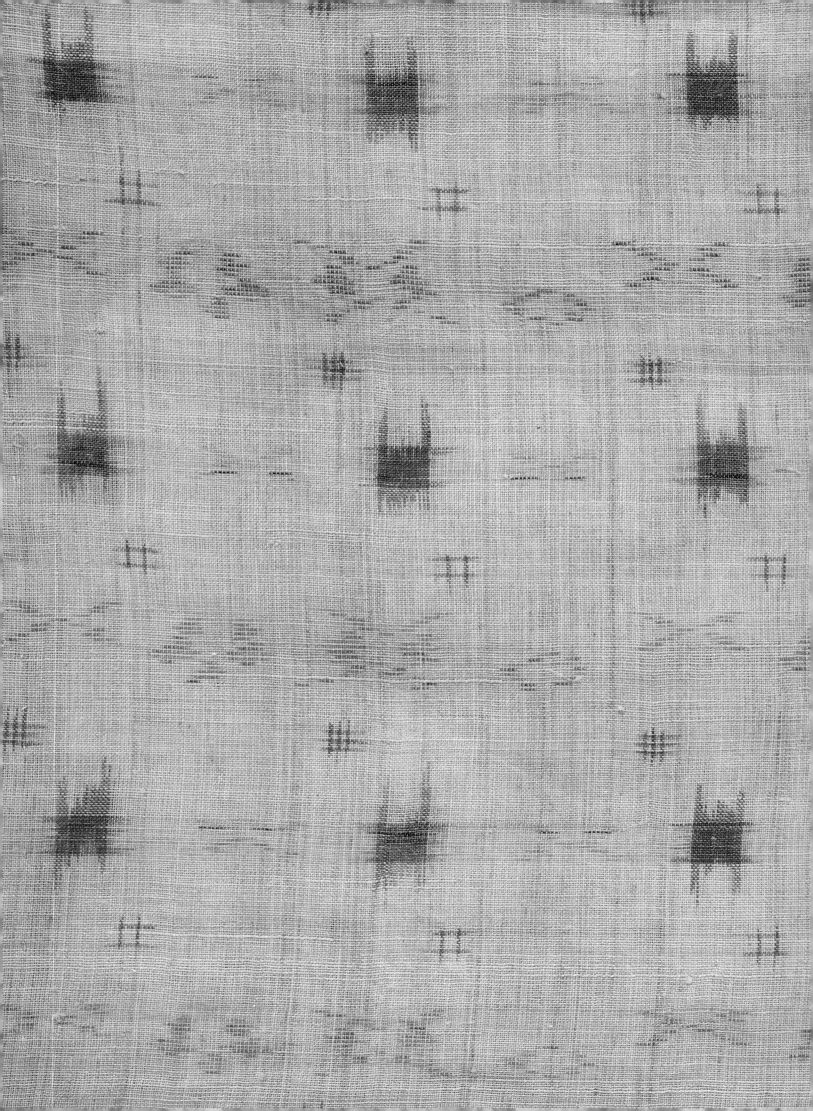

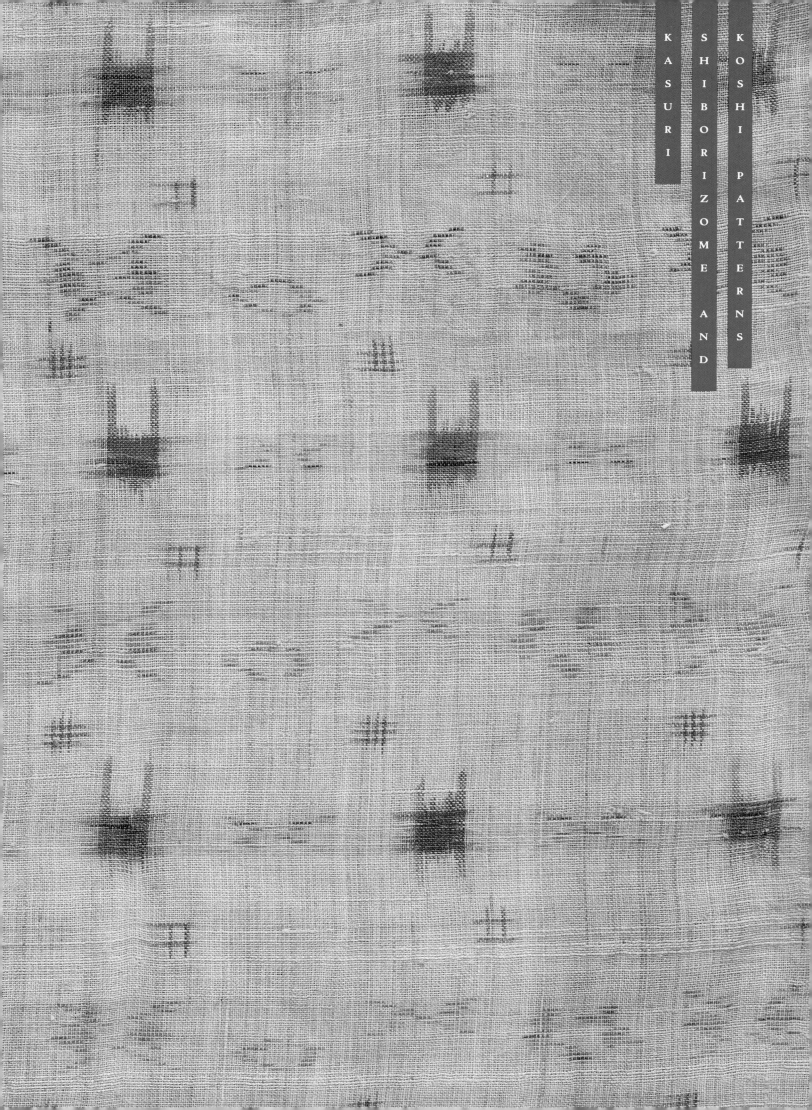

KASURI, SHIBORIZOME, AND KOSHI PATTERNS

WILLIAM JAY RATHBUN

K*ASURI* IS THE JAPANESE TERM FOR IKAT. IN JAPAN KASURI PROVED, IN early modern times, to be a major cultural expression, and these examples of kimono, *futonji*, and other garments will demonstrate the range of technique developed there. They also reflect the major production areas that emerged during the eighteenth and nineteenth centuries.

The kasuri technique requires binding bundles of thread according to prescribed patterns, sometimes involving both the warp and the weft, so that the bound portions remain uncolored when the bundles are dipped into vats of dye. When wefts are woven through warps, the prescribed pattern appears as the undyed portions take their places in the finished fabric. The process is manifestly magical.[1]

Initially kasuri was woven with threads of *asa* and *bashō* (fiber banana of Okinawa).[2] These fibers remained popular even after cotton became readily available in the late seventeenth century. Once available, however, cotton quickly spread in use in the main islands, as it out-performed other fibers in producing fabrics that were not only cheap but warm and comfortable to wear. Cotton fabrics also had ample potential for elaboration in decoration. Among the possible color combinations, blue-and-white kasuri certainly predominated. The ruling elite of the Edo period (1615–1868) jealously guarded their status symbols of colorful clothing and pageantry. In part through a desire to control the economy and in part to maintain Confucian social order, the government promulgated many bans on the use of bright color and expensive fabrics, such as silk. Thus, although indigo was plentiful and thought to have special properties, the choice to use it was to no small degree directed by governmental pressures on the commoners.

In spite of coercion, the choice proved quite a happy one, as Japanese plants produce excellent indigo, and threads are strengthened by the dye, producing a highly reliable, long-wearing fabric; further, it was believed that the smell of indigo repelled insects and that contact with indigo-dyed fabrics could speed recovery from insect and snake bites — an idea which no doubt greatly recommended the dye to the laboring classes, particularly farmers. The great age of blue-and-white kasuri in Japan began in the eighteenth century, and its popularity remained unchallenged until the advent of the chemical aniline dyes and factory-woven fabrics in the late nineteenth century.

The simplest and perhaps most ancient method to achieve kasuri patterns is by manipulating resisted portions of the warp alone. Cloth with patterns made through resisting the vertical yarns is called *tategasuri* (literally,

49.
Child's kimono
Taishō period, early 20th century
Silk cloth with warp ikat *(kasuri),* 40⅜ x 34 in. (100.9 x 85 cm) 89.105

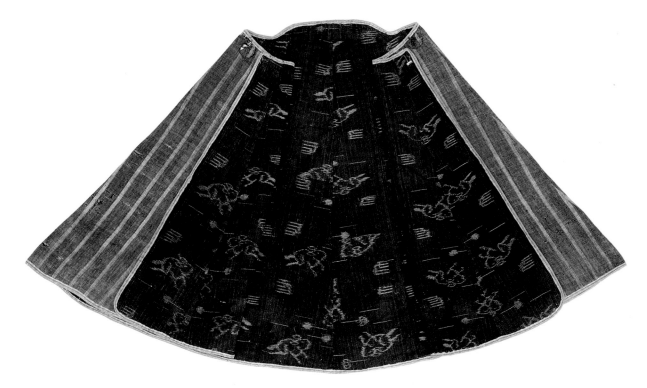

50.
Travel cape (bōzugappa)
Edo period, early 19th
century
Cotton cloth with weft ikat
(yokogasuri or e-gasuri),
33⅛ x 151 in. (84.1 x 377.5 cm)
89.128

warp kasuri). Stripes like those in the fabric of the child's padded silk kimono (cat. 49) were a favorite pattern for tategasuri, and the feathered, wide stripes are called *yagasuri* (literally, arrow-patterned kasuri). This feathered effect can be tied into the warps or created by manipulating the yarns of an ikat-dyed stripe pattern, so that each is pulled a little farther out of line than the one before. This is accomplished mechanically with a device called a *mokuhiki* that makes possible the adjustment of the warps during weaving.[3]

Kyoto has been a major silk-weaving center for centuries, and during the Meiji period (1868–1912), with the disappearance of the sumptuary laws of the former feudal system of government, colorfully patterned silk garments like this kimono became increasingly common in the lives of Japanese.[4]

The strong hues of the fabric and its bright red lining might suggest a garment for a little boy; however, red or pink linings were used without distinction as to the wearer's gender. A clearer understanding of who wore the kimono comes from the closed sleeves below the arm, typical in kimono for little girls. On the back, an amulet (*semamori* or *se-mori*) of embroidered colored threads tells that the kimono definitely belonged to a girl. Believed to protect children against illness and misfortune, it was stitched in the center of the back; at the top, the threads pointed downward to the left for boys and to the right for girls. Lengths of colored thread also sometimes hung down the back.

Kasuri designs achieved solely through resisting weft yarns (*yokogasuri*) create entirely different types of patterns and pose quite different problems for the designer and weaver. The travel cape, or *bōzugappa* (cat. 50) well demonstrates this technique. The garment was adapted from capes worn by Portuguese missionary priests in the sixteenth century, and the term "bōzugappa" derives from the Japanese *bōzu* (priest) and *kappa*, borrowed from the Portuguese word for cape. This cape was initially restricted to use by the military elite, but by the eighteenth century the commoner classes had adopted it as a travel garment; figures wearing such capes appear regularly in travel prints of the nineteenth century, an indication of the garment's popularity.

The cape is made with a kasuri-patterned cotton fabric on one side and a brown-and-white striped cotton fabric on the other. The eighteen pie-shaped panels are laid out in a circular arc with a short, upright collar fitted at the neck, much like the European model; the Japanese version, however, was worn at a longer length than was fashionable in sixteenth-century Europe. Between the two cloth faces, these capes often incorporated a layer of paper treated with persimmon tannin or some other waterproofing agent. This paper layer not only added a measure of protection from rain but brought added warmth by stopping the wind. Capes were usually provided with bone toggles to fasten at the neck; this cape was given fancier ivory fasteners.

A pattern of darting hares with clouds and moon and accompanied by a stylized character is done entirely in weft kasuri. The use of pictorial motifs is called *e-gasuri*, or picture kasuri, and the combination of e-gasuri and geometric motifs was very frequently employed. The basic motif is a hare leaping to the right alternating with one leaping to the left; between them is a circular moon and horizontal lines which can be taken to represent clouds, in reference to the hare who resides in the moon and who pounds special rice to make *mochi* (rice cakes) for the New Year celebration. The striped-fabric side is actually the exterior, and in itself was rather stylish, as striped patterns were among the first well-known imported fabrics.[5]

The hare-in-the-moon motif aside, a darting hare was an image which no doubt offered inspiration for a weary traveler; however, given the libidinous reputation of hares, the choice might reflect an amorous nature on the part of the wearer. A clear point of romantic association in the pattern lies in the stylized character of the type called *genjikō*. These had their origin in the scoring system for the ancient game of correctly naming incense fragrances; eventually these patterns came to be used to identify the different chapters of the *Genjimonogatari*.[6] Careless weaving or resist-tying has led to varying shapes of the woven genjikō as well as to mistakes where motifs overlap; such a seemingly casual attitude underscores the likelihood that this fabric was probably homemade.

Related to the bōzugappa is the *amagappa*, a raincoat that also derives from the capes worn by the Portuguese who came to Japan in the sixteenth century.[7] While the bōzugappa resembled the Portuguese cape rather closely, amagappa (literally, rain cape) first developed in the seventeenth century and in profile more fully reflected native Japanese clothing standards with sleeves and overlapping front like a kimono.[8]

Before the introduction of the various kappa, Japanese had worn raincoats made from straw, and even though the straw raincoat was still the provincial standard, the elite and the well-to-do commoners could choose from among amagappa made from cotton, silk, and imported wool. The most affordable raincoat for the majority of townsmen was a *kamiko* paper raincoat like the one illustrated here (cat. 51).[9] The coat has been constructed carefully from multiple sheets of paper called *tōyugami*, mulberry paper treated with persimmon juice as well as a mixture of *e-no-abura* (perilla oil) and *kiri-abura* (tung oil).[10] The oiled paper raincoat is surprisingly resilient and sturdy. The short, upright collar, the only portion that relates to the original cape form, is lined with cotton for the comfort of the wearer. The areas below the openings of the sleeves, under the sleeves, and the upper portion of the front are reinforced with cotton edging.

An amagappa like this would have been worn by a man, as commonly men's amagappa were made from tōyugami and either were light blue or brown in color. Women's amagappa were often deep purple or light red and made from woven fabric.[11] The red seal script character on the back of this coat reads *gan* or *negau* (to wish [for], entreat, implore) and suggests the wearer was a religious pilgrim. It is also possible that the wish was for safe and smooth travel.[12]

Double kasuri occurs when warp and weft yarns join to form one or more parts of the pattern; this was a very popular technique, especially in combination with pictorial elements of e-gasuri. The kimono (cat. 52) illustrates a combination of both weft-generated e-gasuri and warp patterns which occasionally intersect the weft motifs to create a sort of accidental double-kasuri motif.[13]

On this summer garment woven of crisp asa yarns, the pattern incorporates a wonderfully refreshing seashore motif of clams and a clam basket; the dragonfly seasonally refers to late summer. The baskets (or buckets) are marked with a wave pattern reminiscent of Rimpa school stylizations, indicating that the designer of this motif had a wide acquaintance with art forms. The carefully woven motif is characteristic of e-gasuri patterns, which are produced through a variety of techniques that enabled the weaver to produce lengths of cloth more economically in terms of resist-tying. One method uses a guide thread called a *tane-ito*, which is established from a pattern and becomes the model for tying bundles of threads.[14] These techniques are equally important as a means of encouraging the development of the painterly designs that became a hallmark of Japanese kasuri patterns.[15]

In the case of double-kasuri patterns like this one, the warp yarns have been resisted intermittently in apparent disregard of the weft pattern, and they create short, narrow, vertical stripes. In the finished garment, they work on two levels. They make bursts of highlight where the seemingly unintentional double kasuri occurs, and their overall distribution creates a scrim effect through which the main weft kasuri motif is viewed. This combination imparts depth and visual interest, and the simple addition of the random, perhaps pulled-warp motif affords the weaver an element of expressive freedom over the mechanical repeating of the tane-ito pattern.[16]

An example of a double kasuri with a highly complicated pattern is the child's kimono (cat. 53). Motifs woven in weft-generated e-gasuri are of a palace or temple among clouds, blossoming plum branches, and scattered symbols combined with geometric patterns. The geometric patterns appear quite complicated, incorporating rectangles with small squared spirals at the corners and enclosing crisscrossed patterns marked with a single dot. All elements of the pattern, however, are weft-generated except the vertical sides of the rectangles, and the only double kasuri occurs where the vertical and horizontal elements of the geometric pattern meet. Woven of asa threads, the fabric has softened from use and repeated washing, imparting added wearing comfort and subtle draping to the kimono.

Both these examples, woven of asa yarns with complicated motifs created through weft- and warp-woven patterns, are typical of kasuri produced in areas such as Echigo, facing the Japan Sea (present-day Kanazawa and Niigata prefectures), and Omi, the area around Lake Biwa. These major centers produced *jōfu*, the highest quality kasuri.[17]

51.
Traveling coat *(dōchūgi)*
Meiji period, late 19th century
Paper cloth *(kamiko)* pre-pared with persimmon juice and a mixture of perilla oil *(e-no-abura)* and tung oil *(tōyu)*, 43 x 56 in. (107.5 x 140 cm) 89.167

This kimono (cat. 54) is another example of double kasuri woven in central Honshu. Woven of extremely fine asa thread, the kimono was once mistakenly identified as being from Okinawa. This confusion resulted in part because of the fineness of the fiber, a characteristic for which both areas are well known, and the dye colors and motifs, which are all inspired by Okinawan fabrics. Examples of motifs drawn from Okinawan fabrics are the paired stars, weft-pattern clouds, the well-head motif, and a frog.[18] The weaver has consciously recalled traditions of Yaeyama Island in this fabric design, and in the excellent production and use of color and motifs has paid tribute to the home of kasuri techniques in Japan.

Beginning in the eighteenth century, cotton kasuri fabrics became a commonplace among garments and Japanese household items. Not only were these fabrics worn in everyday clothing, they were incorporated into the family's daily routine in other ways, most notably in the decorative cover on the padded comforter, or *kakebuton*. In houses which typically have no draperies, carpets, or wallpaper in the Western sense of decorating, the decorative *futon* cover constituted a major form of interior decor when spread on the *tatami* (mat) for sleeping.

Three, four, sometimes five narrow-width panels of fabric with stripe patterns and weft or double kasuri were sewn together as decorative kakebuton covers. These fabrics were woven throughout much of Japan, but the looms of western Japan became the most famous for kasuri futon covers. Weavers in districts like the Chūgoku in western Honshu and in the islands of Shikoku and Kyūshū were actively producing double kasuri like those in the garments illustrated here (cat. 55-59). These examples show patterns typical of the Chūgoku, the San'in and Sanyō districts, of the Iyo district around Matsuyama on Shikoku, or of Kurume on Kyūshū where weavers also produced kasuri.[19]

52.
Kimono (detail)

52.
Kimono
Meiji-Taishō period, late 19th-early 20th century
Bast fiber *(asa)* cloth with weft ikat *(yokogasuri* or *e-gasuri)* and warp ikat *(kasuri)*, 52 x 46 in. (130 x 115 cm) 89.107

The panels of fabric (cat. 55-57) are fragmentary futon covers; one, at least, is from a dowry futon. The first (cat. 55) is the most elaborate, with intricate patterns conveying a felicitous concern that the owners find happiness in marriage and good fortune in a long life. The pictorial motifs include a dancing crane, a tiny tortoise within a complicated series of concentric squares, a *tai* fish (sea bream) on a bamboo branch, and an open fan with the characters *takasago* written on it and surrounded by a pine bough and a blossoming plum branch. The *tsuru-kame* (crane and tortoise) combination is a doubling of the wish for long life that is conveyed in each of these motifs. The tai fish skewered on a bamboo branch symbolizes good fortune; the name "tai" makes an auspicious pun, as it suggests the word *omedetai*, or congratulations. The reddish color of the tai, though not seen here, associates it with symbols of happiness, and whole tai often appear as a centerpiece at banquets. The rectangular geometric design is a version of the *igeta*, or well-head motif, which, too, suggests the quiet life of a happy home. The name "Takasago" is the theme of Jō and Uba, the archetypal wedded couple whose spirits dwell in ancient pines on Takasago beach. (One panel has been sewn both upside down and reversed, so that the characters *takasago* appear backwards.) Compound images as seen here, especially the tiny *kame* inside the concentric squares, are a common element in many patterns identified as Iyogasuri.

This e-gasuri pattern and that seen in one futon cover (cat. 56) were probably laid out with a tane-ito technique. Of less complicated imagery is the design in the panels, which shows a repeated motif of a carp leaping through waves, the theme of the carp striving to leap the waterfall. A small, stylized pine bough represents the pine branch found in more elaborate versions. The story of a carp who was turned into a dragon moralizes that one should strive to succeed against all odds and is a dramatization of the phrase *risshin shusse* (to succeed in life).

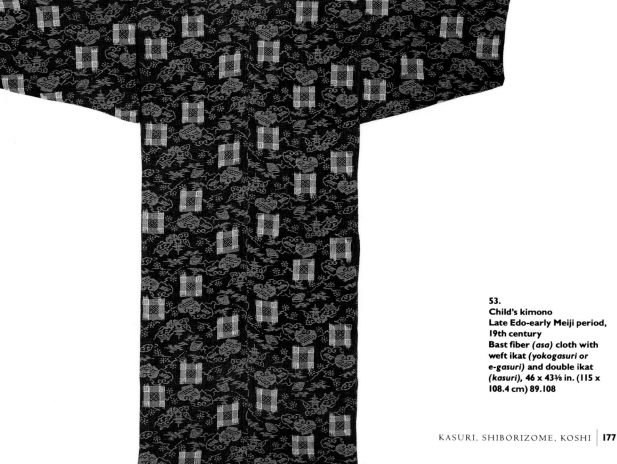

53.
Child's kimono
Late Edo-early Meiji period,
19th century
Bast fiber *(asa)* cloth with weft ikat *(yokogasuri or e-gasuri)* and double ikat *(kasuri)*, 46 x 43⅜ in. (115 x 108.4 cm) 89.108

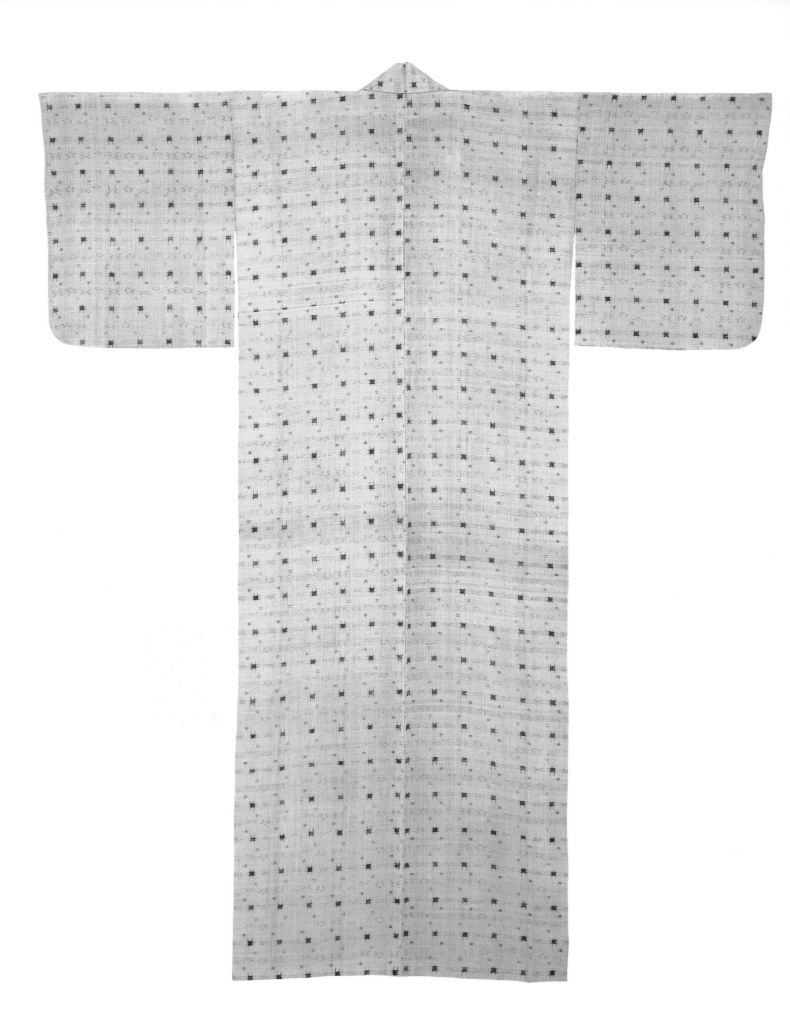

Alternating with this motif is a geometric pattern which derives from the *hachi-jū-hachi* or "88" pattern. Characters for 80 and 8 can be arranged to resemble this general square configuration; however, nothing about this can be read as ideograms. The hachi-jū-hachi pattern is a common wish for longevity, and it is thought that with continued use the motif grew stylized and became elaborated into these familiar geometric patterns. The panels are sewn together so that the hachi-jū-hachi pattern alternates with the pictorial imagery to create a checkerboard pattern across the futon cover. Typically, one of the panels is sewn in the reverse direction of the others. This fabric possibly came from the Sanyō district or perhaps Kyūshū.

On Kyūshū at Kurume, a very distinctive type of kasuri was introduced in the early nineteenth century.[20] Kurume weavers became famous

for kasuri patterns of amazing complexity and, eventually, very large scale. The third of the futon cover panels (cat. 57) shows typical small-scale Kurume geometric patterns. The hachi-jū-hachi pattern with blossoms at the four corners and enclosing a fifth blossom in the center, which is surrounded by a diamond of small squares, alternates with a diamond of small squares surrounding a petaled blossom. These patterns were so standardized that although the third panel in this set has motifs with blossom forms that differ from those in the other two panels, the difference goes almost unnoticed. The frugal homemaker likely substituted this similar, though differing, panel as an economy.

By the end of the nineteenth century, the weavers at Kurume were specializing in such tour-de-force compositions as appear in two large futon covers (cat. 58 and 59).[21] Caught up in the fervor to emulate modern Western technological feats, Kurume weavers produced fantasies of iron bridges, railway trains, and steamboats. Sometimes immense stylized landscapes appeared, such as the settings for the shrine (cat. 58) and the castle (cat. 59).

54. (opposite)
Kimono
Meiji-Taisho period, early 20th century
Bast fiber (asa) cloth with weft ikat (yokogasuri) and double ikat (kasuri), 62¼ x 48¼ in. (155.6 x 120.6 cm)
89.139

55. (above, left)
Portion of a bedding cover (futonji)
Meiji period, late 19th-early 20th century
Cotton cloth with weft ikat (yokogasuri or e-gasuri) and double ikat (kasuri), 58⅛ x 25⅜ in. (145.3 x 63.4 cm)
89.151

56. (above, center)
Bedding cover (futonji)
Meiji-Taishō period, late 19th-early 20th century
Cotton cloth with weft ikat (yokogasuri or e-gasuri) and double ikat (kasuri), 55¾ x 38 in. (139.4 x 95 cm) 89.150

57. (above, right)
Bedding cover (futonji)
Meiji-Taishō period, late 19th-early 20th century
Cotton cloth with double ikat (kasuri), 60½ x 38 in. (151.3 x 95 cm) 89.149

Though not identified by inscription, the shrine is reminiscent of Kotohiragū on Shikoku Island. Perched high up on the mountainside, Kotohiragū is reached by a long stone staircase bordered by innumerable stone lanterns, as might be suggested here with the crosslike forms at every step. The sailing ship at the bottom, afloat on its pale blue sea, furthers the idea this might be Kotohiragū, the shrine that from ancient times was a landmark for navigation, bringing protection to seafarers — a beacon once shone from its precincts. Clearly the design shows a torii flanked by lanterns before the shrine building.

At either side of the shrine are large characters and geometric motifs. The stylized characters are abbreviated, perhaps for the convenience of the weaver. At the top left appear concentric squares and a form of hachi-jū-hachi, followed by the character *fuku* (good fortune) and then, perhaps, *man* (10,000, or myriad) which combine into a wish for great good fortune. At the right, the topmost character, too abbreviated or too stylized, has so far defied translation; the others read *hashi* (bridge) and *yorokobi* (delight). Below this is another set of concentric squares showing the locations of the *tachibana* and the plum tree, while above, stars shine in the inky sky.[22]

Perhaps these giant futon covers were intended as souvenir items, but the haze of cotton wadding clinging to the back of this piece and the needle-holes and creases where the edges were turned under indicate that this one was actually used. The process of resisting, dyeing, and then weaving this piece across five panels is made the more complex by incorporation of the light blue ground in the lower portion.

The castle pattern futon cover (cat. 59) combines traditional and modern motifs. A large medieval castle with a many-storied keep rising from stone foundations almost completely fills the space of the fabric. The weaving is highly accurate, the image clearly continuous across the five panels. The red of the Japanese flags has been added by hand. The castle is usually identified as Kumamoto Castle.[23]

In the sky above the castle where usually appear paired birds or cranes, the weaver has substituted a pair of diving airplanes.[24] Surprise at this unexpected motif, combined with the aircraft's rather ungainly shape, brings a reaction of mirth, perhaps; the appearance of the airplanes, however, is a serious reflection of the mood for westernization of the Meiji period and militarization of the Taishō (1912–26) and early Shōwa (1926–89) periods, when the spirit of the samurai was being transferred to modern warfare.

Related to kasuri as a tied-thread resist technique is *shibori* or *shiborizome*, the tie-dye techniques of decorating textiles. In Japan the technique dates back to the eighth century. One of the *sankechi* (resist-dyeing) techniques, *kōkechi* was a method of tie-dye resist. *Tsujigahana*, a stitch-resist technique producing designs in color which are given hand-painted details, and sometimes details in embroidery, was the ultimate in elegant tie-dyed fabrics in the late Muromachi (1392–1568) and Momoyama (1568–1615) periods. Other types of elaborate patterning on silk fabrics were devised for the elite classes, and Kyoto was a center of this industry.

58. (opposite, top)
Bedding cover *(futonji)*
Meiji-Taishō period, late 19th-early 20th century, Kurume
Cotton cloth with double ikat *(kasuri)*, 85 1/16 x 62 in. (212.7 x 155 cm) 89.154

59. (opposite, bottom)
Bedding cover *(futonji)*
Meiji-Taishō period, early 20th century, Kurume
Cotton cloth with double ikat *(kasuri)*, 91 x 64 1/4 in. (227.5 x 160.6 cm) 89.152

60.
Informal kimono *(yukata)*
Meiji period, 19th century
Cotton cloth with thread-
resist decoration *(shibori)*,
49¾ x 46⅛ in. (124.4 x
115.9 cm) 89.117

Classic tie-dyed fabrics available to common people of the Edo and Meiji periods were made by the dyers of the towns of Narumi and nearby Arimatsu in Owari prefecture, around present-day Nagoya. Their designs captured the public imagination, and their fabrics led the field as the typical expression of the art. As testimony to the clear identification of the towns in which the art of tie dyeing was practiced, Andō Hiroshige (1797–1858), in his woodblock series *Tōkaidō gojūsantsugi*, showed dyers' shops attracting the attention of travelers with their displays of *yukata* (informal kimono) and lengths of cloth ready to be made up, a scene no doubt repeated in these towns on countless days during the latter part of the Edo period. The two towns Narumi and Arimatsu were in strong competition, and despite attempts by Arimatsu dyers to protect their technical and design innovations, the dyers of Narumi seem to have been very skillful at moving into the market; at this distance in time, it is difficult to distinguish between fabrics from these two sources.[25]

The informal kimono (cat. 60) is typical of yukata fabric produced at Narumi and Arimatsu. Tie-dyed fabric is either stitched or tied to resist the dye, and as patterns are often devised to cover the entire garment, they can achieve, as in this example, much bolder effects than the meticulously woven repeated patterns of kasuri.

Made up for a lady, as indicated by the closed sleeve-back, the decoration of this yukata, or *yuage* (for after the bath), combines several different shibori techniques. The motif combining *kiri* (paulownia blossom) and *ajiro* (diaperwork, a pattern resembling woven mats or wall panels) alternate with panels of undulating lines called *tatewaku*. These motifs are interrupted by a broad diagonal panel which reverses the white on blue color scheme. The kiri, ajiro, and tatewaku patterns are created by the *orinui* technique, in which a threaded needle is slipped through the fabric in a line and tightened to create in the dyeing a series of dots along a thin blue line.[26] The tips of the kiri blossom are simple wrapped-thread resisted spots.

The diagonal white band was created by a technique called *shirokage* (literally, white shadow).[27] Typically, shirokage is used to generate overall linear patterns. In this instance, the undyed area is marked with small designs stitched in the *nuishibori* technique. The small oval patterns are a variation of *shippō*, or linked circles, and the central sunburst motif, a variation on *hinode*. The combination of large dark areas with the shirokage panel marked with nuishibori patterns makes this an exceptional example of tie-dyed fabric.[28] The fashion for shibori yukata, said to have originated at Arimatsu in the late seventeenth century, soon swept through the nation and has endured as a summer garment in countless numbers to the present.[29]

Traditional groupings for textiles in Japan usually place kasuri and shibori with striped (*shima*) or lattice patterns (*koshi*), and the plaid silk fabric of this kimono (cat. 61) is an example of a popular type known as *hachijōjima*, or stripe pattern of Hachijō Island. A volcanic dot several hundred miles south of Tokyo in the Pacific Ocean, Hachijō was otherwise known as a place of banishment. Weaving has been a tradition there from ancient times, and a silk industry has flourished on the island since perhaps the late fifteenth century. Administered from Tokyo today, the island's economy has been tied to the capital since the Edo period. Lattice or plaid patterns became a local favorite in Edo, it is said, after the fabric caught the eye of the wife of one of the shoguns, who then dressed the palace maids in them. The fashion among both men and women for plaid weaves in silk fabric spread widely, and hachijōjima became a standard item in drapers' shops in the eighteenth and nineteenth centuries.

The yellow silk plaid, termed *kihachijō*, is only one of many colors from the natural dyes developed for the weaving industry on the island. Yellow, however, was considered the most typical of the island weavers' work. The kihachijō fabric of this kimono is a twill weave (*aya*) that textures the surface of the fabric and imparts a reflective character to it; Hachijō Island weaving is more usually described as without texture.[30] Dyers and weavers were still producing complicated lattice patterns in these wonderful colors well into the twentieth century.[31]

This kimono incorporates embroidered panels from a *katabira* of the late eighteenth century. The pattern of dancing cranes and sheaves of ripened rice is executed in a combination of satin-stitch silk threads and couched gold thread. The panels on which the embroidery is sewn are woven of asa.[32]

Regardless of the blurred history of the origins for kasuri weaving in Japan, Edo-period artisans triumphed in the technique, moving from amateur cottage industry to full-scale factory production by the late Edo period. Along the way they invented elaborations on the basic technology that created a truly unique medium capable of dynamic artistic expression. Similarly in shiborizome, dyers at Narumi and Arimatsu not only originated a new kimono type in the yukata but reached heights of ingenuity and established standards for dramatic patterning that remain unexcelled.

61. (overleaf)
Kimono, perhaps for dance
Yoke: Edo period, late 18th century
Body: Meiji-Taishō period, early 20th century, Hachijō Island
Yoke: bast fiber (*asa*) cloth with metallic thread couching and silk thread embroidery
Body: silk cloth with woven plaid pattern (*koshi*), 54 x 47½ in. (135 x 118.8 cm) 89.142

Motifs ranged in scale from incredibly minute dots and dashes in double-kasuri weave to tie-dyed patterns that explode like fireworks in a night sky across an entire garment. Except in the weaving traditions on Hachijō Island, indigo was the predominant color used by the artisans in kasuri weaving and tie-dye production, and these weavers and dyers worked marvels in blue and white, conjuring an endless flow of irresistible pattern and motif that caught the elegance of subtly refined workmanship in a medium easily available to the general populace.

1. See essays in this volume by Mary Dusenbury and Amanda Mayer Stinchecum for technical details on this process.

2. In Japanese, the term "asa" describes any bast fiber; however, it is often taken to mean hemp fibers. Its vagueness results in part from the Japanese penchant for poetic imprecision and in part from respect for hemp as the classical ancient fiber of Japan. It is also very difficult visibly to distinguish hemp and ramie threads in woven fabric. Please see Louise Cort's discussion of asa and fiber banana in this volume.

3. Mary Dusenbury, "Kasuri: A Japanese Textile," *Textile Museum Journal* 19 (1978), p. 57. We are also grateful to Ms. Dusenbury for her additional suggestions regarding these entries.

4. This kimono is characteristic of a type identified as having been woven in Kyoto. Kichiemon Okamura, *Kasuri no michi* (The Art of Kasuri), (Tokyo: Mainichi Shimbunsha, 1984), fig. 28.

5. Notable ancient imported striped fabrics were organized by tea masters during the Edo period as *meibutsugire*, or "famous cloth scraps." Examples imported from the late Muromachi, Momoyama, and early Edo periods were primarily cotton striped fabrics from India and other southern locations and were influential in fabric designs of the late Edo period. The sober brown and white of the cape was a characteristic pattern of the period. By the late Edo period, sample books (*shimachō*) illustrated numerous combinations from which to choose when ordering a fabric.

6. Literary allusions were popular in Edo-period decorative arts, and classic tales like *Ise monogatari* and *Genji monogatari* were often sources for imagery. The genjikō are monograms devised to identify the fragrances of the ancient incense game; during the Edo period, these were used as insignias denoting the different chapters of the *genji monogatari* and evoked references to events of the stories or provided allusions to contemporary situations. Perhaps due to faulty resisting, careless weaving, or possibly inexact information, the specific form of the genjikō used here is not clear; it should perhaps be termed a pseudo-genjikō.

7. Michiyo Morioka provided research and a draft entry for the amagappa, literally, rain cape: ama or *ame* (rain) and kappa or gappa (from the Portuguese *capa*). Travel garments in general, however, are termed *dōchūgi*.

8. A more precise term for this type of coat is *sodegappa*, or kappa with sleeves, to distinguish it from the bōzugappa.

9. The kamiko technique for making clothing employs pieces of tough handmade paper that are joined into large sheets to create a variety of garments, such as kimono, sleeveless jackets, and traveling coats. Paper was used in part because it was cheap and readily available. However, kamiko garments have the added advantage of comfort, as paper is soft and is a good insulator against wind and cold. Paper clothing was decorated variously with paste-resisted and stencil patterns, hand-painted designs, or with dyes.

10. *Tōyu* means "paulownia oil," since the tung tree resembled the paulownia in the shape of its leaf.

11. Tokusaburō Ikeda and the research staff at the Seikatsu Shiryōkan, Tokyo Kasei University Junior College, provided this information. Personal correspondence with Michiyo Morioka, April 15, 1991.

12. During the Edo period, travel was, at least in theory, strictly controlled, and laborers were obliged to have permission to be away from their work. The highway systems were designed for communication and for the convenience of daimyo and their retinues on their travel to and from Edo. However, religious pilgrimages and eventually pleasure travel were very popular among commoners.

13. Mary Dusenbury has suggested in conversation that the vertical motifs were created with the mokuhiki device.

14. The *e-dai* (or *ezu-dai*) and the *kobajōgi* are systems used in preparing kasuri commercially. The e-dai system uses a tane-ito, or guide thread, which becomes a model to bind bundles of wefts. The kobajōgi system uses a stack of thin leaves of wood onto which a pattern has been drawn or stenciled. Each wooden leaf carries dots and dashes of what will become the weft pattern. The weft thread is tied accordingly. As the weft is woven, the pattern as drawn or stenciled on the stack of wooden leaves is reestablished. *Itajimegasuri* was another method used extensively, but it is not a genuine kasuri technique. This is a clamp-resist method in which threads are pressed between boards onto which patterns in mirror image have been carved. See Mary Dusenbury's essay in this volume, or her "Kasuri," p. 58, figs. 12 -14; Okamura, *Kasuri no michi*, p. 199ff, especially no. 14.22, ills. pp. 200, 203, 209; Tomoyuki Yamanobe, ed., *Some, Nihon no bijutsu* 7 (November 1966), 29ff; Katsumi Nakae, ed., *Senshoku no jiten* (Tokyo: Tairyusha, 1981), pp. 46, 151.

15. Mary Dusenbury made this point in conversation; also, see her essay "Kasuri" in this volume.

16. Designed for a young lady, the kimono has typical lining of plain white cotton fabric down the center of the back. Lining inside the sleeve openings comes from a different piece of kasuri and suggests the kimono was worn over a period of years; it also demonstrates a careful attention to preservation and reuse.

17. See Louise Cort's essay in this volume on jōfu.

18. Toshio Tanaka and Reiko Tanaka, *A Study of Okinawan Textiles* (Kyoto: Shikōsha, 1976), pp. 41ff. It has been suggested by many who have examined this kimono that the fabric is Echigo jofu.

19. One should not draw too fine a distinction between the patterns of these areas, as over time the patterns and certainly the techniques traveled.

20. Kurume tradition has it that a young woman, Inoue Den (1788-1869), at age twelve or thirteen originated a distinctive method of tying threads after observing the rubbed and pale tones of used indigo fabric. Kurume kasuri gained wide recognition, and the fortunes of the weavers of the area rose with increased marketing. The history of Kurume kasuri weaving is said to date from Den's work in about 1799. Later Otsuka Taizō added refinements to the technique; in 1839 he perfected the e-dai for creating large-scale e-gasuri. After a period of serious decline in quality, about 1877, the Meiji government established strict supervision of the production of Kurume kasuri, which resulted in a renewed interest in it nationally. The peak of production came in the mid-1920s. See Nakae, *Senshoku no jiten*, p. 169.

21. Large-pattern futon covers were a genre of kasuri weaving termed *futongasuri*. The castle pattern was a favored motif among Kurume weavers, but other areas, like the San'in district, were known for special patterns, such as wedding futon covers with motifs of crane and tortoise. These futongasuri were popular between the late nineteenth century and the mid-1920s. See ibid., p. 359; and *Nihon senshoku chizu, Shirizu: senshoku no bunka*, vol. 3 (Tokyo: Asahi Shimbunsha, 1985), ill. p. 67.

22. The characters are reversed. This indicates the person who assembled the futon had no concern for which face of the panels became the front. It is possible that they were turned at some point to balance wear. It is more probable that the owner felt no difficulty having the characters backwards or perhaps enjoyed displaying the anomaly. Examination of the piece indicates either face of the fabric might have been chosen for the surface.

23. Kumamoto Castle, located not far from Kurume, would have been a source of wonder and pride locally; however, the depiction is quite generic. The association no doubt is purely romantic, heightened by the fact that in the Meiji period the castle was the site of a siege by rebellious former samurai of the Satsuma clan led by Saigō Takamori (1827-77). Takamori was a popular hero of the movement to return governing power to the emperor. He was a respected and important leader in the early Meiji-period government, and his popularity and his memory are still very much alive in Kyūshū. For insights to this interesting man through his letters, see William Theodore de Bary, ed., *Sources of Japanese Tradition* (New York and London: Columbia University Press, 1958), p. 654ff.

24. See Victor and Takako Hauge, *Folk Traditions in Japanese Art* (Washington, D.C.: International Exhibitions Foundation, 1978), ill. no. 136, for a very similar design without the airplanes and without the red dot in the flags.

25. For discussion of kokechi, see Kaneo Matsumoto, *Tōdai-gire: 7th and 8th Century Textiles in Japan from the Shōsō'-in and Horyūji* (Kyoto: Shikōsha, 1984), pp. 207-208, 213; for *tsujigahana*, see Yoshiko Wada, Mary Kellogg Rice, and Jane Barton, *Shibori: The Inventive Art of Japanese Shaped Resist Dyeing* (Tokyo, New York, and San Francisco: Kodansha International Ltd., 1983), p. 20ff. In woodblock prints showing Narumi, the scene with lengths of drying fabrics flapping in the sunshine appears in vertical versions of the series. Narumi was an official stop on the Tokaido, but nearby Arimatsu, a town established in the early seventeenth century, was also a popular spot for travelers to shop. Narumi is shown as no. 41 in the series on the road from Edo to Kyoto. Other print artists, among them Katsushika Hokusai, also produced illustrations showing the tie-dyed fabrics of Narumi. See Tsutomu Shiraishi, ed., *Hiroshige Tōkaidō Gojūsantugi* (Tokyo: Shogakukan, 1988), pp. 102-103. Wada et al., *Shibori: The Inventive Art*, discusses the history of the two towns, p. 27ff, ill. fig. 9, p. 31.

26. See Wada et al., *Shibori: The Inventive Art*, p. 76ff.

27. Ibid., p. 97.

28. Correspondence with Yoshiko I. Wada, Berkeley, California, an authority on Japanese textiles and a noted specialist in the area of tie dye. Ms. Wada examined photographs and kindly suggested the identifications noted here.

29. See Wada et al., *Shibori: The Inventive Art*, p. 29.

30. Considering the festive nature of the motif, Iwao Nagasaki of the Tokyo National Museum has suggested this kimono was used in a provincial Kyogen performance. The original collar is retained, but covered with a new, polished cotton fabric. On the original collar was discovered an inscription which is not readable.

31. Noted author on Asian crafts Elizabeth Bayley Willis has left a poignant description of her visit to the island in the company of Sōetsu (Yoshimune) Yanagi in September 1951. Her "Japan Journals" (unpublished manuscript) contain a wealth of information about the state of the crafts in early post-World War II Japan. A brief selection hints at the depth of the tradition:

> Meyu, the dyer, was in her farmyard when we arrived. We saw her beyond the bamboo racks which held the drying skeins of newly dyed silks. She was a thin, small, barefoot woman in dark blue peasant pants which were pulled up over a dark blue and gray striped kimono blouse. She was running along the row of skeins shaking the drying silks and changing their positions on the poles. There were over two hundred skeins glistening in the bright sun as the wind blew through them: rose-red and all the colors of pink to its palest shade, lustrous whites, dark yellows, yellow-greens, chartreuse, wheat yellow, sun gold, and rose-browns and glistening blacks.
>
> Meyu ran to us smiling and wiping her hands on her pant legs. (p. 46)

32. Iwao Nagasaki, Tokyo National Museum, identified the embroidery. The fabric of the kihachijō seems to have silk wefts and asa warps. Extraneous fabric has been added to the katabira embroidery piece to fill in between the asa panels and the hachijōjima fabric. Judging from the embroidered motifs, this garment may well have been designed as a dance kimono or a costume for the Kyogen theater.

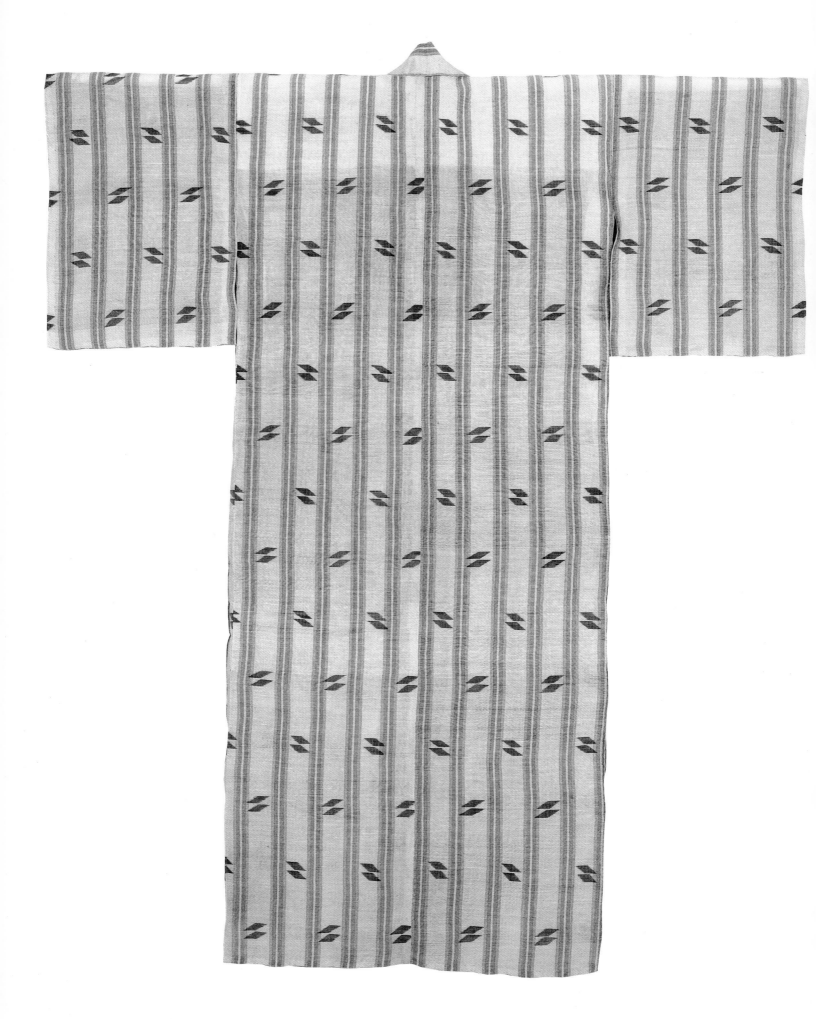

S TRUNG LIKE A GIANT NET AND INTERCEPTING CULTURAL CURRENTS between major centers of eastern and southeastern Asia, the Ryūkyū Islands historically met with myriad foreign influences. Okinawa, the largest island of the group, became an important entrepôt for the trading and transshipping of foodstuffs and merchandise among China, Korea, Japan, the Philippines, Southeast Asia, and Indonesia. Along with material imports came technologies, and among the most important for both the cultural and economic impact were textiles and weaving techniques. Among Okinawan textiles, the two most important imports to Japan were ikat, or *kasuri*, weaving and the paste-resist decoration called *bingata* in Okinawa.[1]

The kasuri woven in silk pongee and ramie became special products of the islands of Kume, Yaeyama, and Miyako. On Okinawa Island, the royal capital of Shuri, too, was a major production center, and its many workshops produced patterned weaves (*monori*), bingata, and kasuri.[2] Communication among the weavers of the various islands was enhanced through a system of *miezuchō*, or pattern books. Fame of the island weavers spread to mainland Japan during the Edo period (1615–1868), when the Satsuma clan from Kyūshū claimed sovereignty over the islands and extracted as tax payment lengths of fabric and garments which were subsequently traded to areas beyond Kyūshū.[3]

The elegant white robe with blue stripes and weft kasuri patterns (cat. 62) represents the quality of kasuri weaving of Shuri workshops. The weaver has manipulated the dyed sections of the warps in a method of weft-shifting termed *hikizurashi*, characterized by a bit of weft left at the selvedge. Hikizurashi creates precise paired-diamond motifs called *mayubichi* in Okinawa. This is one of the patterns that appear in the miezuchō.[4] Woven of silk warps and ramie wefts, the fabric has a rich luster characteristic of the superior Okinawan ramie threads.[5]

The construction of robes of Okinawa and kimono of Japan is similar; however, Okinawan robes often have an added gusset, a triangular piece called a *machi*, where the lower edge of the sleeve joins the garment. The sleeve style of this striped robe, hanging free at the bottom, conforms to Japanese styles.

Another Shuri weaving more typical of Okinawan robe style is the dark blue example with light blue vertical stripes and white weft kasuri patterns (cat. 63). The tubular sleeves, the long *eri*, and the squarish proportion to the garment are typical of *ryūsō*, or Okinawan-style kimono.

62.
Unlined robe
Meiji period, late 19th-20th century, Okinawa
Modified Ryūkyūan construction
Plain weave cloth of raw silk warp and ramie (choma) weft with warp stripes and weft ikat, 55 x 46 in. (137.5 x 115 cm) 89.102

The robe is made from *bashōfu* (fiber-banana cloth), a fabric uniquely Okinawan. The *itobashō* (fiber-banana plant) thrives in the subtropical climate and is cultivated for the fibers obtained from the stalks of the plant, which make several grades of an excellent weaving thread. Bashōfu was used by all classes of society for clothing, though patterns and colors were restricted. The glossy fibers are particularly well suited for garments in the heat and humidity of Okinawa, and this garment, with its sober coloring and minute patterning, is appropriate for the gentry to wear on formal occasions.[6] Cotton threads were used for the vertical stripes and for the weft kasuri patterns.

A variation on double-kasuri patterns is the stencil-dyed version found in another robe (cat. 64). Woven of undyed bashōfu, this modified ryūsō robe displays the rich honey color typical of fine quality bashō threads.

The motifs are stenciled onto one surface only; although guide dots for positioning the stencil are visible, the fabric appears to have been colored directly through the stencil rather than as a paste-resist technique. The motifs were dyed a very deep blue color and are in part variations of traditional patterns.[7]

One other bashōfu robe (cat. 65) combines white silk and colored cotton threads with bashō threads to create a striped pattern. The weaver chose complex arrangements of the white and colored threads, repeating them in alternating stripes; however, change to a different dye batch in some of the cotton threads imparted the appearance of diverse striping.[8]

A modified ryūsō-style robe, the sleeve construction and the eri in this robe adhere to the Okinawan style. The bashō threads are extremely finely divided. Bashō fibers shrink differently from those of silk and cotton when washed, which has caused a notable scalloping wave across the shoulder and along the hem. Summer hemp and ramie robes from central Honshu

63. (above, left)
Unlined robe
Meiji period, late 19th-early
20th century, Okinawa
Ryūkyūan construction
Fiber-banana *(bashō)* cloth
with cotton warp stripes
and weft ikat, 41¾ x 44⅝ in.
(104.4 x 111.6 cm) 89.100

64. (above, right)
Unlined robe
Meiji-Taishō period, early
20th century
Modified Ryūkyūan
construction
Fiber-banana *(bashō)* cloth
with stenciled decoration,
43½ x 43⅜ in. (108.8 x
108.4 cm) 89.99

frequently have a strip of plain cotton or of the same fabric lining the center of the back, on the seat, or as a shoulder yoke. In these Okinawan bashōfu garments, lining is restricted to the yoke. The stencil-decorated robe has a yoke with a delightful floral and vine pattern, also stenciled, on bashōfu that has a woven lattice pattern in brown; the striped robe has a plain yoke of undyed, handspun cotton.

In addition to innovations at Shuri, the royal capital, other locations both on Okinawa and on other islands saw the development of highly distinctive textiles. Amami, Oshima, Yaeyama, Miyako, and Kumejima were among those with important weaving traditions; and on Okinawa, Yùntanza, known today as Yomitan, was the center of spectacular weaves incorporating kasuri and floated weft patterns in contrasting colors.[9]

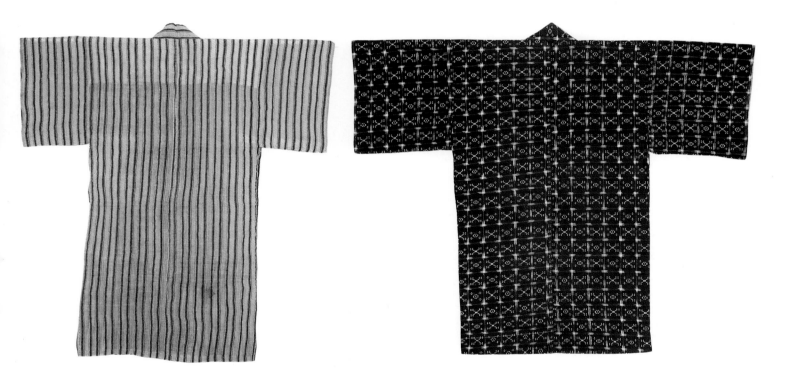

65. (above, left)
Unlined robe
Meiji period, late 19th-early 20th century, Okinawa
Modified Ryūkyūan construction
Fiber-banana (bashō) cloth with cotton and silk warp stripes, 41⅜ x 38⅝ in. (103.4 x 96.6 cm) 89.98

66. (above, right)
Lined over-robe (hanaui aeshi)
Late Edo-Meiji period, 19th century, Yomitan (Oki., Yuntanza), Okinawa
Cotton cloth with check (lattice pattern) warp, weft and double ikat and supplementary wefts (Oki., hanaui); lined with cotton cloth with paste-resist stencil decoration (Oki., bingata), 40½ x 48 in. (101.3 x 120 cm) 89.141

The Yomitan robe (cat. 66), with its red-and-white woven geometric patterns on a blue ground, is a classic example of *ukiori*, better known by the term *hanaori* (Ryū., *hanaui*). The blue fabric is a plain-weave cotton with white double-kasuri motifs and a lattice pattern in red. The intersections of lattice elements are highlighted with white double kasuri, creating a cross-shape. Occasionally, due to incorrect resisting, the cross elements do not intersect, resulting in random white segments along the red line. Within the squares of the lattice pattern are hanaori motifs formed with supplementary weft floats in red-and-white cotton yarns. The motifs are called *jinbana* (coin patterns) and *kajimayabana* (pinwheel patterns).[10]

The lining of the hanaori robe is fabric of hand-spun cotton with pale yellow ground and decorated with bingata paste-resist patterns. A profusion of blossoms in blue and two shades of red pigments, as well as some reserved without color, are scattered across the yellow background, which is interlaced with black lines. Bingata was a technique exclusively for those of the

66.
Lined over-robe
(inside detail)

upper social strata, and small-scale stencil patterns like this were intended for the garments of lesser nobles or samurai. The yellow lining with subdued small patterns contrasts with the deep blue of the exterior, with its lively red-and-white patterns. In addition, this combination of the fancy ukiori patterns of Yomitan weaving with the aristocratic bingata lining conferred on the kimono a special status among garments intended for only the elite.

More than the ukiori of Yomitan, bingata is the textile that best captures the luxury and elegance of the court life of the old kingdom of Ryūkyū. Moreover, unlike kasuri weaving, bingata fabrics remained special to Okinawa and were not exported, nor was their style copied in the main islands. On the contrary, influences apparently came from outside, although they have not yet been clearly traced.[11]

67.
Unlined robe
Late Edo-Meiji period, 19th century, Okinawa
Modified Ryūkyūan construction
Tombian-fiber cloth with paste-resist stencil decoration (Oki., *bingata),* **48¾ x 45 in. (121.9 x 112.5 cm) 89.158**

A second example of Shuri bingata is the deep blue robe with small patterned design (cat. 67). A modified ryūsō type,[12] the small-scale motifs again are those used by lesser nobility. Colored with pigments of red and a greenish yellow, some motifs are left showing the undyed fabric. The motifs include paired redheaded birds (perhaps mandarin ducks) and plum and cherry blossoms. Deep blue dye or possibly sumi was added across the wings of the birds to help distinguish their bodies from the blue of the background. The bright red dots of the birds' heads and the plum blossoms, along with the yellow dots and undyed areas of the flower petals, appear as scattered dots of color when viewed at a distance.[13]

The silk crepe kimono (cat. 68) with strong yellow ground and large-scale stenciled designs represents the premier bingata decorative style. As in China during the Ming and Qing dynasties, yellow was reserved for Okinawan

68. (opposite)
Lined robe, perhaps for dance
Meiji-Taishō period, 20th century, Shuri, Okinawa
Modern modified Ryūkyūan construction
Plain weave silk crepe with paste-resist stencil decoration (Oki., *bingata),* **lined with modern replacement silk broadcloth, 45½ x 42½ in. (113.8 x 106.3 cm) 89.155**

royalty. Moreover, large patterns such as those seen in this robe were reserved for the highest-ranking members of the royal family. It is likely this robe was made subsequent to the demise of the Ryūkyūan throne in the nineteenth century; however, the motifs and large-scale stencils and coloring all represent the royal style.[14]

The motifs of swallows darting among boughs of weeping cherry, its blossoms drifting into a stream where rise Japanese iris, reveal probable influences from the textile patterns of Kyoto. Motifs found in Okinawan textiles usually derived from local flora and fauna; however, in bingata, motifs such as snowflakes (*yukiwa*), weeping cherry, and Japanese iris are mixed variously and without regard to season. Though prunus might bloom in Okinawa, weeping cherries and snowflakes are not known. The delicate hand-shading in the various elements likewise suggests influences from *yūzen* dyeing of Kyoto or Kanazawa.

Typically Okinawan, however, are both the large-scale, symmetrically disposed pattern flowing from shoulder to hem and the brilliant coloring. Magenta, vermillion, pink, purple, green, and reserved elements burst from the dazzling yellow background in a manner known only among Okinawan textiles. The silk crepe lends a delicate draping to the fabric, unequaled in local fabrics like ramie, cotton, or bashōfu, and further emphasizes the voluptuous extravagance of this piece.[15]

These examples display the main types of fabric and, most important, decorative techniques characteristic of textiles produced in Ryūkyūan culture. As elsewhere in traditional cultures, textile materials and dyestuffs were guided by locally available materials. Available in Okinawa were unique materials such as the thread-banana plant used to produce the lustrous fibers for bashōfu weaving; however, while there are numerous excellent plants to produce asa fibers, hemp, so abundantly available in the main islands, is not known. The Ryūkyū Islands host plants, trees, and sea life that all serve as a basis to create special dyestuffs; in addition, contact with overseas cultures gave access to exotic materials denied the artisans of the main islands, and the strongest impression among Ryūkyūan textiles is the joyful coloring of the decoration on bingata pieces. It is tempting to see in these bright colors the influence of tropical sunshine and a lifestyle reflecting white-sand beaches swept by balmy breezes. Surely in response to the climate are distinctive characteristics such as openness of the weave of many fabrics and openness of garment styling. These qualities strongly contrast to much of what was produced in the main islands, where protection from the cold was a primary concern, and Edo-period feudal society injected a special character to life.

Over the past decade, interest among Okinawans has been growing to explore and identify with scholarly discipline not only the richness of these textile traditions but also the unique cultural history expressed through these textiles and embodied in the persons who created them. The enthusiasm and determined effort already at work, it is hoped, will achieve this goal and the wonderful spirit of Okinawan culture will be preserved.

1. Please consult the essays in this catalogue by Amanda Mayer Stinchecum and by Mary Dusenbury on this subject.

2. Amanda Mayer Stinchecum provided helpful direction in preparing this section.

3. The exact manner in which kasuri weaving came to Japan or to Okinawa, and whether the one is debtor to the other, is a matter on which strong and sometimes conflicting opinions are expressed by many seemingly authoritative voices.

4. Toshio Tanaka and Reiko Tanaka, *A Study of Okinawan Woven Textiles* (Kyoto: Shikōsha, 1976), p. 46, no. 57. Transcribing of Okinawan terms varies: Tanaka uses the spelling *bichi*, while other authors, including Amanda Mayer Stinchecum in her essay in this catalogue, use *bichuu*.

5. This robe was considered to be woven, at least in part, of the agave fiber known as *tombian* (also *tunbyan, tonbyan, tonbian*); Amanda Mayer Stinchecum has convincingly demonstrated this robe is woven of ramie and silk yarns. Also see The Japan Textile Color Design Center, ed., *Textile Designs of Japan*, vol. 3, *Okinawan, Ainu, and Foreign Designs* (Tokyo and New York: Kodansha, 1980), p. 9.

6. Please consult essays in this catalogue by Louise Cort and Amanda Mayer Stinchecum for information on these technical points. See also Publication Committee, ed., *The Art of Okinawa*, Shizuko Oshiró and Tashio Uezu, vol. 3, "Textiles" (Naha: Okinawa Times, 1989), pp. 239ff. Mrs. Toshiko Taira, the Okinawan weaver who has been designated a Living National Treasure for rejunvenating the bahsōfu weaving tradition, identified this as a man's robe for formal wear (1989 visit to the Seattle Art Museum).

7. Tanaka and Tanaka, *A Study of Okinawan Woven Textiles*, pp. 41ff.

8. The combining of three different fibers is characteristic of Okinawan taste (conversation with Amanda Mayer Stinchecum).

9. Cotton was introduced to Okinawa in the early seventeenth century from Satsuma on Kyūshū and rapidly became the fabric reserved for nobility. Later in the century, new weaving techniques arrived from China, among them damask weaving, which eventually emerged as the ukiori, or raised-figure weaving, which was produced at Shuri but was perhaps most famous as it was woven at Yomitan. Publication Committee, ed., *The Art of Okinawa*, Oshiro and Uezu, vol. 3, "Textiles," pp. 243ff.

10. Ibid., ill. 102, p. 292. The unidentified author of the commentary to ill. 102 says kimono like this were for ceremonial occasions.

11. Bingata (literally, red stencils or colorful patterns) refers both to paste-resisted stenciled patterns (analogous to *katazome*) and to freehand designs which are applied with the aid of a *tsutsu*, or paste-extruding tube from which the Japanese term *tsutsugaki* derives. Freehand painted resist was seldom used in Okinawan textiles other than for the carrying cloths called *uchikui* in Okinawan. Stenciled patterns derived without color other than indigo are termed *aigata* (Ryū., *e-gata*). Bingata was reserved solely for the royal family and the nobility. Colors and motifs, by type and size, were prescribed for each rank.

12. The robe has been remodeled extensively, no doubt to extend its useful life. It was resewn on a sewing machine; however, all pieces are original. When it was remodeled, the seams were eased to make it slightly larger. We are grateful to Iwao Nagasaki, curator of Japanese textiles, Tokyo National Museum, for this identification.

13. The stencil repeat for this small-scale pattern is the width of the fabric panel and approximately 8 inches high. The fabric of this robe has been considered bashōfu; however, Amanda Mayer Stinchecum indicates that evidence now suggests these dark-blue ground robes are actually tombian fiber, an agave fiber imported from Fujian province in China.

14. Large patterns such as these were made by combining two or more stencils to create a complete pattern. Unlike the present example, use of independent stencils, for instance to create swooping birds, can be noticed on some kimono where the motifs are not strictly symmetrical.

Tradition has it that the Seattle Art Museum kimono was damaged and at some point sent to Kyoto for restoration. The plan, it is said, was to replace missing portions with plain fabric; however, the kimono was ultimately taken apart and remodeled. An extraordinary lining was created by the famed dyer Tsuneo Yoshioka, who used the same sort of natural dyes as were used for the original. When the kimono was reassembled, the back panels were narrowed: the strips which were removed were made into ties that were attached at the waist. Ties for closure are sometimes found on Okinawan kimono but seem restricted to dance or ritual garments. The sleeves, too, were reassembled. The rarity of this type of kimono and the quality of its color and pattern made acquisition irresistible despite its alterations.

15. For similar examples see The Japan Textile Color Design Center, ed., vol. 3, *Okinawan, Ainu and Foreign Designs*, plate 1; also Publication Committee, ed., *The Art of Okinawa*, vol. 3, "Textiles," pls. 29-30, where the commentary (pp. 146-47) discusses a very similar silk crepe kimono (29) which is described as for a member of the royal family. It has been noted by some who examined the Seattle Art Museum kimono that it should have a red eri; however, of the three examples offered for comparison, only one has a red eri.

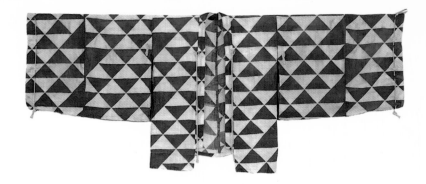

Beyond the Tanabata Bridge
TRADITIONAL JAPANESE TEXTILES

EDITED BY WILLIAM RATHBUN

Tanabata-tsume, the Weaver Maid, is the patron deity of weaving in Japan and the subject of an old and beautiful legend. Devoted to her husband, she neglected her work, and was banished across the River of Heaven (the Milky Way). But once a year birds bridge the river with their wings so the couple can be reunited for one night – the night when women pray for skill in Japan's marvellous textile traditions.

This opulent and authoritative guide to the folk textiles of Japan, based on the collection of the Seattle Art Museum – one of the most comprehensive and significant in America – journeys beyond the Tanabata Bridge on a tour of national and regional cloth-making from the eighteenth to the twentieth century, taking in all major weaving, dyeing and stitchery techniques as well as general themes and local variations in the traditions. Essays from distinguished contributors show how these clothes provide an insight into Japanese culture, and how colour, motif, shape and material reflected the wearer's age, occupation and rank. Specially commissioned colour photographs of the often spectacular and remarkable garments are accompanied by drawings showing how they were worn or used and views of modern weavers at work.
Beyond the Tanabata Bridge displays the splendid fruits of a venerable heritage of fine handicraft. For those interested in the history of dress and textiles, for the specialist who needs a reference, and for anyone fascinated by the arts of Japan, it is essential reading.

William Rathbun is John A. McCone Foundation Curator of Asian Art at the Seattle Art Museum.

With 130 illustrations, 100 in colour

On the cover: Theatrical or Festival robe (hititare), Late Meiji-Taisho-Showa period, 20th Century (see page 141)

THAMES AND HUDSON
30 Bloomsbury Street, London WC1B 3QP

ISBN 0-500-27740-0

9 780500 277409

Printed in Hong Kong